W9-AAI-721

MICROSOFT® OFFICE
Publisher 2003

Introductory Concepts and Techniques

Gary B. Shelly
Thomas J. Cashman
Joy L. Starks

THOMSON
COURSE TECHNOLOGY™

COURSE TECHNOLOGY
25 THOMSON PLACE
BOSTON MA 02210

SHELLY
CASHMAN
SERIES®

Australia • Canada • Denmark • Japan • Mexico • New Zealand • Philippines • Puerto Rico • Singapore
South Africa • Spain • United Kingdom • United States

THOMSON

COURSE TECHNOLOGY

Microsoft Office Publisher 2003
Introductory Concepts and Techniques

Gary B. Shelly

Thomas J. Cashman

Joy L. Starks

Executive Editor:
Cheryl Costantini

Senior Acquisitions Editor:
Dana Merk

Senior Product Manager:
Alexandra Arnold

Associate Product Manager:
Reed Cotter

Editorial Assistant:
Selena Coppock

Print Buyer:
Laura Burns

Signing Representative:
Cheryl Costantini

Series Consulting Editor:
Jim Quasney

Director of Production:
Becky Herrington

Production Editor:
Deb Masi

Production Assistant:
Jennifer Quiambao

Development Editor:
Lyn Markowicz

Copy Editor:
Lyn Markowicz

Proofreader:
Nancy Lamm

Interior Designer:
Becky Herrington

Cover Designers:
Ken Russo
Richard Herrera

Illustrators:
Richard Herrera
Andrew Bartel

Compositors:
Jeanne Black
Andrew Bartel
Kellee LaVars

Indexer:
Cristina Haley

Printer:
Banta Menasha

MICROSOFT® OFFICE

Publisher 2003

Introductory Concepts and Techniques

Contents

Project Three

Publishing a Tri-Fold Brochure

E-Mail Feature

Creating an E-Mail Letter Using Publisher

Appendix A

Microsoft Publisher Help System

Appendix B

Speech and Handwriting Recognition

Appendix C

Publishing Office Web Pages to a Web Server

Appendix D

Changing Screen Resolution and Resetting the Publisher Toolbars and Menus

Preface

The Shelly Cashman Series® offers the finest textbooks in computer education. We are proud of the fact that our series of Microsoft Office 4.3, Microsoft Office 95, Microsoft Office 97, Microsoft Office 2000, and Microsoft Office XP textbooks have been the most widely used books in education. With each new edition of our Office books, we have made significant improvements based on the software and comments made by the instructors and students. The *Microsoft Office Publisher 2003* books continue with the innovation, quality, and reliability that you have come to expect from the Shelly Cashman Series.

In this *Microsoft Office Publisher 2003* book, you will find an educationally sound, highly visual, and easy-to-follow pedagogy that combines a vastly improved step-by-step approach with corresponding screens. All projects and exercises in this book are designed to take full advantage of the Publisher 2003 enhancements. The project material is developed to ensure that students will see the importance of learning Publisher for future coursework. The popular Other Ways and More About features offer in-depth knowledge of Publisher 2003, and the new Q&A feature offers students a way to solidify important desktop publishing concepts. The Learn It Online page presents a wealth of additional exercises to ensure your students have all the reinforcement they need.

Objectives of This Textbook

Microsoft Office Publisher 2003: Introductory Concepts and Techniques is intended for a one-unit course or a portion of a three-unit desktop-publishing course that presents an introduction of Microsoft Office Publisher 2003. No experience with a computer is assumed, and no mathematics beyond the high school freshman level is required. The objectives of this book are:

- To teach the fundamentals of Publisher 2003
- To acquaint students with the proper procedures to design and create professional quality publications suitable for course work, professional purposes, and personal use
- To expose students to practical examples of the computer as a useful desktop publishing tool
- To develop an exercise-oriented approach that allows learning by doing
- To introduce students to new input technologies
- To encourage independent study and help those who are working alone

The Shelly Cashman Approach

Features of the Shelly Cashman Series *Microsoft Office Publisher 2003* books include:

- **Project Orientation:**   Each project in the book presents a practical problem and complete solution using an easy-to-understand methodology.
- **Step-by-Step, Screen-by-Screen Instructions:**   Each of the tasks required to complete a project is identified throughout the project. Full-color screens accompany the steps.
- **Thoroughly Tested Projects:**   Unparalleled quality is ensured because every screen in the book is produced by the author only after performing a step, and then each project must pass Course Technology's award-winning Quality Assurance program.
- **Other Ways Boxes and Quick Reference Summary:**   The Other Ways boxes displayed at the end of many of the step-by-step sequences specify the other ways to perform the task completed in the steps. Thus, the steps and the Other Ways box make a comprehensive reference unit.
- **More About and Q&A Features:**   These marginal annotations provide background information, tips, and answers to common questions that complement the topics covered, adding depth and perspective to the learning process.

- **Integration of the World Wide Web:** The World Wide Web is integrated into the Publisher 2003 learning experience by (1) More About annotations that send students to Web sites for up-to-date information and alternative approaches to tasks; (2) a Publisher 2003 Quick Reference Summary Web page that summarizes the ways to complete tasks (mouse, menu, shortcut menu, and keyboard); and (3) the Learn It Online page at the end of each project, which has project reinforcement exercises, learning games, and other types of student activities.

Organization of This Textbook

Microsoft Office Publisher 2003: Introductory Concepts and Techniques provides basic instruction on how to use Publisher 2003. The material is divided into three projects, an E-Mail Letter feature, four appendices, and a Quick Reference Summary.

Project 1 – Creating and Editing a Publication In Project 1, students are introduced to Publisher terminology and the Publisher screen by preparing an advertising flyer with tear-offs. Topics include starting and quitting Publisher; using the New Publication task pane for color and font decisions; editing text and synchronized objects; using Publisher's zoom features; editing graphics; using the Clip Art task pane; creating bulleted lists; formatting, printing, and saving a publication; opening and modifying a publication; deleting objects; and converting a print publication to a Web publication.

Project 2 – Designing a Newsletter In Project 2, students create a two-page newsletter using a Publisher-designed template. Topics include identifying the advantages of the newsletter medium and the steps in the design process; editing typical newsletter features including mastheads, multi-column articles, sidebars, pull quotes, and graphics; using the Page Navigation control and pagination; importing text and graphic files; using Microsoft Word as an editor; formatting personal information components and attention getters; using WordArt; and moving between foreground and background elements. Finally, students check the publication for spelling, use the Design Checker, and then print the newsletter double-sided.

Project 3 – Preparing a Tri-Fold Brochure for Outside Printing In Project 3, students prepare a tri-fold brochure with three panels displaying text, shapes, graphics, an order form, a price list, and a personalized logo. Topics include the proper use of graphics; inserting a photograph from a file; creating a composite logo using custom shapes; deleting and inserting text boxes; using Smart Tags; grouping, rotating, and overlapping objects; editing form components; and preparing the publication for outside printing by choosing appropriate printing services, paper, and color libraries. This project also illustrates Publisher's Pack and Go feature.

E-Mail Feature – Creating an E-Mail Letter Using Publisher In the E-Mail Letter feature, students are introduced to a new publication type in Publisher 2003, as they create an e-mail letter. Topics include the advantages and disadvantages of sending a publication as an e-mail message versus an attachment; using an e-mail letter design template; editing e-mail letter objects; selecting a logo design; editing logo text; previewing an e-mail letter; using an e-mail address as a hyperlink; and using Publisher's Send E-mail command.

Appendices The book includes four appendices. Appendix A presents an introduction to the Microsoft Publisher Help system. Appendix B describes how to use Publisher's speech and handwriting recognition and speech playback capabilities. Appendix C explains how to publish Web pages to a Web server. Appendix D shows how to change the screen resolution and reset the Publisher toolbars and menus.

Quick Reference Summary In Publisher 2003, you can accomplish a task in a number of ways, such as using the mouse, menu, shortcut menu, and keyboard. The Quick Reference Summary at the back of the book provides a quick reference to each task presented.

End-of-Project Student Activities

A notable strength of the Shelly Cashman Series *Microsoft Office Publisher 2003* books is the extensive student activities at the end of each project. Well-structured student activities can make the difference between students merely participating in a class and students retaining the information they learn. The activities in the Shelly Cashman Series *Microsoft Office Publisher 2003* books include the following.

- **What You Should Know** A listing of the tasks completed within a project together with the pages on which the step-by-step, screen-by-screen explanations appear.
- **Learn It Online** Every project features a Learn It Online page that contains 12 exercises. These exercises include True/False, Multiple Choice, Short Answer, Flash Cards, Practice Test, Learning Games, Tips and Tricks, Newsgroup usage, Expanding Your Horizons, Search Sleuth, Office Online Training, and Office Marketplace.
- **Apply Your Knowledge** This exercise usually requires students to open and manipulate a file on the Data Disk that parallels the activities learned in the project. To obtain a copy of the Data Disk, follow the instructions on the inside back cover of this textbook.
- **In the Lab** Three in-depth assignments per project require students to utilize the project concepts and techniques to solve problems on a computer.
- **Cases and Places** Up to six unique real-world case-study situations, including one small-group activity.

Instructor Resources CD-ROM

The Shelly Cashman Series is dedicated to providing you with all of the tools you need to make your class a success. Information on all supplementary materials is available through your Course Technology representative or by calling one of the following telephone numbers: Colleges and Universities, 1-800-648-7450; High Schools, 1-800-824-5179; Private Career Colleges, 1-800-347-7707; Canada, 1-800-268-2222; Corporations with IT Training Centers, 1-800-648-7450; and Government Agencies, Health-Care Organizations, and Correctional Facilities, 1-800-477-3692.

The Instructor Resources for this textbook include both teaching and testing aids. The contents of each item on the Instructor Resources CD-ROM (ISBN 0-619-20051-0) are described below.

INSTRUCTOR'S MANUAL The Instructor's Manual is made up of Microsoft Word files, which include detailed lesson plans with page number references, lecture notes, teaching tips, classroom activities, discussion topics, projects to assign, and transparency references. The transparencies are available through the Figure Files described below.

LECTURE SUCCESS SYSTEM The Lecture Success System consists of intermediate files that correspond to certain figures in the book, allowing you to step through the creation of an application in a project during a lecture without entering large amounts of data.

SYLLABUS Sample syllabi, which can be customized easily to a course, are included. The syllabi cover policies, class and lab assignments and exams, and procedural information.

FIGURE FILES Illustrations for every figure in the textbook are available in electronic form. Use this ancillary to present a slide show in lecture or to print transparencies for use in lecture with an overhead projector. If you have a personal computer and LCD device, this ancillary can be an effective tool for presenting lectures.

POWERPOINT PRESENTATIONS PowerPoint Presentations is a multimedia lecture presentation system that provides slides for each project. Presentations are based on project objectives. Use this presentation system to present well-organized lectures that are both interesting and knowledge based. PowerPoint Presentations provides consistent coverage at schools that use multiple lecturers.

SOLUTIONS TO EXERCISES Solutions are included for the end-of-project exercises, as well as the Project Reinforcement exercises as described on the next page.

TEST BANK & TEST ENGINE The ExamView test bank includes 110 questions for every project (25 multiple choice, 50 true/false, and 35 completion) with page number references and, when appropriate, figure references. A version of the test bank you can print also is included. The test bank comes with a copy of the test engine, ExamView, the ultimate tool for your objective-based testing needs. ExamView is a state-of-the-art test builder that is easy to use. ExamView enables you to create paper-, LAN-, or Web-based tests from test banks designed specifically for your Course Technology textbook. Utilize the ultra-efficient QuickTest Wizard to create tests in less than five minutes by taking advantage of Course Technology's question banks, or customize your own exams from scratch.

DATA FILES FOR STUDENTS All the files that are required by students to complete the exercises are included. You can distribute the files on the Instructor Resources CD-ROM to your students over a network, or you can have them follow the instructions on the inside back cover of this book to obtain a copy of the Data Disk.

ADDITIONAL ACTIVITIES FOR STUDENTS These additional activities consist of Project Reinforcement Exercises, which are true/false, multiple choice, and short answer questions that help students gain confidence in the material learned.

Online Content

Course Technology offers textbook-based content for Blackboard, WebCT, and MyCourse 2.1.

BLACKBOARD AND WEBCT As the leading provider of IT content for the Blackboard and WebCT platforms, Course Technology delivers rich content that enhances your textbook to give your students a unique learning experience.

MYCOURSE 2.1 MyCourse 2.1 is Course Technology's powerful online course management and content delivery system. MyCourse 2.1 allows nontechnical users to create, customize, and deliver Web-based courses; post content and assignments; manage student enrollment; administer exams; track results in the online grade book; and more.

Acknowledgments

The Shelly Cashman Series would not be the leading computer education series without the contributions of outstanding publishing professionals. First, and foremost, among them is Becky Herrington, director of production and book designer. She is the heart and soul of the Shelly Cashman Series, and it is only through her leadership, dedication, and tireless efforts that superior products are made possible.

Under Becky's direction, the following individuals made significant contributions to these books: Deb Masi, production editor; Jennifer Quiambao, production assistant; Ken Russo, senior Web and graphic designer; Richard Herrera, cover designer; Kellee LaVars, Andrew Bartel, Phillip Hajjar, and Kenny Tran, graphic artists; Jeanne Black, Andrew Bartel, and Kellee LaVars, QuarkXPress compositors; Lyn Markowicz, copy editor; Nancy Lamm, proofreader; and Cristina Haley, indexer.

We also would like to thank Kristen Duerr, executive vice president and publisher; Cheryl Costantini, executive editor; Dana Merk, senior acquisitions editor; Alexandra Arnold, senior product manager; Jim Quasney, series consulting editor; Marc Ouellette and Heather McKinstry, online product managers; Reed Cotter, associate product manager; and Selena Coppock, editorial assistant.

Gary B. Shelly
Thomas J. Cashman
Joy L. Starks

MICROSOFT OFFICE PUBLISHER

MICROSOFT
Office Publisher 2003

MICROSOFT

Office Publisher 2003

Creating and Editing a Publication

PROJECT

1

CASE PERSPECTIVE

Metro University is an urban university with more than 20,000 students. It is located in the heart of the city, close to numerous businesses and Metro High School. Its population is diverse, and its campus is modern, including the latest technology and software and wireless Internet access on campus. The university services traditional students matriculating directly from the high school, students transferring from area community colleges, and others, including older students who are returning to school to finish a degree or those who desire to further their education by taking a few classes. Megan Rivera works in the financial aid office at Metro University. She is in charge of hiring student workers on campus. Megan matches the various departments that need help with students who want part-time work, usually 10 to 15 hours a week.

Megan knows of your interest in Microsoft Publisher and has asked you to design a flyer to advertise openings at the University Library. The library needs student workers with experience in word processing, desktop publishing, and office applications. She would like you to design a flyer that she can post around campus on bulletin boards, in the dormitories, and at the library.

Because of your experience with desktop publishing and the Web, you suggest to Megan that she also might want to post the flyer on the school's electronic bulletin board or send it to the student LISTSERV. Megan agrees. Together, you decide to use a Microsoft Publisher Sale Flyer with a strong bold heading, descriptive text, a sharp graphic, and tear-offs. Megan decides on a color scheme that uses one of Metro's school colors, light blue.

As you read through this project, you will learn how to use Publisher to create, save, and print a publication that includes text, a bulleted list, a graphic, and tear-offs.

Creating and Editing a Publication

PROJECT

1

Objectives

You will have mastered the material in this project when you can:

- Start and quit Publisher
- Describe the Publisher window
- Edit text and graphics
- Use the Best Fit feature to adjust font size
- Edit a synchronized object
- Replace a picture
- Resize and delete objects
- Correct spelling errors
- Save and print a publication
- Open a publication
- Convert to a Web publication and publish
- Use the Publisher Help system to answer questions

What Is Microsoft Office Publisher 2003?

Microsoft Office Publisher 2003 is a powerful desktop publishing (DTP) program that assists you in designing and producing professional, quality documents that combine text, graphics, illustrations, and photographs. DTP software provides additional tools over and above those typically found in word processing packages, including design templates, graphic manipulation tools, color schemes or libraries, advanced layout and printing tools, and multiple templates. For large jobs, businesses use DTP software to design publications that are camera ready, which means the files are suitable for outside commercial printing.

The publishing industry has undergone tremendous change in the past few years due to advancements in hardware and software technology. Books, magazines, and brochures used to be created by slower, more expensive methods such as typesetting — a process that had not changed fundamentally since the days of Gutenberg and his *Bible*. With desktop publishing software, you can create professional looking documents on your own computer and produce work that previously could be achieved only by graphic artists. Both cost and time are significantly decreased. Microsoft Publisher is becoming the choice of people who regularly produce high-quality color publications such as newsletters, flyers, logos, signs, and forms. Saving publications as Web pages or complete Web sites is a powerful feature in Publisher. All publications can be saved in a format that easily is viewed and manipulated using a browser. Some examples of these publications are shown in Figure 1-1.

FIGURE 1-1

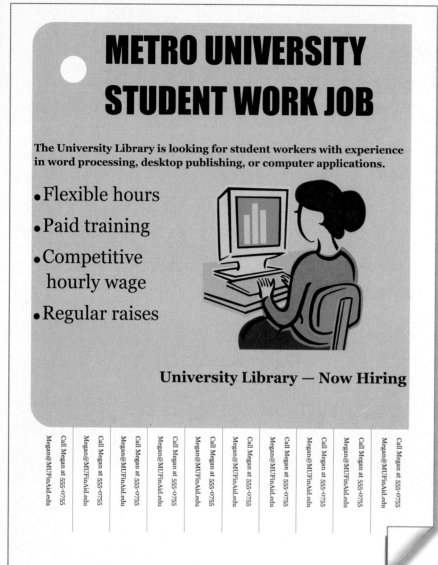

METRO UNIVERSITY STUDENT WORK JOB

The University Library is looking for student workers with experience in word processing, desktop publishing, or computer applications.

- Flexible hours
- Paid training
- Competitive hourly wage
- Regular raises

University Library — Now Hiring

Call Megan at 555-0755 Megan@MUFinAid.edu
Call Megan at 555-0755 Megan@MUFinAid.edu
Call Megan at 555-0755 Megan@MUFinAid.edu
Call Megan at 555-0755 Megan@MUFinAid.edu
Call Megan at 555-0755 Megan@MUFinAid.edu
Call Megan at 555-0755 Megan@MUFinAid.edu
Call Megan at 555-0755 Megan@MUFinAid.edu
Call Megan at 555-0755 Megan@MUFinAid.edu
Call Megan at 555-0755 Megan@MUFinAid.edu
Call Megan at 555-0755 Megan@MUFinAid.edu
Call Megan at 555-0755 Megan@MUFinAid.edu
Call Megan at 555-0755 Megan@MUFinAid.edu

FIGURE 1-2

Project One — Student Work Job Flyer

To illustrate the features of Microsoft Publisher 2003, this book presents a series of projects that use Publisher to create publications similar to those you will encounter in academic and business environments. Project 1 uses Publisher to produce the flyer shown in Figure 1-2. The flyer advertises a student work job opening at the University Library. The heading, METRO UNIVERSITY STUDENT WORK JOB, is designed to draw attention to the flyer, as is the bulleted list describing the job benefits. An eye-catching graphic of a person working at a computer is on the right. Text below the heading explains where the job is located and what kind of experience applicants should have. Finally, in the lower portion of the flyer, is a set of tear-offs with a contact person's name, telephone number, and e-mail address.

Designing an Effective Flyer

A good flyer, or any publication, must deliver a message in the clearest, most attractive, and effective way possible. You must clarify your purpose and know your target audience. You need to gather ideas and plan for the printing of the flyer. Finally, you must edit, proofread, and then publish your flyer.

Table 1-1 outlines the issues to consider during the design process and their application to flyers.

Table 1-1 Design Process

DESIGN ISSUE	FLYER APPLICATION
Purpose	To communicate a single concept, notion, or product in a quick, easy-to read format
Audience	Wide, non-specific audience
Gather data	Content for heading, bulleted list, tear-offs, other text boxes
Plan for printing	Color or black and white; number of copies varies greatly
Layout	Single page with perforated tear-offs
Synthesis	Edit, proofread, and publish both print and Web publications

Starting and Customizing Publisher

If you are stepping through this project on a computer and you want your screen to match the figures in this book, then you should change your computer's resolution to 800 × 600. For more information about how to change the resolution on your computer, read Appendix D.

    To start Publisher, Windows must be running. The following steps show how to start Publisher. You may need to ask your instructor how to start Publisher on your system.

More About

Publisher 2003

For more information about the features of Microsoft 2003, visit the Publisher 2003 More About Web page (scsite.com/ pub2003/more) and click Microsoft Publisher 2003 Features.

To Start Publisher

1

• **Click the Start button on the Windows taskbar, point to All Programs on the Start menu, point to Microsoft Office on the All Programs submenu, and then point to Microsoft Office Publisher 2003 on the Microsoft Office submenu.**

Windows displays the commands on the Start menu above the Start button and displays the All Programs and Microsoft Office submenus (Figure 1-3).

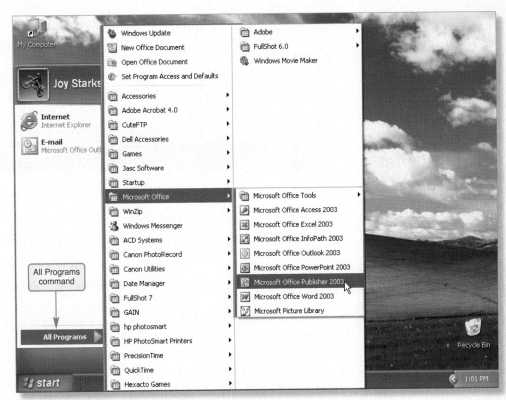

FIGURE 1-3

2

• **Click Microsoft Office Publisher 2003.**

Publisher starts. After a few moments, Publisher displays the Start window and the New Publication task pane (Figure 1-4). The Windows taskbar displays the Publisher program button, indicating Publisher is running.

3

• **If the Publisher window is not maximized, double-click its title bar to maximize it.**

• **If your system displays a different task pane, click the Other Task Panes button and click New Publication in the list.**

Other Ways

1. Double-click Publisher icon on desktop
2. Click Microsoft Office Publisher 2003 on Start menu
3. Click Start button, point to All Programs on Start menu, click New Office Document, click General tab, double-click Blank Document icon

FIGURE 1-4

The screen in Figure 1-4 shows how the Publisher window looks the first time you start Publisher after installation on most computers. As shown, Publisher displays a task pane on the left side of the screen. A **task pane** is a separate window that enables users to carry out some Publisher tasks more efficiently. When you start Publisher, it displays the New Publication task pane, which provides commonly used links and commands that allow you to open new files from design templates, create new files, or open previously created publications.

If the Office Speech Recognition software is installed and active on your computer, the Language bar is displayed on the screen when you start Publisher. The **Language bar** allows you to speak commands and dictate text. It usually is located on the right side of the Windows taskbar next to the notification area, and changes to include the speech recognition functions available in Publisher. In this book, the Language bar is closed because it takes up computer resources. Also, with the Language bar active, the microphone can be turned on accidentally, which can cause your computer to act in an unstable manner. For additional information about the Language bar, see page PUB 21 and Appendix B.

At startup, Publisher sometimes displays multiple toolbars on a single row. Other toolbars also may be displayed. To allow for more efficient use of the buttons, the most commonly used toolbars should be displayed on two separate rows, instead of sharing a single row. The following steps show how to close the Language bar, close extra toolbars, and instruct Publisher to display the commonly used toolbars on two separate rows.

To Customize the Publisher Window

1

• **If the Language bar shows and it indicates that the microphone is on, click the Microphone button to turn it off.**

• **To close the Language bar, right-click it to display a list of commands.**

The Language bar shortcut menu is displayed (Figure 1-5).

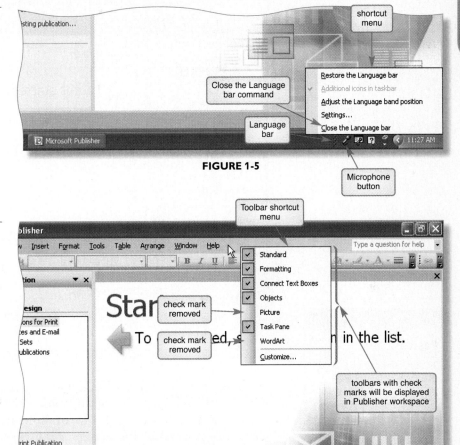

FIGURE 1-5

2

• **Click Close the Language bar.**

• **If Publisher displays a Language Bar dialog box, click its OK button.**

• **Right-click any of the toolbars.**

• **When Publisher displays the shortcut menu, if the Picture command displays a check mark, click Picture.**

• **If the WordArt command displays a check mark, click WordArt.**

The Language bar no longer is displayed. Check marks indicate which toolbars will be displayed in the Publisher window (Figure 1-6).

FIGURE 1-6

3

• **If the toolbars are positioned on the same row, click the Toolbar Options button. If your installation of Publisher already displays the toolbars on two rows, you may skip Steps 3 and 4.**

Publisher displays the Toolbar Options list showing the buttons that do not fit on the toolbars when toolbars are positioned on one row (Figure 1-7).

FIGURE 1-7

4

• **Click Show Buttons on Two Rows.**

Publisher displays the toolbars on two separate rows (Figure 1-8).

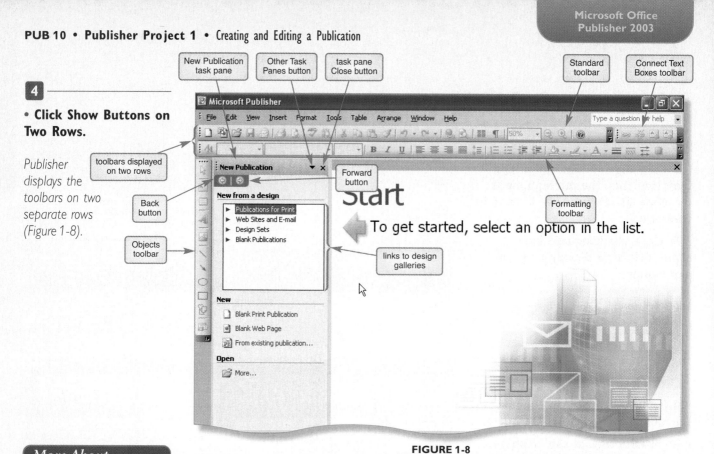

FIGURE 1-8

As an alternative to Steps 3 and 4 above, you can point to the left edge of the second toolbar, and when the mouse pointer changes to a four-headed arrow, drag the toolbar down to create two rows of toolbars.

Each time you start Publisher, the Publisher window is displayed the same way it was the last time you used Publisher. If the toolbar buttons are displayed on one row, then they will be displayed on one row the next time you start Publisher. Typically, three toolbars are displayed on two rows when you first install Publisher: the Standard toolbar, the Connect Text Boxes toolbar, and the Formatting toolbar. These toolbars are discussed later in this project. The Objects toolbar is displayed on the left. You can display or hide toolbars by right-clicking any toolbar and clicking the appropriate check boxes, or by clicking Toolbars on the View menu.

As you work through creating a publication, you will find that other toolbars will be displayed automatically as they are needed in order to edit particular types of objects in Publisher.

When you first start Publisher, the New Publication task pane usually is displayed (Figure 1-8). If it is not displayed, click Options on the Tools menu, and then click Use New Publication task pane at startup in the General sheet.

Additionally, certain Publisher operations will cause other task panes to be displayed. Publisher provides more than 20 additional task panes, in addition to the New Publication task pane shown in Figure 1-8. Some of the more important ones are the Help, Publication Designs, Clipboard, and Clip Art task panes. Throughout the book, these task panes are discussed when they are used.

At any point while working with Publisher, you can open or close a task pane by clicking the Task Pane command on the View menu. You can activate additional task panes by clicking the Other Task Panes button to the left of the Close button on the task pane title bar (Figure 1-8) and then selecting a task pane in the Other Task Panes list. The Back and Forward buttons below the task pane title bar allow you to switch between task panes that you opened during a session.

Creating a Publication

Publisher provides many ways to begin the process of creating a publication. You can:

- Create a new publication from a design
- Create a new publication from a blank publication or Web page
- Create a new publication based on an existing one
- Open an existing publication

Choosing the appropriate method depends upon your experience with desktop publishing and how you have used Publisher in the past. In this first project, as you are beginning to learn about the features of Publisher, a series of steps is presented to create a publication using a design template.

Because composing and designing from scratch is a difficult process for many people, Publisher provides templates to assist in publication preparation. Publisher has more than 2,000 templates to create professionally designed and unique publications. A **template** is a tool that helps you through the design process by offering you publication options and changing your publication accordingly. A template is similar to a blueprint you can use over and over, filling in the blanks, replacing prewritten text as necessary, and changing the art to fit your needs.

Using the New Publication Task Pane

The New Publication task pane displays links to four design galleries in the New from a design area (Figure 1-8):

- Publications for Print
- Web Sites and E-mail
- Design Sets
- Blank Publications

A **gallery** is a collection of publication templates organized by type. As you click a design gallery link in the task pane, the list of publication types expands, and **previews** of the templates are displayed on the right side of the Publisher window, alphabetically (Figure 1-9 on the next page). The gallery previews change based on your choices in the task pane.

Once you choose a publication from the gallery, the task pane will allow you to make choices about the color and font schemes. A **color scheme** is a defined set of colors that complement each other when used in the same publication. Each Publisher color scheme provides a main color and four accent colors. A **font scheme** is a defined set of fonts associated with a publication. A **font**, or typeface, defines the appearance and shape of the letters, numbers, and special characters. For example, a font scheme might be made up of one font for headings, one for body text, and another for captions. Font schemes make it easy to change all the fonts in a publication to give it a new look. Within each font scheme, both a major font and a minor font are specified. Generally, a major font is used for titles and headings, and a minor font is used for body text.

The steps on the next page show how to create a publication using a template from the design gallery.

More About

Templates

For more information about templates, visit the Publisher 2003 More About Web page (scsite.com/pub2003/more) and click Templates.

More About

Maximizing the Publisher Window

The number of previews you see in the gallery (Figure 1-9) may vary depending on the resolution and the size of your window. To make sure you see as many previews as possible, maximize the Publisher window by double-clicking the title bar, or by clicking the Maximize button on the title bar.

To Create a Publication Using a Template

1

• **In the New Publication task pane, click Publications for Print.**

The Quick Publications gallery is displayed on the right (Figure 1-9).

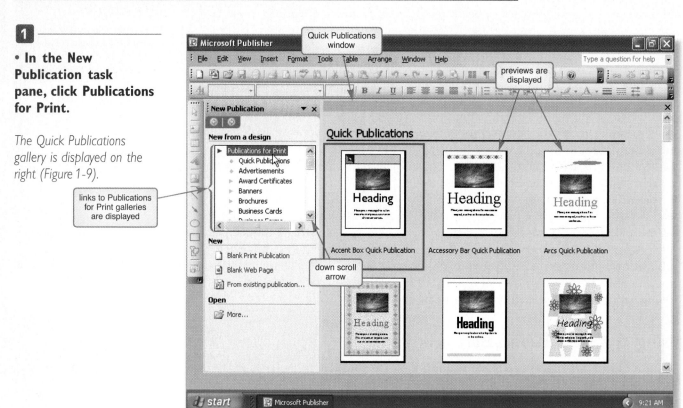

FIGURE 1-9

2

• **Click the down scroll arrow in the New from a design list until Flyers is displayed in the list.**

• **Click Flyers.**

• **When the types of Flyers are displayed, click Sale in the list.**

Publisher displays the Sale Flyers gallery on the right (Figure 1-10). Each category of publication type displays a unique publication gallery.

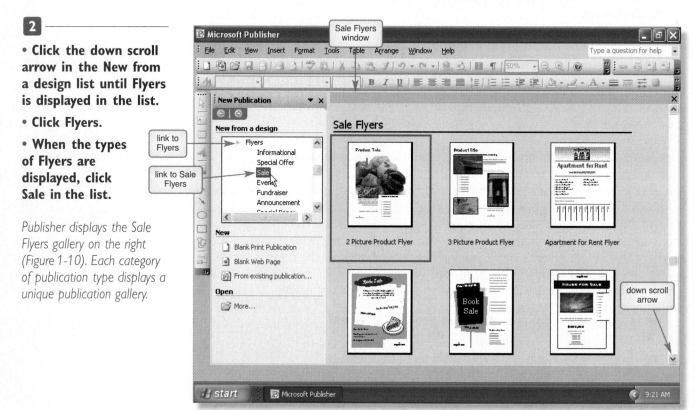

FIGURE 1-10

3

• **Click the down scroll arrow in the gallery until For Sale Flyer 2 is displayed.**

• **Point to the For Sale Flyer 2 preview.**

The For Sale Flyer 2 is displayed (Figure 1-11). Publisher displays a blue box around the flyer as you point to it.

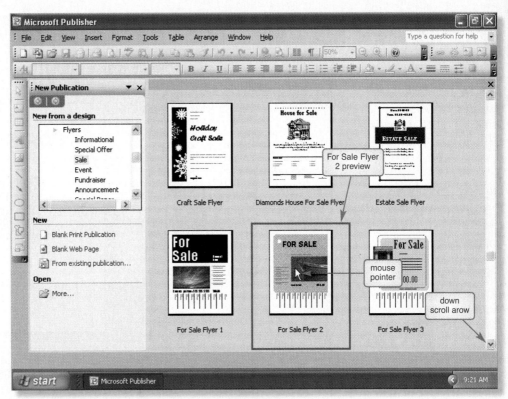

FIGURE 1-11

4

• **Click the For Sale Flyer 2.**

• **If Publisher displays a Personal Information dialog box, click its Close button.**

The gallery window closes, and the flyer is displayed in the Publisher workspace (Figure 1-12). The task pane changes to reflect the current publication's options. The Flyer Options task pane displays links to Publication Designs, Color Schemes, and Font Schemes, as well as options to display the publication with and without a Graphic, a Customer address, and Tear-offs.

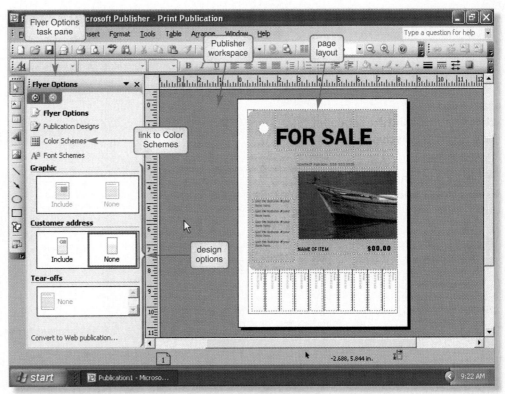

FIGURE 1-12

5

• **Click Color Schemes in the Flyer Options task pane.**

• **When the task pane changes to Color Schemes, click Aqua in the Apply a color scheme list.**

*The Color Schemes task pane appears with a list of color schemes (Figure 1-13). Each color scheme uses colors that complement one another. The **main color** is displayed to the left, and the four **accent colors** are displayed to its right. The Aqua color scheme is applied to the flyer.*

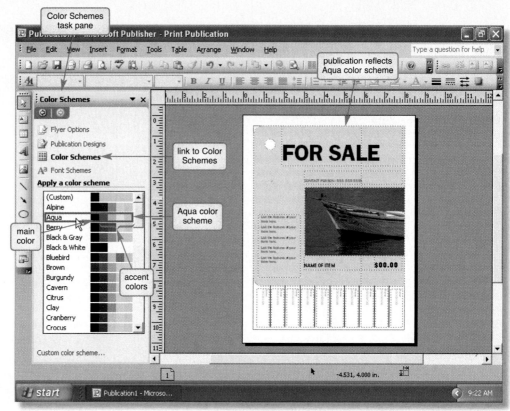

FIGURE 1-13

6

• **Click Font Schemes in the Color Schemes task pane.**

• **When the task pane changes to Font Schemes, scroll until the Impact font scheme is displayed.**

• **Click Impact in the Apply a font scheme list.**

A ScreenTip appears with the name of the scheme, as well as the names of the major and minor fonts used in the scheme (Figure 1-14). The Impact font scheme is applied to the flyer.

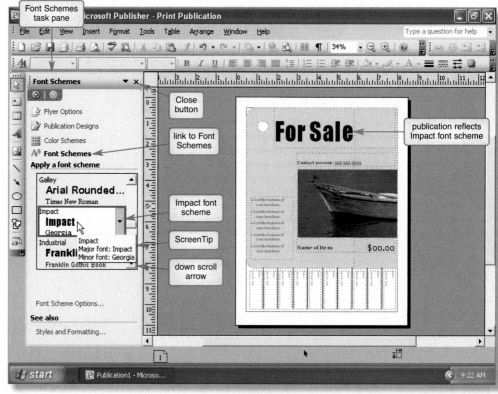

FIGURE 1-14

7

• **Click the Close button in the Font Schemes task pane.**

The task pane closes, and the publication, ready to edit, is displayed in the Publisher workspace (Figure 1-15).

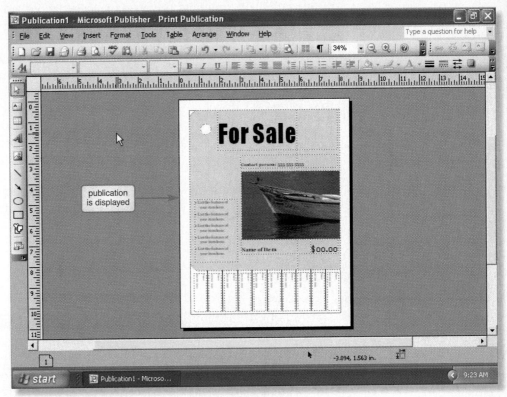

FIGURE 1-15

The **Flyer Options task pane** displays its option links in the upper portion of the task pane and design choices in the lower portion (Figure 1-12 on page PUB 13). Each publication design will differ slightly in its options. The Publication Designs option offers you the ability to apply a different design from the gallery. Publication options can be revisited at any time during the design process by clicking the option in the task pane. If the task pane does not display, click Task Pane on the View menu.

The Publisher Window

The Publisher window consists of a variety of components to make your work more efficient and your publication more professional. The following sections discuss these components, which are identified in either Figures 1-16 or 1-17 on the next page.

The Workspace

The **workspace** contains several elements similar to the document windows in other applications, as well as some elements unique to Publisher. As you create a publication, the page layout, rulers, scroll bars, guides and boundaries, and objects are displayed in the gray workspace (Figure 1-16).

PAGE LAYOUT The **page layout** contains a view of the publication, all the objects contained therein, plus the guides and boundaries for the page and its objects. The page layout can be changed to accommodate multi-page spreads. You also can use the Special Paper command to view your page layout, as it will be printed on special paper, or see the final copy after preparing your publication for a printing service.

RULERS Two rulers outline the workspace at the top and left. A **ruler** is used to measure and place objects on the page. Although the vertical and horizontal rulers display at the left and top of the workspace, they can be moved and placed anywhere you need them. You use the rulers to measure and align objects on the page, set tab stops, adjust text frames, and change margins. Additionally, the rulers can be hidden to show more of the workspace. You will learn more about rulers in a later project.

FIGURE 1-16

SCROLL BARS By using **scroll bars**, you display different portions of your publication in the workspace. At the right edge of the publication window is a vertical scroll bar. At the bottom of the publication window is a horizontal scroll bar. On both the vertical and horizontal scroll bars, the position of the **scroll box** reflects the location of the portion of the publication that is displayed in the publication window.

BOUNDARIES AND GUIDES Publisher's page layout displays the boundaries and guides of the page and its objects. Aligning design elements in relation to each other, both vertically and horizontally, is a tedious task. **Layout guides** create a grid that

More About

The Rulers

If the rulers are not displayed on your screen, click View on the menu bar and click Rulers. To hide the rulers, also click View on the menu bar and click Rulers.

repeats on each page of a publication (Figure 1-17). They define sections of the page and help you align elements with precision. Page **margin guides** are displayed in pink. **Grid guides**, which are displayed in blue, assist you in organizing text pictures and objects into columns and rows to give a consistent look to your publication.

FIGURE 1-17

Boundaries are the gray lines surrounding an object. Boundaries are useful when you want to move or resize objects on the page. Boundaries and guides can be turned on and off using the View menu.

OBJECTS **Objects** include anything you want to place in your publication, such as text, WordArt, tear-offs, graphics, pictures, bullets, lines, and Web tools. You can choose objects from the Objects toolbar, from the Design Gallery, or insert them from original material. You click an object on the page to **select** it; selected objects are displayed with **handles**, at each corner and middle location of the object boundary. Many objects also display a green rotation handle connected to the top of the object or a yellow adjustment handle used to change the shape of some objects. A selected object can be resized, rotated, moved, deleted, or grouped as necessary. To select an object such as a picture, click the picture. The entire object is selected automatically. If you want to select a text box, however, you must click the boundary of the text box rather than the text inside. You will learn more about object manipulation later in the project.

STATUS BAR Immediately above the Windows taskbar at the bottom of the Publisher window is the status bar. In Publisher, the **status bar** contains the page sorter, the Object Position box, and the Object Size box (Figure 1-17). The **page sorter** displays a button for each page of your publication. The current page in a multi-page document will display selected in blue in the page sorter. You may click any page to display it in the workspace or right-click to display the page sorter shortcut menu.

As an alternative to using the rulers, you can use the **Object Position** and **Object Size** boxes as guidelines for lining up objects from the left and top margins. The exact position and size of a selected object is displayed in inches as you create or move it. You may choose to have the measurement displayed in pica, points, or centimeters. If no object is selected, the Object Position box displays the location of the mouse pointer. Double-clicking the status bar will display the Measurements toolbar. You will learn more about the Measurements toolbar in a future project.

Q & A

Q: How do I display a shortcut menu?

A: Right-clicking an object displays a shortcut menu (also called a context-sensitive or object menu). Depending on the object, the commands in the shortcut menu vary.

More About

The Publisher Help System

Need Help? It is no further away than the Type a question for help box on the menu bar in the upper-right corner of the window. Click the box that contains the text, Type a question for help, type help, and then press the ENTER key. Publisher responds with a list of topics you can click to learn about obtaining help on any Publisher-related topic. To find out what is new in Publisher 2003, type what is new in Publisher in the Type a question for help box.

Menu Bar and Toolbars

Publisher displays the menu bar at the top of the screen just below the title bar. The toolbars display below the menu bar and down the left side of the Publisher window (Figure 1-18).

FIGURE 1-18

MENU BAR The **menu bar** is a special toolbar displaying at the top of the window, just below the Publisher title bar (Figure 1-18). The menu bar lists the menu names. When you point to a **menu name** on the menu bar, the area of the menu bar containing the name displays a button. Publisher shades selected buttons in light orange and surrounds them with a blue outline.

When you click a menu name, Publisher displays a menu. A **menu** contains a list of commands that you can use to retrieve, store, print, and manipulate data in the publication. To display a menu, such as the Edit menu, click the Edit menu name on the menu bar. If you point to a command with an arrow to its right, a **submenu** is displayed from which you can choose a command. An ellipsis (…) denotes that Publisher will display a dialog box when you click that menu command. **Keyboard shortcuts**, when available, are displayed to the right of menu commands.

When you click a menu name on the menu bar, Publisher displays a **short menu** listing the most recently used commands (Figure 1-19a). If you wait a few seconds or click the arrows at the bottom of the short menu, the full menu displays. The **full menu** lists all the commands associated with a menu (Figure 1-19b). You also can display a full menu immediately by double-clicking the menu name on the menu bar.

In this book, when you display a menu, always display the full menu using one of the following techniques.

1. Click the menu name on the menu bar and then wait a few seconds.
2. Click the menu name and then point to or click the arrows at the bottom of the short menu.
3. Double-click the menu name.
4. In Voice Command mode, say the name of the menu and then wait a few seconds.

Both short and full menus display some dimmed commands. A **dimmed command** displays gray, or dimmed, instead of black, which indicates it is not available for the current selection. A command with medium blue shading in the rectangle to the left of it on a full menu is called a **hidden command** because it does not display on a short menu. As you use Publisher, it automatically personalizes the short

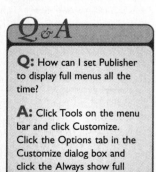

menus for you based on how often you use commands. That is, as you use hidden commands on the full menu, Publisher unhides them and places them on the short menu. You can reset the menus to their original configuration by clicking Customize on the Tools menu, and then clicking the Reset My Usage Data button in the Options sheet. The process is described in greater detail in Appendix D.

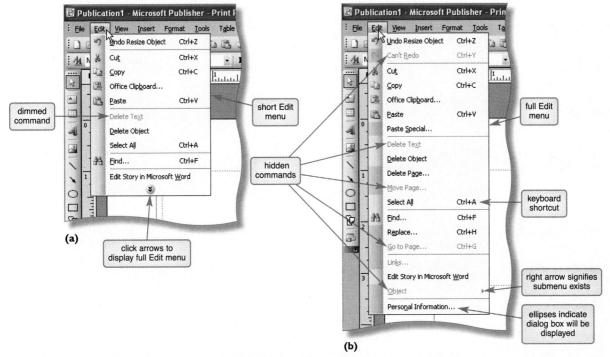

FIGURE 1-19

TOOLBARS **Toolbars** contain buttons and boxes that allow you to perform frequent tasks more quickly than when using the menu bar. For example, to print a publication, you can click the Print button on a toolbar instead of navigating through the File menu to reach the Print command.

Each button on a toolbar has a picture on its face that helps you remember its function. In addition, when you move the mouse pointer over a button or box, the name of the button or box displays below it in a **ScreenTip**. Each button and box is explained in detail as it is used in the projects.

The **Standard toolbar** (Figure 1-20a on the next page) is displayed just below the menu bar. The **Connect Text Boxes toolbar** (Figure 1-20b) is displayed to the right of the Standard toolbar. Immediately below the Standard toolbar is the **Formatting toolbar** (Figure 1-20c). The Formatting toolbar **enables**, or turns on, different buttons depending on the type of object you select. The toolbar changes when you click the object. For instance, in Figure 1-18, the selected text box displays a Formatting toolbar with font options, whereas a graphic object, such as a picture, will not. The **Objects toolbar** (Figure 1-20d) displays on the left edge of the Publisher window and contains buttons for each category of objects you can add to a publication. Additional toolbars, such as the Measurements toolbar, the Picture toolbar, and WordArt toolbar are object-specific, which means they are displayed only when you use that specific type of object. You will learn about other toolbars in future projects. If you do not see a toolbar in the window, click Toolbars on the View menu and then click the name of the toolbar you want to be displayed.

FIGURE 1-20

(a) Standard Toolbar

(b) Connect Text Boxes Toolbar

(c) Formatting Toolbar

(d) Objects Toolbar

More About

Toolbar Buttons

If you have difficulty seeing the small buttons on the toolbars, you can increase their size. Click View on the menu bar, point to Toolbars, click Customize on the Toolbars submenu, click the Options tab, place a check mark in the Large icons check box, and click the Close button.

The Standard and Connect Text Boxes toolbars are preset to display on one row, immediately below the menu bar. The Formatting toolbar is displayed below that (Figure 1-18 on the previous page). Unless the resolution of your display device is greater than 800 × 600, some of the buttons that belong on these toolbars do not display. Use the **Toolbar Options button** to display these hidden buttons (Figure 1-21). If more than one toolbar is displayed on a single row, you can double-click the **move handle** on the left of each toolbar to display more buttons.

FIGURE 1-21

The toolbars initially are displayed **docked**, or attached, to the edge of the Publisher window. Additional toolbars may be displayed either stacked below the Formatting toolbar or floating in the Publisher window. A **floating toolbar** is not attached to an edge of the Publisher window. You can rearrange the order of **docked toolbars** and can move floating toolbars anywhere in the Publisher window by dragging the move handle to the desired location.

Resetting Menus and Toolbars

Each project in this book begins with the menus and toolbars displaying as they did at the initial installation of the software. If you are stepping through this project on a computer and you want your menus and toolbars to match the figures in this book, then you should reset your menus and toolbars. For more information about how to reset menus and toolbars, read Appendix D.

Speech Recognition

With the **Office Speech Recognition software** installed and a microphone, you can speak the names of toolbar buttons, menus, menu commands, list items, alerts, and dialog box controls, such as OK and Cancel. You also can dictate text and numeric entries. To indicate whether you want to speak commands or dictate entries, you use the Language bar.

The Language bar can be in one of four states: (1) **restored**, which means it is displayed somewhere in the Publisher window (Figure 1-22a); (2) **minimized**, which means it is displayed on the Windows taskbar (Figure 1-22b); (3) **hidden**, which means you do not see it on the screen but it will be displayed the next time you start your computer; (4) **closed**, which means it is hidden permanently until you enable it. If the Language bar is hidden or closed and you want it to be displayed, then do the following:

1. Right-click an open area on the Windows taskbar at the bottom of the screen.
2. Point to Toolbars and then click Language bar on the Toolbars submenu.

More About

Speech Recognition

If Office Speech Recognition software is installed on your computer, you can speak instructions to Publisher including toolbar button names, menu names and commands, and items in dialog boxes and task panes. You also can dictate so Publisher writes exactly what you say. The microphone picks up others' voices and background sounds, so speech recognition is most effective when used in a quiet environment.

(a) **Language Bar in Publisher Window with Microphone Enabled**

(b) **Language Bar Minimized on Windows Taskbar**

FIGURE 1-22

If the Language bar command is dimmed on the Toolbars submenu or if the Speech command is dimmed on the Tools menu, the Office Speech Recognition software is not installed.

In this book, the Language bar is not displayed in the figures. If you want to close the Language bar so your screen is identical to what you see in the book, right-click the Language bar and then click Close the Language bar on the shortcut menu. Additional information on Office Speech Recognition is available in Appendix B.

Microsoft Office
Publisher 2003

Entering Text

Most of the templates in the design galleries come with text already inserted into text boxes. A **text box** is an object in a publication designed to hold text in a specific shape, size, and style. Text boxes also can be drawn on the page using the **Text Box button** on the Objects toolbar. Text boxes can be formatted from the menu, on the Formatting toolbar, or on the shortcut menu displayed by right-clicking the text box.

To enter text into a text box you can type on the keyboard or speak into the microphone. To replace **placeholder text**, or text supplied by the template, you click the placeholder text and then enter the new text.

A text box has changeable properties. A **property** is an attribute or characteristic of an object. Within text boxes, you can **edit**, or make changes to, the following properties: font, spacing, alignment, fill color, and margins, among others.

Zooming

Sometimes the size of the text box or other Publisher object is small and, therefore, difficult to edit. Publisher provides several ways to **zoom in**, or increase the magnification of an object, to facilitate viewing and editing.

Table 1-2 shows several zoom methods.

Editing small areas of text is easier if you use zooming techniques to enlarge the view of the publication. When viewing an entire printed page, 8½-by-11 inches, the magnification is approximately 34%, which makes reading the small text difficult. You may press the F9 key to enlarge selected objects to 100% magnification. Pressing the F9 key a second time returns the layout to its previous magnification. Publisher also allows you to zoom using the **Zoom box** on the Standard toolbar (Figure 1-23). Clicking the Zoom box arrow displays a list of magnifications, such as Whole Page, Page Width, and various magnifications. Whole Page displays the complete page layout at approximately 34%. Page Width displays at approximately 86%, filling the workspace. Additionally, the **Zoom In button** on the Standard toolbar allows you to increase magnification. If you click an object before zooming in, Publisher displays the selected object magnified, in the center of the workspace, when you zoom.

Table 1-2 Zoom Methods

NUMBER	METHOD	RESULT
1	Press the F9 key on the keyboard.	Selected object is displayed centered in the workspace at 100% magnification.
2	Click the Zoom box arrow on the Standard toolbar. Click desired magnification.	Objects are displayed at selected magnification.
3	Click the Zoom In button on the Standard toolbar.	Objects display at increased magnification.
4	Right-click object, point to Zoom on shortcut menu, click desired magnification.	Objects display at selected magnification.
5	On View menu, point to Zoom, click desired magnification.	Objects display at selected magnification.
6	Using a microphone, say "Zoom in."	Objects display at increased magnification.

Editing Publisher Text Boxes

The next series of steps show how to edit the placeholder text in the heading, sub-heading, the bulleted list, the tear-offs, and other text boxes. Flyers typically display a **heading**, or title, in the upper portion of the page layout using the major font from the font scheme. A heading is designed to identify, with just a few words, the purpose of the flyer and to draw attention to the flyer.

Each text entry in a bulleted list is preceded by a **bullet** which is a dot or other symbol that is placed before the text to add emphasis. A bulleted list identifies key elements related to the publication in an easy to read format. When editing a bulleted list, each time you press the ENTER key, a bullet displays at the beginning of the next line or paragraph.

Tear-offs are small, ready-to-be scored text boxes with some combination of name, telephone, fax, e-mail, or address. Designed for customer use, tear-offs typically are perforated so a person walking by can tear off a tab to keep, rather than having to stop, find a pen and paper, and write down the name and telephone number. Traditionally, small businesses or individuals wanting to advertise something locally used tear-offs; but more recently, large companies are mass-producing advertising flyers with tear-offs to post at shopping centers, display in offices, and advertise on college campuses. Publisher tear-offs are **synchronized**, which means when you finish editing one of the tear-off text boxes, the others change to match it automatically. You may undo synchronization by clicking the Undo button on the Standard toolbar.

The following steps illustrate how to edit placeholder text.

To Edit Placeholder Text

1

• **Click For Sale in the heading of the flyer.**

• **If your page layout is not centered in the workspace, you may drag the horizontal scroll box at the bottom of the workspace.**

The text box is displayed with its text selected (Figure 1-23). Handles indicate the object can be resized. Publisher displays a ScreenTip immediately below the object.

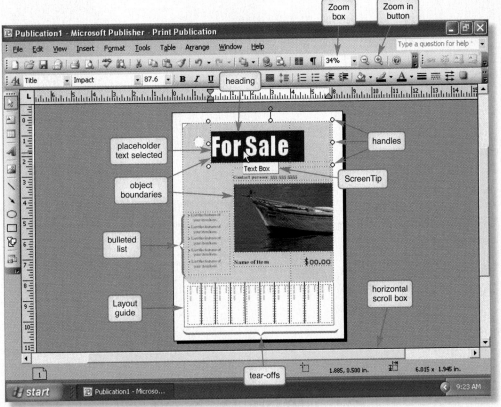

FIGURE 1-23

2

• **Type** METRO UNIVERSITY STUDENT WORK JOB **in the text box.**

The selected text is replaced automatically (Figure 1-24). Publisher automatically resizes the text so it fits into the allotted amount of space. The Impact major font from the font scheme is used for the text. The font size has been reduced to accommodate the new, longer phrase.

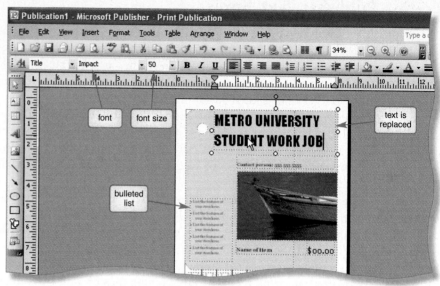

FIGURE 1-24

3

• **Click the bulleted list on the left side of the flyer to select it and then press the F9 key to zoom in on the object.**

The selected bulleted list is displayed at 100% magnification in the middle of the screen (Figure 1-25).

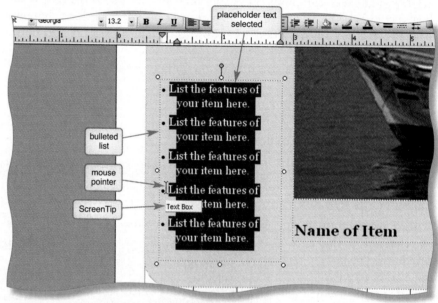

FIGURE 1-25

4

• **Type** Flexible hours **in the text box.**

The new text displays in a bulleted format (Figure 1-26). The minor font displays in the Font box on the Formatting toolbar.

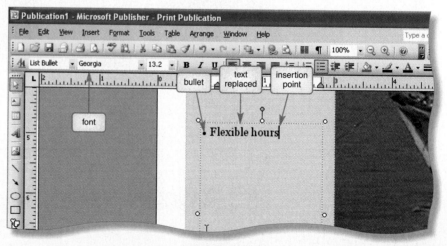

FIGURE 1-26

5

• **Press the ENTER key.**

• **Enter the remaining lines of text from Figure 1-27.**

The bulleted list is complete.

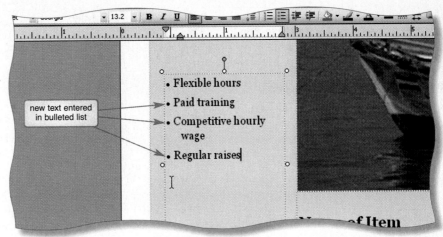

FIGURE 1-27

6

• **Click the Zoom box arrow on the Standard toolbar.**

The Zoom list is displayed (Figure 1-28).

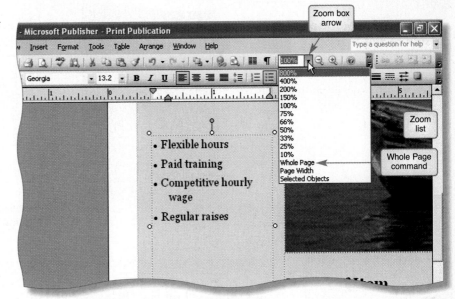

FIGURE 1-28

7

• **Click Whole Page in the Zoom list.**

• **Click the text in the first tear-off text box on the left to select it.**

The placeholder text in the tear-off is selected (Figure 1-29).

FIGURE 1-29

8

• **Press the F9 key to increase the magnification.**

• **Type** Call Megan at 555-0755 **and then press the ENTER key.**

• **Type** Megan@MUFinAid.edu **to enter the e-mail address.**

The new text appears in the first tear-off (Figure 1-30).

FIGURE 1-30

9

• **Click the gray workspace area, outside of the tear-offs.**

The other tear-off text boxes synchronize and display the newly edited text (Figure 1-31).

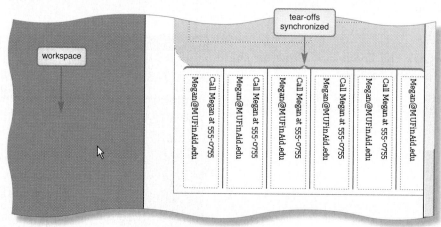

FIGURE 1-31

In Figure 1-24 on page PUB 24, the font size is 50. **Font size** specifies the size of the characters and is determined by a measurement system called points. A single **point** is about 1/72 of one inch in height. Thus, a character with a font size of 12 is about 12/72 or 1/6 of one inch in height.

As you type to replace placeholder text, Publisher will change the font size and wrap the text. **Wordwrap** allows you to type words continually without pressing the ENTER key at the end of each line. When the insertion point reaches the right side of the text box, Publisher automatically positions the insertion point at the beginning of the next line. As you type, if a word extends beyond the right margin, Publisher also automatically positions that word on the next line with the insertion point.

Deleting Objects

Recall that a Publisher object includes anything you want to place in your publication, such as text boxes, graphics, or shapes. Sometimes you may want to **delete**, or permanently remove, an object. In order to delete an object, the object must be selected.

Publisher provides four different ways to delete an object:

- Right-click the object and click Delete Object on the shortcut menu.
- Select the object and click Delete Object on the Edit menu.

- Select the object (not the text inside) and press the DELETE key.
- Select the object and click the Cut button on the Standard toolbar.

Deleting Objects in the Flyer

The text box below the graphic that displays a dollar amount is unnecessary in this flyer. Therefore, you will delete it.

The following steps show how to delete an object using the shortcut menu.

Q&A

Q: How do I delete multiple objects?

A: Click an object, SHIFT-click subsequent objects, and then press the DELETE key.

To Delete an Object

1

• **Right-click anywhere in the Publisher workspace and then point to Zoom on the shortcut menu.**

The Zoom submenu appears with magnification choices (Figure 1-32).

FIGURE 1-32

2

• **Click Whole Page on the Zoom submenu.**

• **When the entire page layout is displayed, right-click the dollar amount text box below the graphic.**

A shortcut menu appropriate for text box editing is displayed (Figure 1-33). Shortcut menus vary depending upon the selected object.

3

• **Click Delete Object on the shortcut menu.**

The text box is deleted.

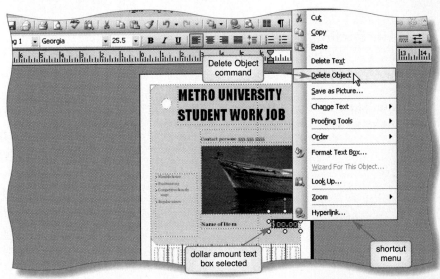

FIGURE 1-33

Other Ways

1. On Edit menu, click Delete Object
2. Press DELETE key
3. On Standard toolbar, click Cut button

More About

Flagged Words

Recall that the commands on a shortcut menu differ depending on the object. If you select a word and then right-click it, you can cut, copy, or paste the word from the shortcut menu; however, if the selected word has a red wavy underline below it, you can only spell check it from the shortcut menu.

More About

Correcting Spelling

As you type, Publisher automatically corrects some misspelled words. For example, if you type recieve, Publisher automatically fixes the misspelling and displays the word, receive, when you press the SPACEBAR or type a punctuation mark. To see a complete list of automatically corrected words, click Tools on the menu bar, click AutoCorrect Options, click the AutoCorrect tab, and scroll through the list of words near the bottom of the dialog box.

If you delete an object accidentally, you can click the Undo button on the Standard toolbar to retrieve it. Or, if you used the Cut button, you can click the Paste button to retrieve the deleted object.

You delete text in a similar manner to deleting an object. First you select the text, and then you can use the Delete Text command on a menu, the DELETE key on the keyboard, or the Cut button on the Standard toolbar.

Checking Spelling as You Type

As you type text in a publication, Publisher checks your typing for possible spelling and grammar errors. If a word you type is not in the dictionary, a red wavy underline is displayed below the word. Similarly, if text you type contains a possible grammar error, a green wavy underline is displayed below the text. Although you can check the entire document for spelling and grammar errors at once, you also can check these flagged errors immediately.

To verify that the Check spelling as you type feature is enabled, point to Spelling on the Tools menu, then click Spelling Options on the Spelling submenu. If a check mark does not display beside Check spelling as you type, click the check box.

When a word is flagged with a red wavy underline, it is not in Publisher's dictionary. To display a list of suggested corrections for a flagged word, you right-click the word. A flagged word, however, is not necessarily misspelled. For example, many names, abbreviations, and specialized terms are not in Publisher's main dictionary. In these cases, you tell Publisher to ignore the flagged word. As you type, Publisher also detects duplicate words. For example, if your document contains the phrase, to the the store, Publisher places a red wavy underline below the second occurrence of the word, the.

In the following example, the word, library, has been misspelled intentionally as libray to illustrate Publisher's Check spelling as you type feature. If you are completing this project on a personal computer, your flyer may contain different misspelled words, depending on the accuracy of your typing. The following steps illustrate how to check spelling as you type.

To Check Spelling as You Type

1

• **Click the Name of Item text box below the graphic.**

The text is displayed selected (Figure 1-34).

FIGURE 1-34

2

• **Press the F9 key.**

• **Type** University Libray **and then press the SPACEBAR.**

• **Right-click the flagged word, Libray.**

Publisher flags the misspelled word, Libray, by placing a red wavy underline below it (Figure 1-35). The shortcut menu lists suggested spelling corrections for the flagged word.

FIGURE 1-35

3

• **Click Library on the shortcut menu.**

Publisher replaces the misspelled word with the word selected on the shortcut menu and removes the red wavy underline (Figure 1-36).

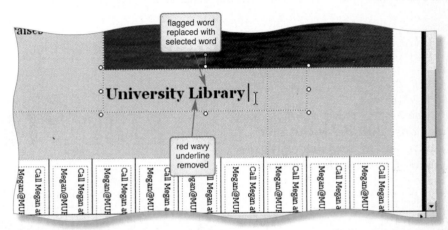

FIGURE 1-36

If a flagged word actually is spelled correctly and, for example, is a proper name, you can right-click it and then click Ignore All on the shortcut menu (Figure 1-35). If when you right-click the misspelled word, your desired correction is not in the list on the shortcut menu, you can click outside the shortcut menu to close the menu and then retype the correct word, or you can click Spelling on the shortcut menu to display the Spelling dialog box. You will learn more about the Spelling dialog box in a later project.

The next step is to type the remainder of text in the text box, as described in the following steps.

To Enter More Text

1 **Press the END key to move the insertion point to the end of the line.**

2 **Type** - Now Hiring **as the rest of the entry.**

The text box is complete (Figure 1-37).

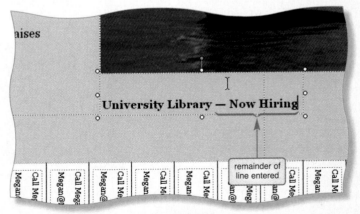

FIGURE 1-37

Table 1-3 Selecting Text	
TYPE OF SELECTION	ACTIONS
Character	Drag through character or press SHIFT+RIGHT ARROW
Word	Drag through word or double-click word
Line	Press SHIFT+END or SHIFT+DOWN ARROW
Paragraph	Drag through paragraph or triple-click paragraph
Placeholder text	Click
Multiple placeholder text items	Click first item, SHIFT-click second item
All text in text box	Press CTRL+A

Selecting Text

The final text box to edit in the flyer contains two occurrences of placeholder text in the same text box. To replace the text, you could click and delete each, one at a time, or you can select both and then type. Publisher provides ways to select portions of text, as shown in Table 1-3.

The following steps illustrate using the SHIFT key to make multiple selections of the placeholder text items and then insert new text.

To Select and Replace Multiple Placeholder Text Items

1

• **If necessary, zoom to whole page and then click the words, Contact person, in the text box above the graphic to select the placeholder text.**

• **Press the F9 key.**

The first placeholder text is displayed selected (Figure 1-38).

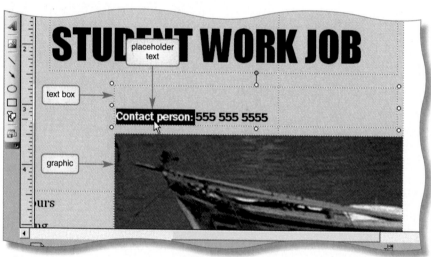

FIGURE 1-38

2

• **SHIFT-click the phone number, 555 555 5555.**

Both placeholder text items are selected (Figure 1-39).

Other Ways

1. Select text box, press CTRL+A
2. On Edit menu, click Select All, press DELETE key

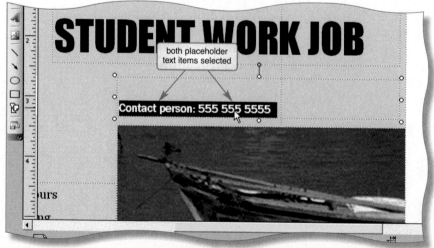

FIGURE 1-39

To select multiple areas of text that are not next to each other, make your first selection, hold down CTRL, and then select any other items you want.

Fitting Text

The Contact person text box above the graphic does not adjust the font size automatically to fit new text. Because this box will hold many words in the flyer, you need to change the way Publisher will fit text in the text box. The Format menu contains an AutoFit Text command. When you point to the AutoFit Text command, the AutoFit Text submenu displays three choices, Do Not Autofit, Best Fit, and Shrink Text On Overflow. **Do Not Autofit** will retain the font size, even if you type more words than will fit in the text box. Publisher stores the extra text in **overflow**, meaning that the text is hidden until it can be formatted to a smaller font size, flowed into a new text box, or until the text box itself is enlarged. **Best Fit** allows Publisher to change the font size so all text will fit in the text box. Sometimes that means reducing the font size, but it also might mean increasing short text to a very large font to create the best fit. An additional feature of Best Fit resizes the font whenever the text box itself changes in size. **Shrink Text On Overflow** means that Publisher will change the font only if necessary to display all of the text.

You will select Best Fit to allow for more words in the Contact person text box, as shown in the following steps. Additionally, you will choose the Best Fit option for the text box containing the bulleted list and the University Library – Now Hiring text box.

Q: Why is using Best Fit better than changing the font size?

A: When you use Best Fit, the font size automatically changes every time you resize the text box.

To Use Best Fit

1

• **With both of the placeholder text items still selected, click Format on the menu bar and then point to AutoFit Text.**

The AutoFit Text submenu displays the three options (Figure 1-40).

FIGURE 1-40

2

• **Click Best Fit on the AutoFit Text submenu.**

• **Type** The University Library is looking for student workers with experience in word processing, desktop publishing, or computer applications.

As you type, the font size reduces to allow all of the text to be displayed (Figure 1-41).

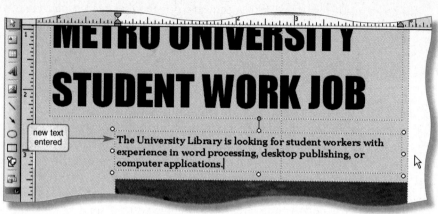

FIGURE 1-41

Other Ways

1. Right-click text box, point to Change Text, point to AutoFit Text, click Best Fit

Alternately, you can right-click a text box to display a shortcut menu with a Change Text command. The Change Text submenu displays an AutoFit Text command with the three fit options.

The final step in editing text is to choose Best Fit for the bulleted list and the University Library – Now Hiring text boxes.

To AutoFit Other Text Boxes

1 Press the F9 key to display the whole page.

2 Right-click the bulleted list in the text box to the left of the graphic. Point to Change Text on the shortcut menu. When the Change Text submenu is displayed, point to AutoFit Text.

The three AutoFit Text options are displayed on the AutoFit Text submenu (Figure 1-42).

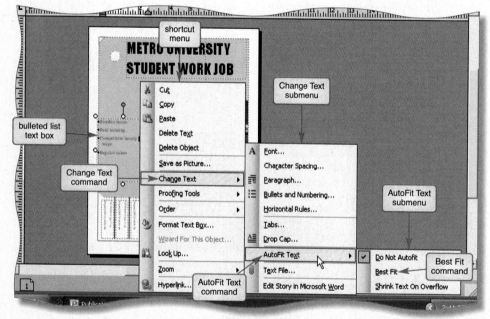

FIGURE 1-42

3 Click Best Fit on the AutoFit Text submenu.

4 Right-click the University Library – Now Hiring text box below the graphic. Point to Change Text on the shortcut menu. When the Change Text submenu is displayed, point to AutoFit Text. When the AutoFit Text menu is displayed, click Best Fit.

The text now is sized as large as possible for the size of the text box.

Using Best Fit allows you to change the size of the text box at a later time without worrying about changing the size of the font.

Saving a New Publication

The text changes in your publication now are complete. Because you have made so many changes, now is a good time to save a copy of your work. You may click either the Yes button or the No button when Publisher reminds you to save. The next series of steps illustrates how to save a publication on a floppy disk inserted in drive A using the Save button on the Standard toolbar.

To Save a New Publication

1

• **With a formatted floppy disk in drive A, click the Save button on the Standard toolbar.**

Publisher displays the Save As dialog box (Figure 1-43). Publisher uses a default file name on unsaved publications. Your default file name may differ. With this file name selected, you can change it by immediately typing the new file name.

FIGURE 1-43

2

• **With the default file name selected, type the file name** Student Work Job Flyer **in the File name text box.**

• **Do not press the ENTER key after typing the file name.**

FIGURE 1-44

*The file name, Student Work Job Flyer, replaces the text in the File name text box (Figure 1-44). Notice that the current save location is the My Documents folder (Figure 1-43). A **folder** is a specific location on a disk. To change to a different save location, you use the Save in box.*

3

• **Click the Save in box arrow.**

The Save in list displays the available save locations (Figure 1-45). Your list may differ depending on your system configuration.

FIGURE 1-45

4

• **Click 3½ Floppy (A:) in the Save in list.**

The 3½ Floppy (A:) drive becomes the selected location (Figure 1-46). The names of existing files that are stored on the floppy disk in drive A are displayed. In Figure 1-46, no files currently are stored on the floppy disk. Your list may differ.

FIGURE 1-46

5

• **Click the Save button in the Save As dialog box.**

The saved publication displays the new file name, Student Work Job Flyer, on the title bar and on the taskbar (Figure 1-47). Although the publication is saved on a floppy disk, it also remains in memory and is displayed in the workspace.

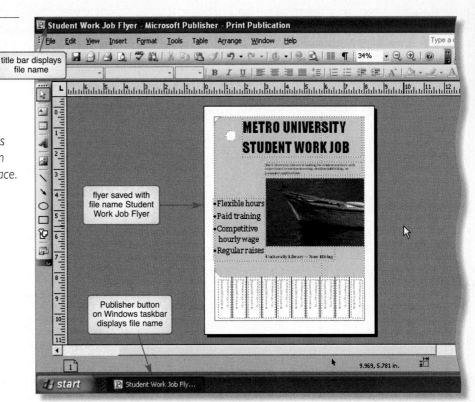

title bar displays file name

flyer saved with file name Student Work Job Flyer

Publisher button on Windows taskbar displays file name

METRO UNIVERSITY STUDENT WORK JOB

•Flexible hours
•Paid training
•Competitive hourly wage
•Regular raises

FIGURE 1-47

You can use the seven buttons at the top of the Save As dialog box (Figure 1-45) and the five icons along the left edge to change the save location and other tasks. Table 1-4 on the next page lists the function of the buttons and icons in the Save As dialog box.

When you click the **Tools button** in the Save As dialog box, a list is displayed. The **General Options command** in the list allows you to save a backup copy of the publication, create a password to limit access to the publication, and carry out other functions that are discussed later. Saving a backup publication means that each time you save a publication, Publisher copies the current version of the publication on disk to a file with the same name, but with the words, Backup of, appended to the front of the file name. In the case of a power failure or some other problem, use the backup version to restore your work.

You also can use the General Options command on the Tools list to assign a **password** to a workbook so others cannot open it. A password is case-sensitive and can be up to 15 characters long. **Case-sensitive** means Publisher can differentiate between uppercase and lowercase letters. If you assign a password and forget the password, you cannot access the publication.

The five buttons on the left of the Save As dialog box in Figure 1-43 on page PUB 33 allow you to select often used folders. The My Recent Documents button displays a list of shortcuts to the most recently used files in a folder titled Recent. You cannot save publications to the Recent folder.

When creating file names, you should make them as meaningful as possible. A **file name** can contain up to 255 characters and can include spaces.

Q&A

Q: How can I help prevent wrist injury while working on a computer?

A: Typical computer users frequently switch between the keyboard and the mouse during a word processing session, an action that strains the wrist. To help prevent wrist injury, minimize switching. If your fingers already are on the keyboard, use keyboard keys to scroll. If your hand already is on the mouse, use the mouse to scroll.

Table 1-4	Save As Dialog Box Toolbar Buttons	
BUTTON	**BUTTON NAME**	**FUNCTION**
	Default File Location	Displays contents of default file location
	Up One Level	Displays contents of next level up folder
	Search the Web	Starts browser and displays search engine
	Delete	Deletes selected file or folder
	Create New Folder	Creates new folder
	Views	Changes view of files and folders
Tools	Tools	Lists commands to print or modify file names and folders
My Recent Documents	My Recent Documents	Displays contents of My Recent Documents in Save in list (you cannot save to this location)

Table 1-4	Save As Dialog Box Toolbar Buttons	
BUTTON	**BUTTON NAME**	**FUNCTION**
Desktop	Desktop	Displays contents of Windows desktop folder in Save in list to save quickly to the Windows desktop
My Documents	My Documents	Displays contents of My Documents in Save in list to save quickly to the My Documents folder
My Computer	My Computer	Displays contents of My Computer in Save in list to save quickly to another drive on the computer
My Network Places	My Network Places	Displays contents of My Network Places in Save in List to save quickly to My Network Places

Using Graphics

Files containing graphical images, also called **graphics**, are available from a variety of sources. Publisher includes a series of predefined graphics such as drawings, photographs, sounds, videos, and other media files called clips. A **clip** is a single media file, including art, sound, animation, or movies, that you can insert and use in print publications, Web publications, and other Microsoft Office documents.

You can find, add, and organize media clips by displaying the **Clip Art Task Pane** (Figure 1-48). **Clip art** is an inclusive term given to a variety of predefined graphics such as images, artwork, and draw-type images that are created from a set of instructions (also called object-based or vector graphics). You can search for clip art based on descriptive keywords, file name, file format, or clip collection. The **clip collection** is a hierarchical organization of media clips. You can create your own clip collections; import clip collections; or add, move, or copy clips from one collection to another. The Search in box arrow displays three areas in which to search: My Collections, Office Collections, and Web Collections. The Results should be box arrow displays four types of media to include the search results: Clip Art, Photographs, Movies, and Sounds. More information on graphics, animation, and sound is presented in later projects.

At the bottom of the Clip Art task pane is a link to Organize clips, which opens the Microsoft Clip Organizer. You can use the **Clip Organizer** to browse through clip collections, add clips, or catalog clips in ways that make sense to you. For example, you can create a collection to group the clips you use most frequently, or let Clip Organizer automatically add and catalog clips on your hard disk.

If you have an Internet connection established, clip art search results automatically will include content from the Microsoft Office Online Web site. Or, you can visit the site yourself by clicking the **Clip art on Office Online** link at the bottom of the Clip Art task pane.

Using the Clip Art Task Pane

Because this flyer is advertising for a computer-related job, it is more appropriate to choose a graphic related to computers and workers rather than the picture of the boat supplied by the template. A graphic should enhance the message of the publication.

The following steps illustrate how to retrieve an appropriate graphic using the Clip Art task pane to replace the supplied graphic. If you cannot access the graphic described, choose a suitable replacement from your system's clip art.

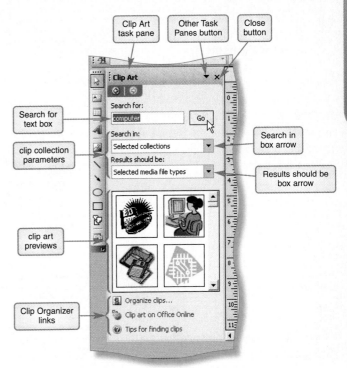

FIGURE 1-48

To Replace a Graphic Using the Clip Art Task Pane

1

• **If necessary to view the whole page, click the Zoom box arrow, and then click Whole Page in the Zoom list.**

• **Double-click the graphic of the boat.**

• **When the Clip Art task pane is displayed, if the Search for text box contains text, drag through the text to select it.**

• **Type** computer **in the Search for text box.**

Publisher displays the Clip Art task pane at the left edge of the Publisher window (Figure 1-49). Recall that a task pane is a separate window that enables you to carry out some Publisher tasks more efficiently. When you enter a description of the desired graphic in the Search for text box and click the Go button, Publisher searches the clip collection for clips that match the description. Publisher also may display the Picture toolbar.

FIGURE 1-49

• **Click the Go button.**

Publisher displays a list of clips that match the description, computer (Figure 1-50). Your pictures may vary depending on the installation of Publisher or the files on your network. Choose an appropriate image from your clip collection.

FIGURE 1-50

• **Click the desired picture in the task pane.**

Publisher inserts the clip art into the publication (Figure 1-51). The new image replaces the previous boat picture. The size of your graphic may differ.

• **Close the Clip Art task pane by clicking its Close button.**

• **Close the Picture toolbar by clicking its Close button.**

FIGURE 1-51

A graphic is any object in Publisher other than a text box. Graphics may include objects from the clip collection, imported images and pictures, drawings, tables, WordArt, shapes, lines, and arrows. A full installation of Publisher copies thousands of graphics including clip art, pictures, sounds, video clips, and animation to the computer's hard disk. For network installations, ask your instructor for the location of the graphic files.

Graphic files also are available from a variety of other sources. If you have a scanner or digital camera attached to your system, Publisher can insert the graphic directly from the scanner or camera. Alternatively, you can save the graphic in a file and then insert it into the publication at a later time. Some users purchase photographs from local software retailers, have their film developed on a CD-ROM, or locate pictures on the Web.

You can use the Clip collection to organize your clips by category or keyword so that finding the one you want is made easier. Some graphics are more suitable for display on the Web, while others print better on color printers. Future projects discuss the various types of graphics files in detail, including their advantages and disadvantages.

Moving and Resizing Objects

A key feature of desktop publishing software is its capability to move objects around and resize them on the page layout. You **move** an object by dragging its boundary to a new location. You **resize**, or change the width and height of an object, by dragging one of its handles.

Moving an Object

In general, moving an object requires you to select it and then drag it to the desired position. Unless a specific effect is desired, you usually move objects to a blank portion of the page layout. While you drag an object, the mouse pointer changes to a four-headed arrow, as shown in the following steps.

To Move an Object

- **If necessary, click the Zoom box arrow on the Standard toolbar and then click Whole Page in the Zoom list.**
- **Click the bulleted list text box and then point to its boundary.**

The mouse pointer changes to a four-headed arrow (Figure 1-52).

2

- **Drag the text box up so that its top boundary is approximately even with the top boundary of the graphic.**

FIGURE 1-52

Publisher has a special feature called **snapping**, which adjusts the placement of an object automatically so it aligns to rulers, boundaries, or guides. You may turn on and off the snapping feature by pointing to Snap on the Arrange menu, and then clicking the appropriate choice. If you want objects moved close to but not adjacent to other objects, you should turn off the snapping feature. You will learn more about snapping in a later project.

Resizing Objects

You easily can change the size of objects to fit your needs. Resizing includes both enlarging and reducing the size of an object. You can reshape an object by clicking a handle and dragging. Recall that a handle is one of several small shapes displayed around an object when the object is selected.

Two text boxes are resized in the steps on the next page. In a later project, you will learn how to resize objects in other ways.

To Resize an Object

- **Click the University Library – Now Hiring text box.**
- **Point to the middle handle on the right side of the text box.**

Publisher selects the text box, which displays with eight small circle handles in its boundary at each corner and middle location (Figure 1-53). The mouse pointer shape changes to a two-headed arrow when it is positioned over a handle.

FIGURE 1-53

- **Drag the middle-right handle to the right until the dotted boundary is even with the right guide of the page layout.**

The text box is resized, and the text automatically resizes to Best Fit (Figure 1-54). Publisher displays a dotted line while you are resizing.

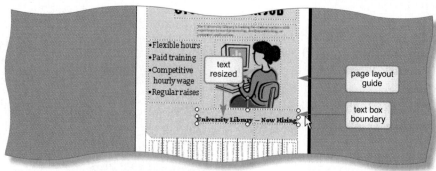

FIGURE 1-54

3

- **Select the text box above the graphic that begins with the phrase, The University Library is looking for student workers.**
- **Drag the middle-left handle to the left guide of the page layout.**

The text box is resized, and the text automatically resizes to Best Fit (Figure 1-55).

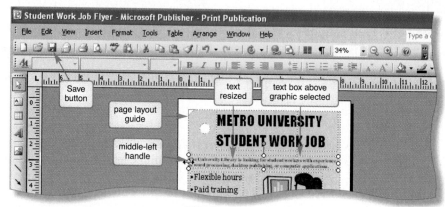

FIGURE 1-55

When you drag a corner handle instead of a middle handle, you can change both the width and height of the object. Special care should be taken if the object is a graphic, because dragging the middle handle sometimes may cause the graphic to look distorted.

Instead of resizing a selected object by dragging with the mouse, you also can use the Size sheet displayed by clicking the object's Format command on the Format menu. Later, you also will learn how to resize an object using the Measurements toolbar. Either way, you can enter exact height and width measurements.

Saving an Existing Publication with the Same File Name

The print version of the flyer now is complete. To transfer the formatting and graphic changes to your floppy disk in drive A, you must save the publication again. When you saved the publication the first time, you assigned the file name, Student Work Job Flyer. Publisher assigns this same file name automatically to the publication each time you subsequently save it, if you use the following procedure. The following step saves the publication using the same file name.

To Save an Existing Publication with the Same File Name

1 **Click the Save button on the Standard toolbar.**

Publisher saves the publication on a floppy disk inserted in drive A using the current file name, Student Work Job Flyer. The publication remains in memory and is displayed on the screen.

If for some reason, you want to save an existing publication with a different file name, click Save As on the File menu to display the Save As dialog box. Then, fill in the Save As dialog box as discussed in Steps 2 through 5 on pages PUB 33 through PUB 35 using a different file name in the File name text box.

Other Ways

1. On File menu click Save
2. Press CTRL+S
3. In Voice Command mode, say "Save"

Printing a Publication

Once you have created a publication and saved it, you might want to print it. A printed version of the publication is called a **hard copy** or printout. The following steps print the publication created in Project 1.

Other Ways

1. On File menu click Print, click OK button
2. Press CTRL+P, click OK button
3. In Voice Command mode, say "Print"

To Print a Publication

1

• **Ready the printer according to the printer instructions.**

• **Click the Print button on the Standard toolbar.**

A dialog box briefly appears indicating it is preparing to print the publication. A few moments later, the publication begins printing on the printer. The tray status area displays a printer icon while the publication is printing (Figure 1-56).

2

• **When the printer stops, retrieve the printout.**

FIGURE 1-56

More About

Healthy Computing

For more information about healthy computing, visit the Publisher 2003 More About Web page (scsite.com/pub2003/more) and click Healthy Computing.

When you use the Print button to print a publication, Publisher prints the entire publication automatically. You then may distribute the hard copy or keep it as a permanent record of the publication.

If you want to cancel a job that is printing or waiting to be printed, double-click the printer icon in the tray status area (Figure 1-56 on the previous page). In the Print dialog box, right-click the job to be canceled and then click Cancel Printing on the shortcut menu.

Quitting Publisher

After you create, save, and print the publication, you are ready to quit Publisher and return control to Windows. The following step shows how to quit Publisher.

To Quit Publisher

Other Ways

1. On File menu, click Exit
2. Press ALT+F4
3. In Voice Command mode, say "File, Exit"

1 **Click the Close button in the upper-right corner on the title bar (Figure 1-56 on the previous page). If a Microsoft Office Publisher dialog box is displayed asking if you want to save the changes, click the No button.**

If you made changes to the publication since the last save, Publisher displays a dialog box asking if you want to save the changes. Clicking the Yes button saves changes; clicking the No button ignores the changes; and clicking the Cancel button returns to the publication. If you did not make any changes since you saved the publication, this dialog box does not display.

Closing a publication is different from quitting Publisher. Closing a publication, by clicking Close on the File menu, leaves any other Publisher publications open and Publisher running. If no other publication was open, the Close command displays the New Publication task pane.

As you created the flyer, you edited the template, resized text boxes and changed the way they fit text, inserted a picture from the clip collection, printed the publication, and saved it. You might decide, however, to change the publication at a later date. To do this, you must start Publisher again and then retrieve your publication from the floppy disk in drive A.

More About

Opening Files

In Publisher, you can open a recently used file by clicking File on the menu bar and clicking the file name on the File menu. To instruct Publisher to show the recently used publications on the File menu, click Tools on the menu bar, click Options, click the General tab, click Recently used file list to place a check mark in the check box, and click the OK button.

Opening a Publication

Once you have created and saved a publication, you often will have reason to retrieve it from disk. For example, you might want to revise the publication or print it again. Earlier, you saved the publication created in this project on a floppy disk using the file name, Student Work Job Flyer. The following steps illustrate how to open the file from a floppy disk in drive A, and make changes to the Publication to prepare it for publishing on the Web.

To Open a Publication

1

• **With your floppy disk in drive A, click the Start button on the Windows taskbar, point to All Programs on the Start menu, point to Microsoft Office on the All Programs submenu, and then click Microsoft Office Publisher 2003 on the Microsoft Office submenu.**

Publisher starts. The Open area of the New Publication task pane lists up to four of the most recently used files (Figure 1-57).

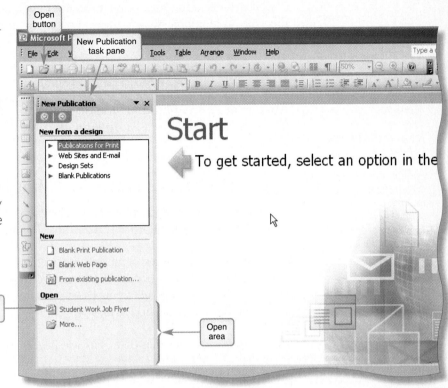

FIGURE 1-57

2

• **Click Student Work Job Flyer in the New Publication task pane.**

Publisher opens the document, Student Work Job Flyer, from the floppy disk in drive A and displays it in the Publisher window (Figure 1-58).

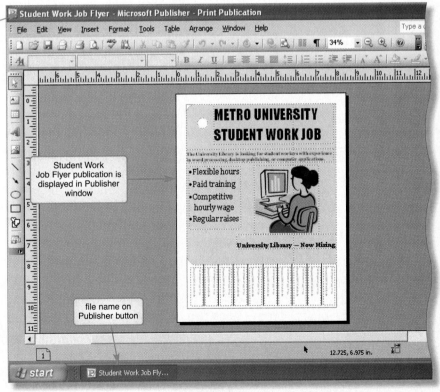

FIGURE 1-58

If you want to open a publication other than one of the four most recently opened ones, click the Open button on the Standard toolbar or the More link at the bottom of the New Publication task pane. Clicking the Open button or the More link displays the Open dialog box, which allows you to navigate to a document stored on disk.

Modifying a Publication

After creating a publication, you often will find that you must make changes to it. Changes can be required because the document contains an error or because of new circumstances.

Types of Changes Made to Publications

The types of changes made to publications normally fall into one of the three following categories: additions, deletions, or modifications.

ADDITIONS Additional text, objects, or formatting may be required in the publication. Additions occur when you are required to add items to a publication. For example, in this project you would like to insert a text box that will display when the flyer is published to the Web.

DELETIONS Sometimes deletions are necessary in a publication because objects are incorrect or are no longer needed. For example, to place this advertising flyer on the electronic bulletin board at the college, the tear-offs no longer are needed. In that case, you would delete them from the page layout.

MODIFICATIONS If you make an error in a document or want to make other modifications, normal combinations of inserting, deleting, and editing techniques for text and graphics apply. Publisher provides several methods for correcting errors in a document. For each of the text error correction techniques, you first must move the insertion point to the error. For graphic modification, the object first must be selected.

Modifying the Flyer

If this flyer displays on an electronic bulletin board, the tear-offs are unnecessary and should be deleted. Additionally, a new text box should be inserted, with a hyperlink, in preparation for creating a Web version of the publication. The following steps show how to delete the tear-offs.

To Delete the Tear-Offs

1. **If necessary, right-click the workspace. Point to Zoom on the shortcut menu and then click Whole Page.**

2. **Right-click any of the tear-offs, and then click Delete Object on the shortcut menu.**

tear-offs are deleted

FIGURE 1-59

The tear-offs are deleted (Figure 1-59).

If you delete an object accidentally, you can restore it by clicking the Undo button on the Standard toolbar. If you want to cancel your undo, you can use the Redo button. Some actions, such as saving or printing a document, cannot be undone or redone.

Inserting a Text Box

The final step in modifying the flyer is to create a new text box. Recall that the Objects toolbar contains buttons for many different kinds of objects that you can insert into publications. In the case of a text box, you click the Text Box button and then drag in the publication to create the text box. Once it is created, you can type in the text box just as you did with those created by the template. You will use a font from the font scheme of the publication, as well as the Best Fit option.

The following steps illustrate how to insert a text box in the publication.

To Insert a Text Box

1

• **Click the Text Box button on the Objects toolbar and then move the mouse to the lower portion of the flyer where the tear-offs were located.**

• **Drag a rectangle approximately 5.5 inches wide and 1.5 inches tall.**

The empty text box is inserted (Figure 1-60). The width and height are displayed on the status bar as you drag. The mouse pointer changes to a cross hair.

FIGURE 1-60

2

• **Press the F9 key to zoom in.**

• **Type** Call Megan at 555-0755 **and then press the ENTER key.**

• **Type** Megan@MUFinAid.edu **to complete the text box.**

• **Right-click the text box. On the shortcut menu, point to Change Text.**

• **Point to AutoFit Text on the Change Text submenu.**

The AutoFit Text submenu displays three choices (Figure 1-61).

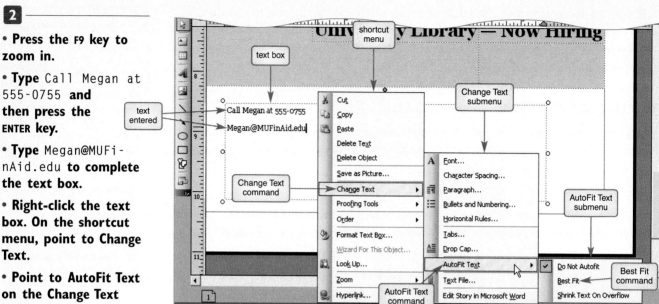

FIGURE 1-61

3

• **Click Best Fit on the AutoFit Text submenu.**

Publisher increases the font size of the text to fill the text box (Figure 1-62).

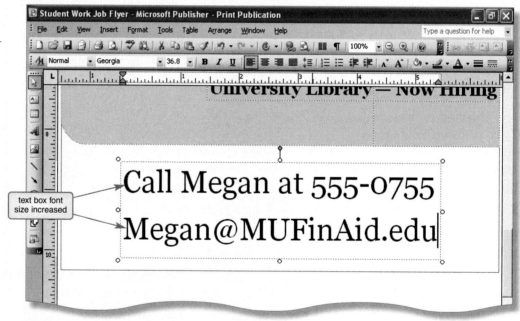

FIGURE 1-62

Inserting a Hyperlink

The final modification in preparation for converting this publication to a Web publication is inserting a hyperlink. A **hyperlink** is colored and underlined text or a graphic that you click to go to a file, a location in a file, a Web page, or an e-mail address. When you insert a hyperlink, you select the text or object and then click the Insert Hyperlink button on the Standard toolbar. The **Insert Hyperlink dialog box** allows you to select options and enter Web addresses, as shown in the following steps.

To Insert a Hyperlink

1

• **Select the text, Megan@MUFinAid.edu, by dragging through it in the text box.**

Publisher displays the e-mail address selected (Figure 1-63).

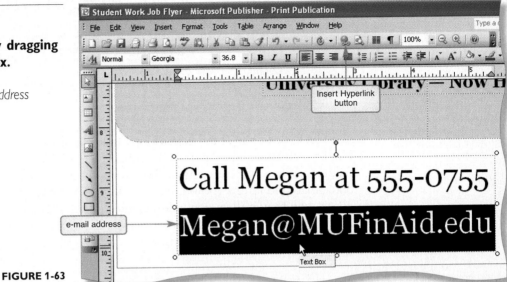

FIGURE 1-63

2

• **Click the Insert Hyperlink button on the Standard toolbar.**

The Insert Hyperlink dialog box is displayed (Figure 1-64). Publisher displays Link to locations on the Link to bar on the left.

FIGURE 1-64

3

• **Click E-mail Address on the Link to bar in the Insert Hyperlink dialog box.**

• **Type** Megan@MUFinAid.edu **in the E-mail address text box. Press the TAB key.**

• **Type** Student Work Job Web Flyer Inquiry **in the Subject text box.**

The mailto: prefix automatically is placed before the e-mail address (Figure 1-65). The Subject text box entry will be entered as the e-mail subject line when users click the link.

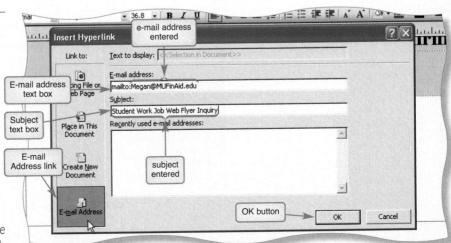

FIGURE 1-65

4

• **Click the OK button.**

The Insert Hyperlink dialog box closes, and the e-mail address is displayed as a hyperlink (Figure 1-66).

FIGURE 1-66

The Link to bar in the Insert Hyperlink dialog box displays links to an Existing File or Web Page, Place in This Document, Create New Document, and E-mail Address. When you click one of these links on the Link to bar, the dialog box displays text boxes and information unique to the type of link. The **E-mail Address link** allows you to edit the e-mail address and provides a subject line to be inserted in the resulting e-mail message. It also displays a list of recently used e-mail addresses (Figure 1-65 on the previous page).

Creating a Web Page from a Publication

Publisher can create a Web page from your publication. It is a three-step process. First, Publisher uses a **Design Checker** to look for potential problems if the publication was transferred to the Web. After saving the publication with a new file name, it will be converted to a Web Publication using the Convert to Web Publication command on the File menu. Finally, Publisher publishes the Web page.

Running the Design Checker

If your publication contains a layout that is not appropriate, such as overlapping objects, the Design Checker will alert you. If you use links or hot spots to other Web pages within your publication, Design Checker will verify the addresses. The following steps show how to run the Design Checker.

To Run the Design Checker

1

• **Click Tools on the menu bar.**

The Tools menu is displayed (Figure 1-67).

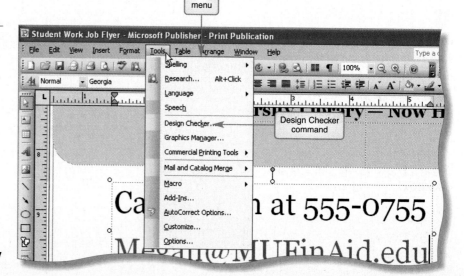

FIGURE 1-67

2

- Click Design Checker.
- When Publisher displays the Design Checker task pane, if any problems are listed in the Select an item to fix text box, click the problem.
- When Publisher selects the object, fix the error.
- When no design errors exist, Publisher displays a message, indicating there are no problems in the publication.

A progress bar appears as the Design Checker checks the publication (Figure 1-68).

3

- Click the Close Design Checker button in the Design Checker task pane.

The task pane closes.

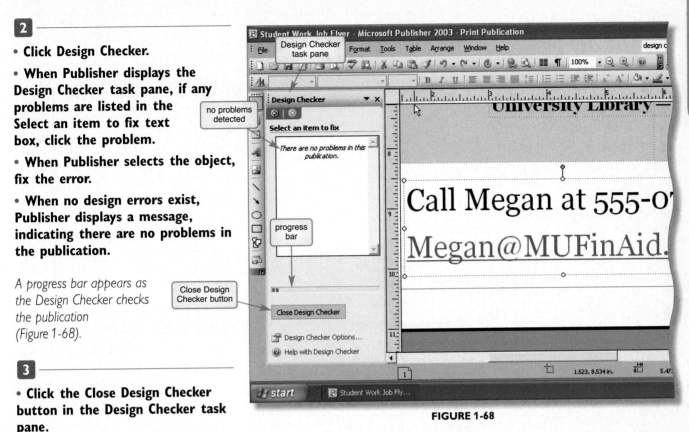

FIGURE 1-68

If your publication had problems or contained design errors, you would have been given the option to go to the error, ignore, continue, or obtain more information about the problems. The Design Checker looks for appropriate layouts. If text overlaps an object, the Design Checker offers to convert the text box to a graphic so it will display properly. The Design Checker looks at all graphics and may display suggestions on those that load slowly. More about the Design Checker and information on types of graphics will be covered in future projects.

Saving a Publication with a New File Name

The steps on the next page illustrate how to save the publication with a new file name in preparation for converting it to a Web publication. It is important to save the publication before converting it to a Web publication so you can make changes at a later time, if necessary.

To Save a Publication with a New File Name

1

• **Make sure a floppy disk is inserted in drive A. Click File on the menu bar and then click Save As.**

• **When the Save As dialog box displays, type** Student Work Job Web Flyer **in the File name text box. Click the Look in box arrow and then click 3½ Floppy (A:) in the Look in list.**

The Save As dialog box is displayed (Figure 1-69).

2

• **Click the Save button.**

The saved file is stored with a new file name on the disk in drive A.

FIGURE 1-69

Normally, Publisher saves a file with the three-letter extension, .pub. The **.pub extension** allows Publisher easily to open your formatted file and assign a recognizable icon to the shortcut on your disk.

Converting a Print Publication to a Web Publication

You can create two types of publications with Microsoft Publisher: print publications and Web publications. A **Web publication** is one suitable for publishing to the Web with certain objects, formatting options, hyperlinks, and other features specific to Web pages.

A command on Publisher's File menu converts publications from one type to another. Up to now, you have worked on a print publication as noted in the title bar (Figure 1-68 on the previous page). Once you convert the file, you work in **Web mode**. The options available to you in Web mode are tailored specifically to Web publications so you can create a publication that is optimized for display in a Web browser. A **browser** is a piece of software that interprets and formats files into Web pages and displays them. A Web browser, such as Microsoft Internet Explorer, can follow hyperlinks, transfer files, and play sound or video files that are embedded in Web pages. You always can determine which publication mode you are in by looking at the title bar of your open publication, which will display either Print Publication or Web Publication, depending on the publication type.

When you convert a publication from one type to the other, Publisher copies the text and graphics from your original publication into the new publication type. Because certain print features are not available in Web mode, and certain Web features are not available in Print mode, your publication may undergo formatting changes when you convert it from one publication type to the other.

The following steps illustrate how to convert a print publication to a Web publication. A two-step wizard helps you through the conversion process. A **wizard** is a series of dialog boxes and questions to help you make choices and format publications based on your responses.

More About

Print Preview

To view a publication before you print it, click the Print Preview button on the Standard toolbar. To return to the workspace window, click the Close Preview button on the Print Preview toolbar.

To Convert a Print Publication to a Web Publication

1

• **Click File on the menu bar.**

Publisher displays the File menu (Figure 1-70).

FIGURE 1-70

2

• **Click Convert to Web Publication.**

• **When Publisher displays the Convert to Web Publication dialog box with the Save Your Current Print Publication step, click the No option button to select it.**

The first dialog box reminds you to save the publication (Figure 1-71). Because you previously saved the file, you will choose not to save the file again.

FIGURE 1-71

3

• **Click the Next button. When Publisher displays the Add a Navigation Bar step, click the No option button to select it.**

This single page Web page will not use a navigation bar (Figure 1-72). If Publisher displays the Web Tools toolbar, click its Close button.

4

• **Click the Finish Button.**

FIGURE 1-72

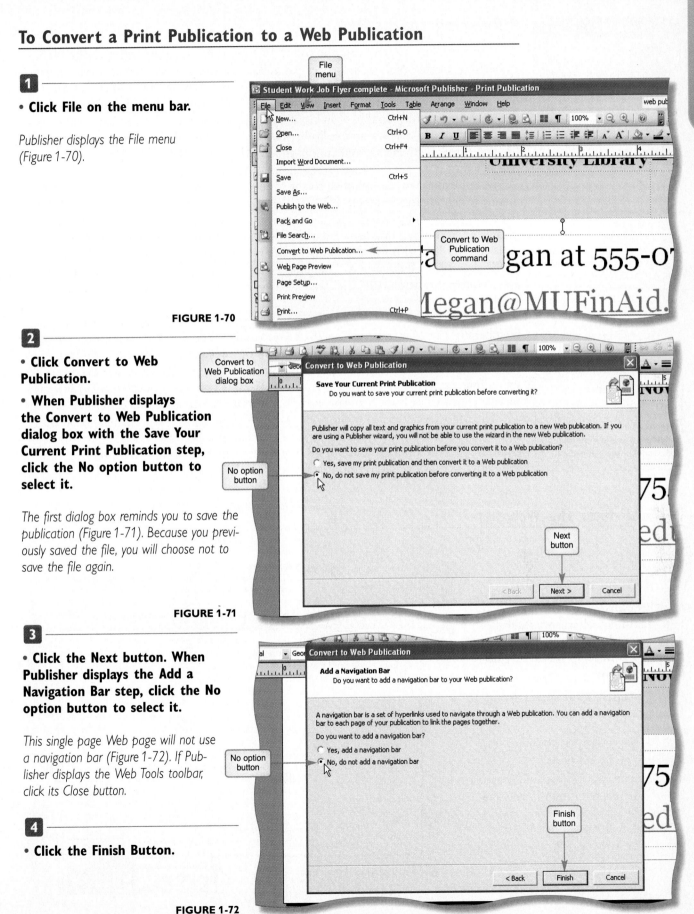

More About

HTML

For more information about HTML, visit the HTML Web page (scsite.com/html) and click More About.

Publishing to the Web

The final step in preparing the flyer's Web presence is to publish it to the Web. **Publishing to the Web** is the process of making Web pages available to others, for example on the World Wide Web or on a company's intranet. Files intended for use on the Web, however, need a different format. A **Hypertext Markup Language** (**HTML**) file is a file capable of being stored and transferred electronically on a file server in order to display on the Web. When you publish, Publisher can save your file in a **filtered HTML format** that is smaller than regular HTML files. It can be published to, and downloaded from, the Internet quickly.

In Publisher, you can publish to the Web using a wizard accessed through the File menu, which creates a filtered HTML file; or, you can save a publication as a Web page to a Web folder, which creates a traditional HTML file. Either way, Publisher creates an accompanying folder for each separate publication intended for the Web. A **folder** is a logical portion of a disk created to group and store similar documents. Inside this folder, Publisher will include copies of the associated graphics. Once created, your publication can be viewed by a Web browser, such as Microsoft Internet Explorer.

The concept of a Web folder facilitates integration of Publisher with other members of the Microsoft Office 2003 Suite and Windows. With Windows, you can choose to use Web style folders on your desktop, which means that the desktop is interactive, and all your folders look like Web pages. Publisher also will take care of uploading, or transferring, your files to the Web, if you are connected to an Internet service provider or host. See Appendix C for more information on Web folders.

The following steps show how to use the Publish to the Web command on the File menu to create a Web site from your publication. Because not all systems are connected to the Internet and not all users subscribe to a Web hosting service, the following steps store the resulting Web files on the floppy disk.

More About

Using Web Folders

For more information about publishing to the Web using a Web folder, see Appendix C.

To Publish to the Web

1

• **Click File on the menu bar.**

• **Click Publish to the Web on the File menu. If a Microsoft Publisher dialog box displays reminding you about Web hosting services, click its OK button.**

• **Type** Student Work Job Web Flyer **in the File name text box.**

Publisher displays the Publish to the Web dialog box (Figure 1-73). The Save in location, file name, and file type are displayed. You will save the publication in the same location and with the same file name; the Save as type box will change the publication's file name extension.

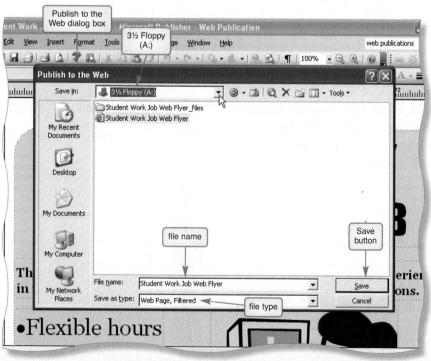

FIGURE 1-73

2

• **Click the Save button in the Save As dialog box.**

Publisher displays a Microsoft Office Publisher dialog box describing filtered HTML files (Figure 1-74).

3

• **Click the OK button.**

The saved files are ready to send to the Web.

FIGURE 1-74

To preview what the Web publication looks like, you can click the Web Page Preview button on the Standard toolbar, as shown in the following step.

To Preview the Web Publication in a Browser

1 Click the Web Page Preview button on the Standard toolbar. When the browser window opens, if necessary, maximize it by clicking the Maximize button on the title bar.

2 Click the Close button on the browser title bar.

Microsoft Internet Explorer displays the Publisher Web publication (Figure 1-75). Your browser may be different.

FIGURE 1-75

More About

**The Quick
Reference**

For a table that lists how to
complete the tasks covered in
this book using the mouse,
menu, shortcut menu, and
keyboard, see the Quick
Reference Summary at the
back of this book, or visit
the Publisher 2003 Quick
Reference Web page
(scsite.com/pub2003/qr).

Closing the Entire Publication

Sometimes, everything goes wrong. If this happens, you may want to close the publication entirely and start over. You also may want to close a publication when you are finished with it so you can begin your next publication.

To Close the Entire Publication and Start Over

1 Click File on the menu bar and then click Close.

2 If Publisher displays a dialog box, click the No button to ignore the changes since the last time you saved the publication.

3 Click the Blank Print Publication link on the New Publication task pane.

You also can begin a new publication by clicking the New button on the Standard toolbar.

More About

**The Publisher
Help System**

The best way to become
familiar with the Publisher
Help system is to use it.
Appendix A includes detailed
information on the Publisher
Help system and exercises
that will help you gain confidence in using it.

Publisher Help System

At any time while you are using Publisher, you can get answers to questions by using the **Publisher Help system**. You activate the Publisher Help system by using the Type a question for help box on the menu bar, the Microsoft Publisher Help button on the Standard toolbar, or the Help menu. Used properly, this form of interactive assistance can increase your productivity and reduce your frustrations by minimizing the time you spend learning how to use Publisher.

The following section shows how to get answers to your questions using the Type a question for help box. Additional information about using the Publisher Help system is available in Appendix A.

Using the Type a Question for Help Box

Through the Type a question for help box on the right side of the menu bar, you type free-form questions, such as *how do I save* or *how do I create a Web page*, or you can type terms, such as *copy*, *save*, or *formatting*. Publisher responds by display-ing a list of topics related to what you entered. The following steps show how to use the Type a question for help box to obtain information on color schemes.

To Use the Type a Question for Help Box

1

• **Click the Type a question for help box on the right side of the menu bar and then type** color schemes **(Figure 1-76).**

FIGURE 1-76

2

• **Press the ENTER key.**

• **When Publisher displays the Search Results task pane, scroll to display the topic, About color schemes and fill effects.**

Publisher displays the Search Results task pane with a list of topics relating to the phrase, color schemes (Figure 1-77).

FIGURE 1-77

3

• **Click the About color schemes and fill effects link.**

• **When the Microsoft Publisher Help window opens, double-click its title bar to maximize the window.**

• **Click the Show All link in the upper-right corner of the window to expand the links in the window.**

Publisher opens a Microsoft Publisher Help window that provides information about color schemes (Figure 1-78). The Show All link becomes the Hide All link.

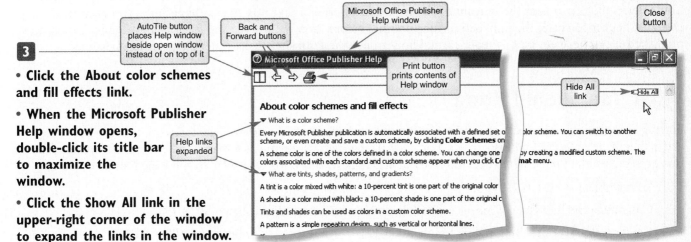

FIGURE 1-78

4

• **Click the Close button on the Microsoft Publisher Help window title bar.**

• **Click the Close button in the Search Results task pane.**

Publisher closes the Microsoft Publisher Help window. The Publisher window again is active.

Use the buttons in the upper-left corner of the Microsoft Publisher Help window (Figure 1-78) to navigate through the Help system, change the display, and print the contents of the window.

You can use the Type a question for help box to search for Help about any topic concerning Publisher. As you enter questions and terms in the Type a question for help box, Publisher adds them to the Type a question for help list. Thus, if you click the Type a question for help box arrow, Publisher displays a list of previously asked questions and terms.

Quitting Publisher

The final step in this project is to quit Publisher, as shown in the following step.

To Quit Publisher

1 **Click the Close button on the title bar (Figure 1-78 on the previous page). If a Microsoft Office Publisher dialog box is displayed, click the No button.**

The Publisher window closes, and the Windows desktop is displayed.

Project Summary

In creating the Student Work Job Flyer publication in this project, you gained a broad knowledge of Publisher. First you were introduced to starting Publisher. You learned about the Publisher workspace. You chose a flyer publication and replaced the template-supplied text in text boxes. You deleted objects, resized objects, moved objects, and changed how the text fit within the text box.

Once you saved the print publication, you learned how to replace a graphic using the Clip Art task pane. You deleted the tear-offs at the bottom of the flyer and inserted a text box with a hyperlink. You used the Design Checker to check the publication for potential errors. You then saved the flyer as a Web publication and published it on the Web. Finally, you learned how to use the Publisher Help system to answer questions.

What You Should Know

Having completed this project, you should be able to perform the tasks below. The tasks are listed in the same order they were presented in this project. For a list of the buttons, menus, toolbars, and commands introduced in this project, see the Quick Reference Summary at the back of this book and refer to the Page Number column.

1. Start Publisher   (PUB 7)
2. Customize the Publisher Window   (PUB 9)
3. Create a Publication Using a Template   (PUB 12)
4. Edit Placeholder Text   (PUB 23)
5. Delete an Object   (PUB 27)
6. Check Spelling as You Type   (PUB 28)
7. Enter More Text   (PUB 29)
8. Select and Replace Multiple Placeholder Text Items   (PUB 30)
9. Use Best Fit   (PUB 31)
10. AutoFit Other Text Boxes   (PUB 32)
11. Save a New Publication   (PUB 33)
12. Replace a Graphic Using the Clip Art Task Pane (PUB 37)
13. Move an Object   (PUB 39)
14. Resize an Object   (PUB 40)
15. Save an Existing Publication with the Same File Name   (PUB 41)
16. Print a Publication   (PUB 41)
17. Quit Publisher   (PUB 42)
18. Open a Publication   (PUB 43)
19. Delete the Tear-Offs   (PUB 44)
20. Insert a Text Box   (PUB 45)
21. Insert a Hyperlink   (PUB 47)
22. Run the Design Checker   (PUB 48)
23. Save a Publication with a New File Name (PUB 50)
24. Convert a Print Publication to a Web Publication (PUB 51)
25. Publish to the Web   (PUB 52)
26. Preview the Web Publication in a Browser (PUB 53)
27. Close the Entire Publication and Start Over (PUB 54)
28. Use the Type a question for help Box   (PUB 54)
29. Quit Publisher   (PUB 56)

Learn It Online

Instructions: To complete the Learn It Online exercises, start your browser, click the Address bar, and then enter the Web address scsite.com/pub2003/learn. When the Publisher 2003 Learn It Online page is displayed, follow the instructions in the exercises below. Each exercise has instructions for printing your results, either for your own records or for submission to your instructor.

1 Project Reinforcement TF, MC, and SA

Below Publisher Project 1, click the Project Reinforcement link. Print the quiz by clicking Print on the File menu for each page. Answer each question.

2 Flash Cards

Below Publisher Project 1, click the Flash Cards link and read the instructions. Type 20 (or a number specified by your instructor) in the Number of playing cards text box, type your name in the Enter your Name text box, and then click the Flip Card button. When the flash card is displayed, read the question and then click the ANSWER box arrow to select an answer. Flip through Flash Cards. If your score is 15 (75%) correct or greater, click Print on the File menu to print your results. If your score is less than 15 (75%) correct, then redo this exercise by clicking the Replay button.

3 Practice Test

Below Publisher Project 1, click the Practice Test link. Answer each question, enter your first and last name at the bottom of the page, and then click the Grade Test button. When the graded practice test is displayed on your screen, click Print on the File menu to print a hard copy. Continue to take practice tests until you score 80% or better.

4 Who Wants To Be a Computer Genius?

Below Publisher Project 1, click the Computer Genius link. Read the instructions, enter your first and last name at the bottom of the page, and then click the PLAY button. When your score is displayed, click the PRINT RESULTS link to print a hard copy.

5 Wheel of Terms

Below Publisher Project 1, click the Wheel of Terms link. Read the instructions, and then enter your first and last name and your school name. Click the PLAY button. When your score is displayed, right-click the score and then click Print on the shortcut menu to print a hard copy.

6 Crossword Puzzle Challenge

Below Publisher Project 1, click the Crossword Puzzle Challenge link. Read the instructions, and then enter your first and last name. Click the SUBMIT button. Work the crossword puzzle. When you are finished, click the Submit button. When the crossword puzzle is redisplayed, click the Print Puzzle button to print a hard copy.

7 Tips and Tricks

Below Publisher Project 1, click the Tips and Tricks link. Click a topic that pertains to Project 1. Right-click the information and then click Print on the shortcut menu. Construct a brief example of what the information relates to in Publisher to confirm you understand how to use the tip or trick.

8 Newsgroups

Below Publisher Project 1, click the Newsgroups link. Click a topic that pertains to Project 1. Print three comments.

9 Expanding Your Horizons

Below Publisher Project 1, click the Articles for Microsoft Publisher link. Click a topic that pertains to Project 1. Print the information. Construct a brief example of what the information relates to in Publisher to confirm you understand the contents of the article.

10 Search Sleuth

Below Publisher Project 1, click the Search Sleuth link. To search for a term that pertains to this project, select a term below the Project 1 title and then use the Google search engine at google.com (or any major search engine) to display and print two Web pages that present information on the term.

11 Publisher Online Training

Below Publisher Project 1, click the Publisher Online Training link. When your browser displays the Microsoft Office Online Web page, click the Publisher link. Click one of the Publisher courses that covers one or more of the objectives listed at the beginning of the project on page PUB 4. Print the first page of the course before stepping through it.

12 Office Marketplace

Below Publisher Project 1, click the Office Marketplace link. When your browser displays the Microsoft Office Online Web page, click the Office Marketplace link. Click a topic that relates to Publisher. Print the first page.

Apply Your Knowledge

1 Editing a Publication

Instructions: Start Publisher. Open the publication, Apply 1-1 Music Lessons Flyer, on the Data Disk. See the inside back cover of this book for instruction for downloading the Data Disk or see your instructor for information about accessing files required in this book.

The publication on the Data Disk is a flyer that contains some template text, a graphic that needs to be replaced, and spelling errors. You are to fix the spelling mistake, replace the template text, use the Best Fit option on the information text box, resize the information text box, and change the font and color scheme so that it looks like Figure 1-79.

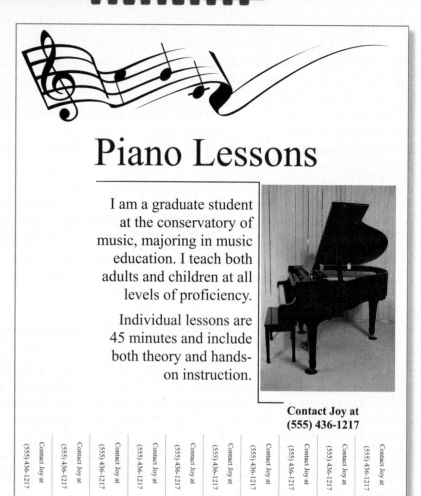

FIGURE 1-79

1. Correct each spelling error by right-clicking the flagged word and then clicking the appropriate correction on the shortcut menu, so the flyer text matches Figure 1-79. The flyer contains three spelling errors (indicated by a red wavy underline).
2. If the task pane is not displayed, click View on the menu bar and then click Task Pane. Click the Other Task Panes button in the task pane title bar (see Figure 1-8 on page PUB 10 for the location of the Other Task Panes button). Select Font Schemes from the list. Scroll to and then select the Versatile font scheme.
3. Click the Other Task Panes button again and select Color Schemes from the list. Scroll to and then select the Clay color scheme.
4. Double-click the graphic. When the Clip Art task pane is displayed, type piano in the Search for text box. Click the Go button. When the clip selections display, scroll to find a photograph of a piano similar to the one in Figure 1-79.
5. Close the task pane by clicking the Close button in the task pane title bar.
6. Right-click the information text box that displays to the left of the graphic. On the shortcut menu, point to Change Text, then point to AutoFit Text, and then click Best Fit on the AutoFit Text submenu.
7. Drag the middle-right handle of the information text box so the right boundary is positioned closer to the graphic.
8. Click the Contact person placeholder text and type Contact Joy at to replace the text.
9. Click the phone number placeholder text and type (555) 436-1217 to replace the text.

Apply Your Knowledge

10. Click the text in any one tear-off and type Contact Joy at and then press the ENTER key. Type (555) 436-1217 and then click outside the tear-offs to synchronize them all.
11. Fix any other spelling errors you might have made while typing the text. Right-click any words with red wavy underlines below them and then choose a correct spelling on the shortcut menu. Run the Design Checker and fix any errors that Publisher displays.
12. Click File on the menu bar and then click Save As. Save the publication using Apply 1-1 Music Lessons Flyer Revised as the file name.
13. Print the revised publication.

In the Lab

1 Creating a Flyer with Tear-Offs

Problem: A friend of yours would like to get some part-time work as a tutor for mathematics courses. He has asked you to create a flyer advertising his services. He would like his name, e-mail, and telephone number on tear-offs at the bottom, along with an eye-catching graphic. A big, bold heading should attract passers-by.

You prepare the publication shown in Figure 1-80. *Hint:* Remember, if you make a mistake while editing the publication, you can click the Undo button on the Standard toolbar to undo your last action.

1. Start Publisher.
2. In the New Publication task pane, click Publications for Print, click Flyers, click Sale. When the previews are displayed, scroll to and then click For Sale Flyer 1.
3. When the correct flyer is displayed, click the Close button on the Flyer Options task pane.

FIGURE 1-80

(continued)

Creating a Flyer with Tear-Offs *(continued)*

4. Click the heading, For Sale. Type Need a Math Tutor? to replace the placeholder text.
5. Click the text in the Name of Item text box. Type All Math Courses to replace the placeholder text.
6. Click the bulleted list to the right of the graphic. Type the following list:
   * Senior math major
   * Tutoring experience
   * Flexible hours
   * Meet at the library
   * Algebra
   * Trigonometry
   * Calculus
7. Click the placeholder text, Contact person. Type Call Mike at: to replace the text. Click the phone number placeholder text. Type (555) 852-7226 to replace the phone number.
8. Click the dollar amount text box. Type $10/hour to replace the text.
9. Click the text in one of the tear-offs. Type Mike (555) 852-7226 and press the ENTER key. Type mike@mathtutor.com to complete the text.
10. Double-click the graphic. When Publisher displays the Clip Art task pane, type math in the Search for text box. Click the Go button.
11. Scroll through the available clips and choose a graphic that is similar to the one in Figure 1-80 on the previous page. Click the clip in the Clip Art task pane to replace the graphic in the publication. Click the Close button in the Clip Art task pane.
12. Fix any spelling errors you might have made while typing the text. Right-click any words with a red wavy underline below them and then choose the correct spelling on the shortcut menu. Run the Design Checker and fix any errors that Publisher displays.
13. Click File on the menu bar and then click Save As. Save the publication with the file name, Lab 1-1 Math Tutor Flyer.
14. Print the publication.

2 Planning and Creating a Flyer Using Font and Color Schemes

Problem: You have taken a part-time job as an intern at the Ponderosa Realty company. Your first assignment is to create a flyer about a special piece of land that the realty company is trying to sell. Your boss has given you the details about the acreage.

You prepare the publication shown in Figure 1-81. *Hint:* Remember, if you make a mistake while editing the publication, you can click the Undo button on the Standard toolbar to undo your last action.

1. On a piece of paper, fill in the following table to plan for the publication (Table 1-5). See page PUB 6 for information about each of the design issues.
2. Start Publisher.
3. In the New Publication task pane, click Publications for Print, click Flyers, click Sale. When the previews are displayed, click Borders House For Sale Flyer.
4. In the Flyer Options task pane, click Color Schemes. Click Tuscany in the list of color schemes.

In the Lab

5. In the Color Schemes task pane, click Font Schemes. Click Online in the list of font schemes.

6. Right-click the Organization logo at the top of the publication and then click Delete Object on the shortcut menu.

7. Replace the placeholder text in the heading with the words, Land for Sale as the new heading.

8. Replace the other text boxes with the text shown in Figure 1-81.

9. Double-click the graphic. When the Clip Art task pane displays, type scenery in the Search for text box. Click the Go button. Choose an appropriate graphic, similar to the one in Figure 1-81.

10. If you choose a graphic that is different from the one in Figure 1-81, choose a complementary color scheme by clicking the Other Task Panes button on the Clip Art task pane title bar. Click Color Schemes in the list. Choose a color scheme whose second accent color closely matches one of the colors in the graphic.

11. Fix any spelling errors you might have made while typing the text. Right-click each word with a red wavy underline below it and then choose the correct spelling on the shortcut menu. Run the Design Checker and fix any errors that Publisher displays.

12. Click File on the menu bar and then click Save As. Save the publication with the file name, Lab 1-2 Land For Sale Flyer.

13. Print the publication. On the back of the printout, list five places that you might post the flyer in your community if you actually were trying to sell the land. Turn in the planning table and the printout to your instructor.

Land for Sale

- 5 acres
- 8 miles from schools and shopping
- Zoned residential and/or farm
- Horses OK
- Well on property
- Lush vegetation

A beautiful, five-acre setting with mountains on the horizon.

$125,000

Call Chandra at 555 903-8642

Ponderosa Realty

9753 Smiley Lane
Gilbert, CA 94558

Phone: (555) 903-8642
Fox (555) 903-8643
E-mail: Chandra@ponderosarealty.com

FIGURE 1-81

Table 1-5 Planning a Flyer	
DESIGN ISSUE	REALTY FLYER PUBLICATION
Purpose	
Audience	
Gather data	
Plan for printing	
Layout	
Synthesis	

In the Lab

3 Creating a Flyer and Converting it to a Web Publication

Problem: As the resident assistant (RA) in your dormitory, you have been approached by a tour company hoping to schedule a kayak trip for an upcoming weekend. You decide to use your Publisher skills to create a flyer to hang on the bulletin boards in each of the dorms. You also want to post the flyer on the school's electronic bulletin board in hopes of getting 10 people to go, thereby receiving a discount.

Instructions Part 1: Perform the following tasks to create the publication shown in Figure 1-82a:

1. Start Publisher.
2. In the New Publication task pane, click Publications for Print, click Flyers, click Announcement, and then click Baby-Sitting Announcement Flyer.
3. In the Flyer Options task pane, click Color Schemes. Click Sapphire in the list of color schemes.
4. One at a time double-click each of the two graphics. When the Clip Art task pane displays, type kayak in the Search for text box. Click the Go button. When the clips are displayed, click a clip that closely matches the one in Figure 1-82a.
5. Close the Clip Art task pane.
6. Click the heading, Baby-Sitting. Type Kayak Trip to replace the text.
7. Click the text in the description text box. Type Kayak the New River! and then press the ENTER key. Type With 10 students, we can get a discounted rate. Call or e-mail today! to complete the description.
8. Click the text in the hourly rate text box. Type October 23-24, 2004 to replace the text.

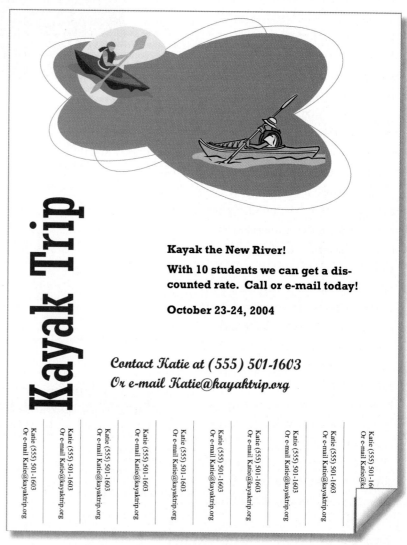

FIGURE 1-82a

9. Click the Contact person placeholder text. SHIFT-click the telephone number placeholder text so both are selected. Type Contact Katie at (555) 501-1603 and then press the ENTER key. Type Or e-mail Katie@kayaktrip.org to complete the contact information.

In the Lab

10. Click the text in any one of the tear-offs. Type `Katie (555) 501-1603` and then press the ENTER key. Type `Or e-mail Katie@ kayaktrip.org` as the entry.

11. Fix any spelling errors you might have made while typing the text. Run the Design Checker, and fix any errors that Publisher displays.

12. Save the publication on your floppy disk with the file name, Lab 1-3 Kayak Trip Flyer.

13. Print the print publication.

Instructions Part 2: Perform the following tasks to convert the flyer to a Web publication shown in Figure 1-82a:

1. When Publisher displays the Kayak Trip Flyer, right-click the tear-offs and then click Delete Object on the shortcut menu.

2. In the contact information text box, select the text, Katie@ kayaktrip.org, by dragging through it. Click the Insert Hyperlink button on the Standard toolbar. When the Insert Hyperlink dialog box is displayed, click E-mail Address on the Link to bar. Type `Katie@kayaktrip.org` in the E-mail address text box. Press the TAB key. Type `Kayak Trip Web Flyer Inquiry` in the Subject text box. Click the OK button.

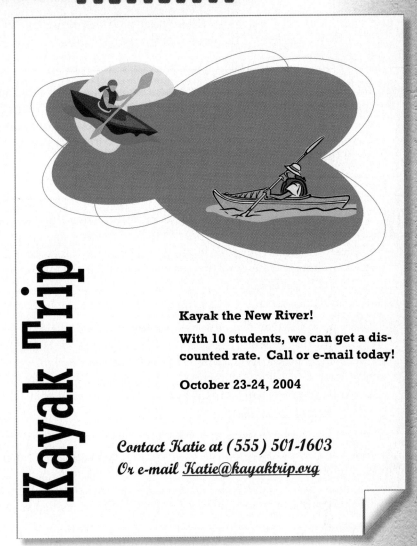

Kayak the New River!

With 10 students, we can get a discounted rate. Call or e-mail today!

October 23-24, 2004

Contact Katie at (555) 501-1603
Or e-mail <u>Katie@kayaktrip.org</u>

FIGURE 1-82b

3. Run the Design Checker and fix any errors that Publisher displays.

4. Click Save As on the File menu and save the file on your floppy disk with the file name, Lab 1-3 Kayak Trip Web Flyer.

5. Click File on the menu bar and then click Convert to Web Publication. When Publisher displays the Saves Your Current Print Publication step, click the No option button to select it. When Publisher displays the Add a Navigation Bar step, click the No option button to select it. Click the Finish button.

6. Click File on the menu bar and then click Publish to the Web. If a Microsoft Office Publisher dialog box is displayed, click its OK button. Save the file as, Lab 1-3 Kayak Trip Web Flyer.

7. When the Publish to the Web dialog box is displayed, click the Save button. When the Microsoft Office Publisher dialog box that describes filtered HTML files is displayed, click the OK button.

8. Preview the Web Flyer by clicking the Web Page Preview button on the Standard toolbar. When you are done previewing, click the browser's Close button. Print the Web publication.

Cases and Places

The difficulty of these case studies varies:
■ are the least difficult and ■■ are more difficult. The last exercise is a group exercise.

1 ■ Use the Flyers Fundraiser template titled Car Wash Fundraiser Flyer 2 to create a flyer for your club's upcoming 5K walk-a-thon for charity. Select the Crocus color scheme and the Casual font scheme in the Flyer Options task pane. The walk-a-thon is Saturday, September 18 from 10:00 a.m. to 2:00 p.m. Use the name of your own school and address in the appropriate areas. The starting location is the College Library parking lot.

2 ■ Your high school has asked you to create a flyer for the upcoming 10-year class reunion. Create a table similar to Table 1-1 on page PUB 6. Once you are satisfied with your planning, create the flyer with information from your high school. Be sure to include at least two bulleted items in a list, and insert an appropriate graphic from the Media Gallery or the Web.

3 ■■ Start the Play Announcement Flyer template to create a flyer for a local dramatic production. Use the Cranberry color scheme and the Fusion font scheme. Look through a local newspaper to find a community theater production. Use the techniques in Project 1 to edit the flyer with the local information. Include the name of the play, the author, the dates, the time, the location, and the ticket prices. Choose an appropriate graphic from the Clip Art task pane. Delete any unused or unnecessary objects.

4 ■■ Many communities offer free Web page hosting for religious organizations. Using a Flyers template, create a flyer for a local house of worship. Include the name, address, telephone, worship and education hours, as well as the name of a contact person. If possible, include a photo of the building. Run the publication through the Design Checker and then save it as a Web publication.

5 ■■ Your Internet service provider maintains an electronic bulletin board where customers may post one-page business announcements. Create an advertising flyer for the place where you work or want to work. You may use one of Publisher's templates, or design the flyer from scratch. Use color and graphics to attract attention. Use a bulleted list to describe your company's services. Instead of tear-offs, use a text box that includes the company's e-mail address as a hyperlink. Use words in your text boxes that will produce many hits during Web searches. Save the flyer as a Web publication.

6 ■■ **Working Together** Schools, churches, libraries, grocery stores, and other public places have bulletin boards for flyers and other postings. Often, these bulletin boards have so many flyers that some go unnoticed. Look at a local bulletin board and find a posted flyer that you think might be overlooked. Copy the text from the announcement and distribute it to each team member. Each member then independently should use this text to create an announcement that would be more likely to catch a reader's eye. Be sure to check the spelling and run the Design Checker. As a group, critique each flyer and have each member redesign his or her flyer based on the group's recommendations. Hand in printouts of each team member's original and final flyer.

Designing a Newsletter

PROJECT

2

CASE PERSPECTIVE

Extreme Sports Club is a student organization at Ventana State College. The club's membership includes students who are interested in playing, watching, and learning more about extreme sports. The members meet once each month and plan extreme activities such as gravity games, bungee jumping, and various forms of biking, skating, and board sports. The campus is close to the beach, so many of the club's members are interested in surfing, as well. Extreme Sports Club has 30 members, both male and female, from freshmen to seniors, who represent many different academic majors on campus. Ventana State College provides student organizations, such as Extreme Sports Club, with a place to meet and a faculty sponsor.

Each month, the club sends a newsletter via e-mail to its members, other interested students, and people who subscribe to the athletics listserv. It also distributes a printed version on paper around campus. Several students submit monthly articles for the newsletter after they are approved by the faculty sponsor, Mr. Sullivan. Some of the members are graduating, so the club needs help with the publication of the newsletter.

Because you are both a member of Extreme Sports Club and a computer and information technology major, Mr. Sullivan has asked you to use Publisher to create the newsletter this year. You agree, as your assignments for your desktop publishing class include similar projects. Together, you and Mr. Sullivan decide on a color scheme and font that matches the flair and personality of this club. Because the club does not have a large budget, the newsletter will be just two pages, printed front and back.

As you read through this project, you will learn how to use Publisher to create, save, and print a newsletter that includes a masthead, imported text and graphics, a pull quote, and WordArt.

Designing a Newsletter

Objectives

You will have mastered the material in this project when you can:

- Describe the advantages of using a newsletter medium and identify the steps in its design process
- Edit a newsletter template
- Insert, delete, and navigate pages in a newsletter
- Edit a masthead
- Import text files and graphics

- Edit personal information components, design sets, attention getters, styles, and sidebars
- Insert a WordArt object and pull quote
- Add page numbers to the master page
- Identify foreground and background elements
- Check a newsletter for spelling and design errors
- Print a two-sided page

Introduction

Desktop publishing is becoming the most popular way for businesses of all sizes to produce their printed publications. The desktop aspects of design and production make it easy and inexpensive to produce high-quality documents in a short time. **Desktop** implies doing everything from a desk, including the planning, designing, writing, layout, cutting, and pasting, as well as printing, collating, and distributing. With a personal computer and a software program such as Publisher, you can create a professional document from your computer without the cost and time of sending it to a professional publisher.

Project Two — Designing a Newsletter

Project 2 uses a Publisher Newsletter template to produce *Extreme News*, the newsletter shown in Figures 2-1a and 2-1b. This semi-monthly publication informs a college community about events sponsored by the Extreme Sports Club on campus. The club's two-page newsletter contains articles, features, event dates, and graphics.

Extreme News

Extreme Sports Club

Special points of interest:

- Surfing Championship Tour, September 15
- X-Meeting Mondays, 7:00 p.m. Student Center
- Gravity Games at Back to Campus Days, October 1-2

Volume 3, Issue 1   September 2, 2005

Surfing Championship Tour

Are you ready to see Doug, Ross, Spiel, Freddie, and Nate the Great mix it up? The Surfing Championship Tour (SCT) is coming to town Thursday, September 15.

The world's top-rated professional surfers will be making their only local appearance next week. A 10-day waiting period from September 5-14 will guarantee the best surfing conditions possible as the top-25 surfers in the world battle it out for $250,000 in total prize money.

The last time the SCT visited our bea newcomer Doug pulled off a big victo over Jon Redmond. Now Doug retur with veteran Nate the Great to mix it

with rising superstars like Australians Freddie Mantel and Spiel Connor. Nate and Ross are relying on local knowledge to give them an advantage over the international field.

Nate the

The proximity of the event to the Extreme Expo will attract the surfing world's top luminaries and put added pressure on contestants to perform at their high-

"Mountain biking isn't just great exercise, it's a great way to take a break from everything!"

Mountain Bik

It's a whole new world when you're mountain biking," says Ken Jones, biking enthusiast and V.P. of the Extreme Sports Club. "You have so much more stimulus with the trees and the terrain." Although he still puts the miles on his road bike, Jones says that when he is on his mountain bike,

he gets amoun

Jones i made th In fact, terrain the fast ing to t

1

Extreme Sports Club

Campus Student Union
Ventana State College
Big Sur, California

Phone: 831-555-1234
Fax: 831-555-1235
E-mail: extremesports@vsc.edu

Everything Extreme!

Do you march to the beat of a different drummer? Do you push the boundaries? Are you an adrenaline junkie?

In the Extreme Sports Club, we understand your passion for that tingling feeling. We understand why you ignore that faint voice in your head that asks, "Why am I doing this?" We know what it is like to have folks shake their heads in bewilderment.

Breathe deeply. You are now among friends. Whether it is battling gravity on the side of a rock, punching through life's less than peaceful waters, or wheeling over a poorly maintained trail, just choose an extreme and go! In the Extreme Sports Club, we will keep you up-to-date with awesome information, cool locations, local accommodations, and just plain nonsensical verbiage. After all, life is WAY too short to be normal.

Mondays, Student Center, 7 p.m.

Up for Gravity Games?

The 2005 Campus Gravity Games will be held October 1-2, at the Campus Arena during the annual Back to Campus days. The campus TV station will broadcast this year's games.

The Campus Gravity Games competitions will be held in the following categories: Inline Vert, Bike Vert, Bike Street, Skateboarding Street, and Skateboarding Vert.

In general, gravity games include any kind of extreme sport in which participants leave the ground, such as skateboarding or trick biking, although recently it has started to include wakeboarding and wake skating.

Last year, more than 250 people participated in the games, which drew a huge crowd from students, the community, and parents who were on campus for Back to Campus days.

The Campus Gravity Games are both invitational (some of the

Skateboarding tricks thrill the audience at last year's event.

local stars will compete) and open for rookie qualifiers. You can pick up an application at the Student Union. All participants need to supply their own helmets, as well as knee and elbow pads, which are required.

Qualification rounds begin at 8:00 a.m. Music, food, and fun begin at 10:00 a.m. Several local bands are scheduled to perform.

Tickets are $5.00 for students and children and $8.00 for adults. After defraying the cost of the arena and judges, all proceeds from this year's Campus Gravity Games will benefit the Extreme Sports Club on campus.

2

FIGURE 2-1

Starting Publisher

To start Publisher, Windows must be running. The following steps explain how to start Publisher.

To Start Publisher

1 Click the Start button on the Windows taskbar, point to All Programs on the Start menu, point to Microsoft Office on the All Programs submenu, and then click Microsoft Office Publisher 2003 on the Microsoft Office submenu.

2 If the Publisher window is not maximized, double-click its title bar to maximize it.

3 If Publisher does not display the New Publication task pane, click View on the menu bar and then click Task Pane. If the Publication Designs task pane is displayed, click the Other Task Panes button in the task pane title bar, and then click New Publication.

4 If the Language bar displays, click its Minimize button.

You may recall that Publisher's New Publication task pane displays publication types, commands to begin new publications, and the names of previously opened publications on your computer.

The Newsletter Medium

Newsletters are a popular way for offices, businesses, and other organizations to distribute information to their clientele. A **newsletter** usually is a double-sided multi-page publication with newspaper features such as columns and a masthead, and the added eye appeal of sidebars, pictures, and other graphics.

Newsletters have several advantages over other publication media. They are easy to produce. **Brochures**, designed to be in circulation longer as a type of advertising, usually are published in greater quantities and on more expensive paper than newsletters and are, therefore, more costly. Additionally, newsletters differ from brochures in that they commonly have a shorter shelf life, making newsletters a perfect forum for dated information.

Newsletters are narrower and more focused in scope than newspapers; their eye appeal is more distinctive. Many organizations and companies distribute newsletters inexpensively to interested audiences, although that is beginning to change. Newsletters are becoming an integral part of many marketing plans because they offer a legitimate medium by which to communicate services, successes, and issues.

Table 2-1 lists some benefits and advantages of using the newsletter medium.

Table 2-1 Benefits and Advantages of Using a Newsletter Medium

AREA	BENEFITS AND ADVANTAGES
Exposure	An easily distributed publication — office mail, bulk mail, electronically A pass-along document for other interested parties A coffee table reading item in reception areas
Education	An opportunity to inform in a nonrestrictive environment A directed education forum for clientele An increased, focused feedback — unavailable in most advertising
Contacts	A form of legitimized contact A source of free information to build credibility An easier way to expand a contact database than other marketing tools
Communication	An effective medium to highlight the inner workings of a company A way to create a discussion forum A method to disseminate more information than a brochure
Cost	An easily designed medium using desktop publishing software An inexpensive method of mass production A reusable design

Designing a Newsletter

Designing an effective newsletter involves a great deal of planning. A good newsletter, or any publication, must deliver a message in the clearest, most attractive, and effective way possible. You must clarify your purpose and know your target audience. You need to gather ideas and plan for the printing of the newsletter. Finally, you must determine the best layout for eye appeal and reliable dissemination of content.

Table 2-2 Design Process Issues

DESIGN ISSUE	NEWSLETTER APPLICATION
Purpose	To communicate and to educate readers about the organization
Audience	Local interested clientele or patrons, both present and future
Gather data	Articles, pictures, dates, figures, tables, discussion threads
Plan for printing	Usually mass-produced, collated, and stapled
Layout	Consistent look and feel; simple, eye-catching graphics
Synthesis	Edit, proofread, and publish

Table 2-2 outlines the issues to consider during the design process and their application to newsletters.

Creating a Newsletter Template Using a Template

You can type a newsletter from scratch by choosing a blank publication from the task pane, or you can use a template that Publisher preformats with appropriate headings, graphics, and spacing. You can customize the resulting newsletter by filling in the blanks, and selecting and replacing objects.

Many design planning features are built into Publisher, including 65 different newsletter templates from which you may choose, each with its own set of design, color, font, and layout schemes. The Newsletter Options task pane provides options for double-sided printing and customer address, color and font schemes links, and page content design choices.

The steps on the next page illustrate how to choose a newsletter template and make design choices.

To Choose a Newsletter Template and Change Options

1

• **In the New Publication task pane, click Publications for Print in the New from a design area. When the types of publications are displayed, scroll as necessary to display Newsletters.**

• **Click Newletters.**

• **Scroll to display the Banded Newsletter preview.**

Publisher displays the New Publication task pane on the left and the previews on the right in the Newsletters pane (Figure 2-2). The list of previews may display differently on your computer. The Banded Newsletter preview displays a blue box around it when you point to it.

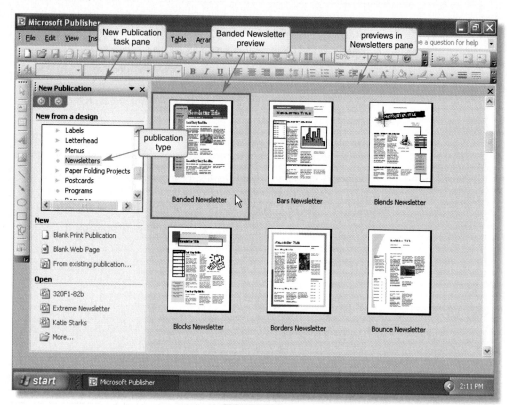

FIGURE 2-2

2

• **Click the Banded Newsletter preview. If Publisher displays a Personal Information dialog box, click its Cancel button.**

The Newsletter Options task pane is displayed on the left. In the workspace, page 1 of the Banded Newsletter displays (Figure 2-3). Newsletter options include both the choice of one- or two-sided printing and whether or not to include a customer address.

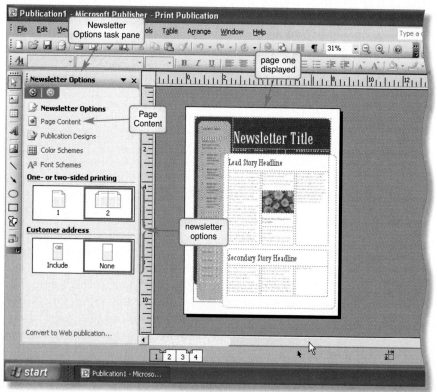

FIGURE 2-3

3

• **In the Newsletter Options task pane, click Page Content. When the Page Content task pane is displayed, click Mixed in the Columns area.**

*The page content of the newsletter will display a **mixed** variety of 1, 2, and 3 columns of text (Figure 2-4).*

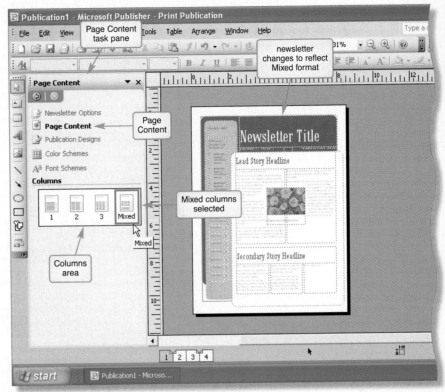

FIGURE 2-4

4

• **Click Color Schemes. In the Apply a color scheme list, click Cranberry.**

The newsletter is displayed with the Cranberry color scheme (Figure 2-5).

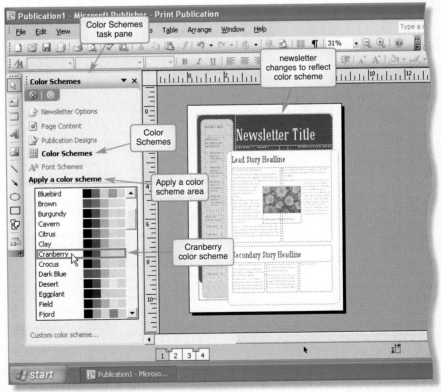

FIGURE 2-5

Microsoft Office Publisher 2003

5

• **Click Font Schemes. In the Apply a font scheme list, if necessary, scroll down and then click the Basis font scheme.**

Publisher displays the newsletter with the Basis font scheme (Figure 2-6).

FIGURE 2-6

6

• **Click the Close button in the Font Schemes task pane.**

The publication displays the options, content layout, color, and font choices selected from the task panes (Figure 2-7).

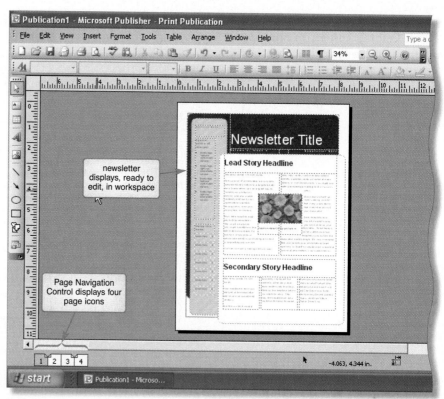

FIGURE 2-7

You can revisit newsletter options to make changes by clicking View on the menu bar and then clicking Task Pane.

Any publication you choose in the Publications list is a Publisher-designed publication. You may use these publications, of course, as part of Publisher's licensing agreement. Using proven design strategies, Publisher places text and graphics in the publication at appropriate places for a professional looking newsletter.

Editing the Newsletter Template

As the first step in the design process, the purpose of a newsletter is to communicate and educate its readers. Publisher places the lead story in a prominent position on the page and uses a discussion of purpose and audience as the default text.

The following pages discuss how to edit various articles and objects in the newsletter.

Pagination

Publisher's Newsletter template creates four pages of text and graphics. This template is appropriate for some applications, but the Extreme Sports Club wants to print a single sheet, two-sided newsletter. Page 4 of the newsletter contains objects typically used on the back page, so you will delete pages 2 and 3. The following steps show how to change and delete pages.

To Change and Delete Pages in a Newsletter

1

• **Click the Page 2 icon on the Page Navigation Control.**

Pages 2 and 3 are displayed in the workspace (Figure 2-8). The Page Navigation Control displays the selected pages in light orange on the status bar.

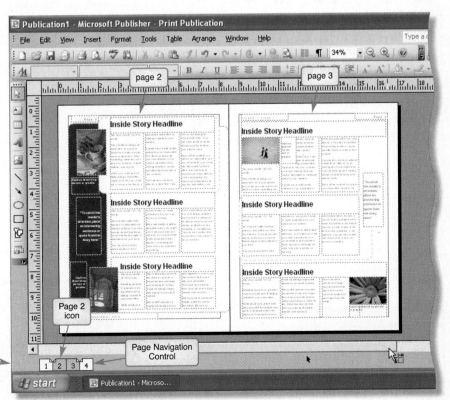

FIGURE 2-8

2

• **Click Edit on the menu bar and then click Delete Page.**

• **When the Delete Page dialog box is displayed, if necessary, click Both pages to select it.**

Publisher displays a dialog box with options for deleting either or both pages (Figure 2-9).

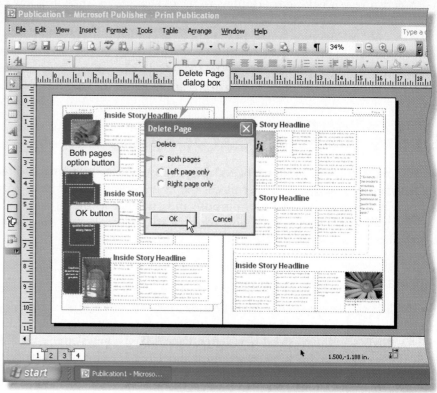

FIGURE 2-9

3

• **Click the OK button in the Delete Page dialog box.**

• **If a Microsoft Publisher dialog box displays to confirm deleting all the objects, click the OK button.**

Publisher deletes pages 2 and 3 and displays the back page as the new page 2 (Figure 2-10).

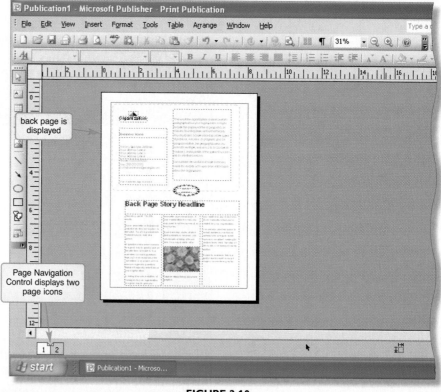

FIGURE 2-10

Other Ways

1. To change pages, on Edit menu click Go to Page
2. To change pages, press CTRL+G
3. To change pages, press F5
4. To delete pages, on Edit menu, click Delete Page

Inserting pages in a newsletter is just as easy as deleting them. The Page command on the Insert menu provides the option of inserting a left- or right-hand page, as well as choices in the types of objects to display on the page. When you choose to insert or delete, when working on the first or last page, Publisher will warn you of pagination problems and will offer you a confirmation dialog box.

With the newsletter containing two pages, you are ready to edit the masthead, graphics, and articles.

Editing the Masthead

Most newsletters and brochures contain a masthead similar to those used in newspapers. A **masthead** is a box or section printed in each issue that lists information, such as the name, publisher, location, volume, and date. The Publisher-designed masthead, included in the Banded Newsletter template, contains several text boxes and color-filled shapes that create an attractive, eye-catching graphic that complements the Banded Newsletter design set. You need to edit the text boxes, however, to convey appropriate messages.

Publisher incorporates three text boxes in the Banded Newsletter masthead (Figure 2-11 on the next page). The newsletter title is displayed in a text box layered on top of a rectangle. Two text boxes are displayed in the lower portion of the masthead for the volume/issue and date.

Editing Techniques

Recall that Publisher uses text-editing techniques similar to most word processing programs. To insert text, position the insertion point and type the new text. Publisher always inserts the text to the left of the insertion point. The text to the right of the insertion point moves to the right and downward to accommodate the new text.

The BACKSPACE key deletes text to the left of the insertion point. To delete or change more than a few characters, however, you should select the text. Publisher handles selecting text in a slightly different manner than word processing programs. In Publisher, you select unedited default text, such as placeholder titles and articles in the newsletters, with a single click. To select large amounts of text, click the text and then press CTRL+A to select all the text in the text box, or drag through the text. To select individual words, double-click the word, as you would in word processing.

The steps on the next page demonstrate some of these techniques as text is selected and edited.

More About

Design Issues

The steps in good design and attractive layout are similar to the steps in designing any new product, program, or presentation. For more information on design, visit the Publisher 2003 More About Web page (scsite.com/pub2003/more) and click Design Issues.

More About

Design Sets

Each Publisher-designed newsletter is part of a design set, which is a collection of related publication types that share a consistent color scheme, design, and look. For example, a master set includes a business card, a company letterhead, and a company brochure, each with a matching design. To view design sets and their elements, click the Design Gallery Object button, and then click the Objects by Design tab.

More About

Deleting

Whether to delete using the BACKSPACE key or the DELETE key is debated in word processing circles. It really depends on the location of the insertion point in the publication. If the insertion point already is positioned left of the character you want to delete, it makes more sense to press the DELETE key rather than reposition the insertion point just to use the BACKSPACE key.

To Edit the Masthead

1

• **Click the Page 1 icon on the Page Navigation Control.**

• **Click the text, Newsletter Title. Press the F9 key to view the masthead more closely.**

Publisher enlarges the masthead and selects the entire title's text because it is placeholder text (Figure 2-11).

FIGURE 2-11

2

• **Type** Extreme News **in the text box.**

• **Click the placeholder text in the volume/issue text box.**

Publisher replaces the selected text using the font from the design set (Figure 2-12). Because fonts sometimes are printer-dependent, your font may differ from the one shown. Publisher selects the placeholder text in the volume/issue text box.

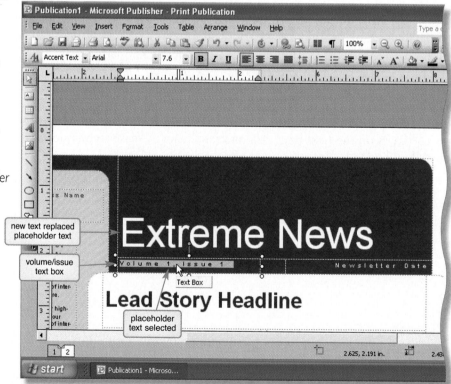

FIGURE 2-12

3

- **Type** Volume 3, Issue 1 **to replace the selected text.**
- **Click the placeholder text, Newsletter Date.**

Publisher selects the entire date because it is placeholder text, designed to be replaced (Figure 2-13). The new volume and issue information is entered.

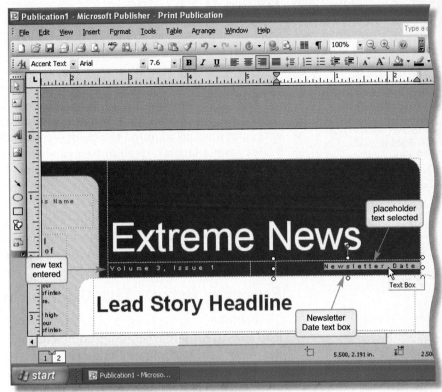

FIGURE 2-13

4

- **Type** September 2, 2005 **in the text box.**

The masthead edits are complete (Figure 2-14).

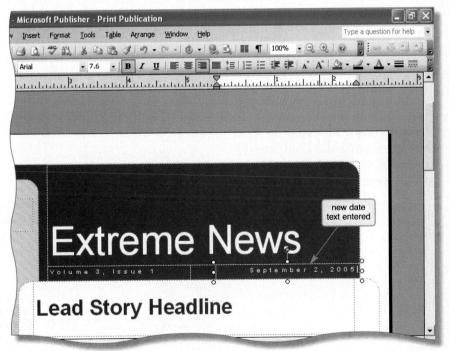

FIGURE 2-14

Different newsletter templates may include other shapes and text boxes in their mastheads, such as a text box that displays the organization name.

More About

Importing Files

In order to import all manner of word processing documents, you must have chosen to perform a full installation of Microsoft Publisher. Publisher will remind you to reinsert the Publisher CD-ROM if it needs more information about the type of file you are trying to import.

Importing Files

Publisher allows users to import text and graphics from many sources into its publications. Publisher accepts imported objects from a variety of different programs and in many different file formats. Gathering data of interest to the readers is an important phase in the design process. The stories for the newsletter are provided on the Data Disk associated with this textbook. See the inside back cover for instructions for downloading the Data Disk or see your instructor for information on accessing the files required in this book. **Downloading** means moving data or programs from a larger computer to a smaller one. Publisher uses the term **importing** to describe inserting text or objects from any other source into the Publisher workspace.

Publisher uses the term, **story**, to mean text that is contained within a single text box or a chain of linked text boxes. Each newsletter template provides **linked text boxes**, or text boxes whose text flows from one to another. In the templates, two or three text boxes may be linked automatically; however, if a story is too long to fit in the linked text boxes, Publisher will offer to link even more text boxes for easy reading.

Replacing Default Text Using an Imported File

Publisher suggests that 175 to 225 words will fit in the space allocated for the lead story. This Publisher-designed newsletter uses a two-column text format that **connects**, or wraps, the running text from one linked text box to the next.

This edition of *Extreme News* has three stories that previously have been typed and stored using Microsoft Word. The stories, stored on the Data Disk that accompanies this textbook, are ready to be used in the newsletter.

The following steps first edit the Lead Story Headline placeholder text and then import a text file from a floppy disk to replace the Publisher-supplied default text.

To Edit a Headline and Import a Text File

1

• **With the Data Disk in drive A, scroll down until the Lead Story Headline is displayed. Click the headline text to select it.**

The placeholder text is selected (Figure 2-15).

FIGURE 2-15

2

• **Type** Surfing Championship Tour **to replace the selected placeholder text.**

• **Click the story below the headline. Read the story.**

Publisher displays the new headline and selects the entire story (Figure 2-16). Reading the story will provide you with valuable suggestions about the design process of newsletter publications.

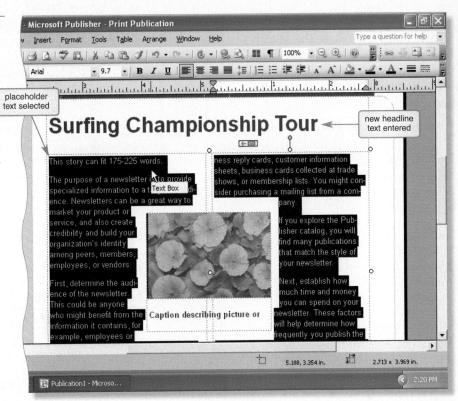

FIGURE 2-16

3

• **Click Insert on the menu bar.**

Publisher displays the Insert menu (Figure 2-17).

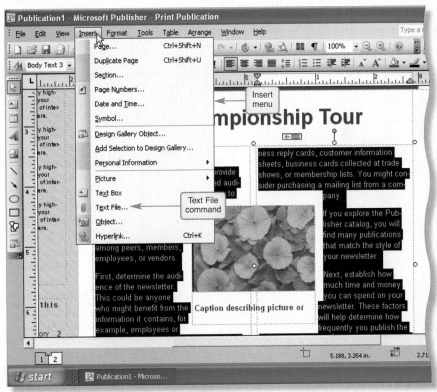

FIGURE 2-17

Microsoft Office
Publisher 2003

4

• **Click Text File. When the Insert Text dialog box is displayed, click the Look in box arrow, and then click 3½ Floppy (A:) in the Look in list.**

• **Double-click the Project 2 folder.**

The data files on the floppy disk are displayed below the Look in box (Figure 2-18). Your list of files may differ.

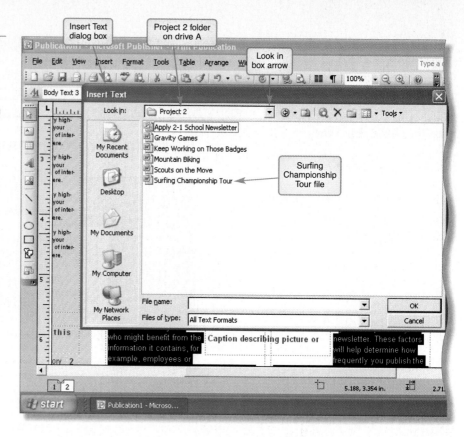

FIGURE 2-18

5

• **Double-click the Surfing Championship Tour file name.**

The story is inserted in the newsletter (Figure 2-19).

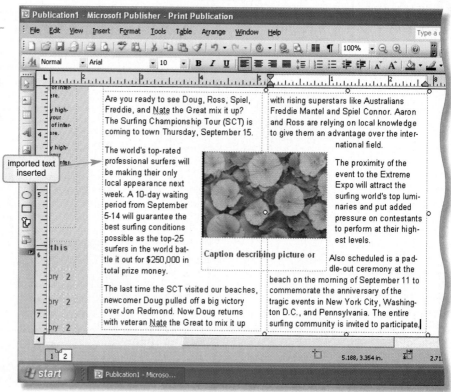

FIGURE 2-19

Other Ways

1. Right-click story, point to Change Text on shortcut menu, click Text File

Continuing a story across columns or text boxes is one of the features that Publisher performs for you. If the story contains more text than will fit in the default text box, Publisher displays a message to warn you. You then have the option of connecting to another box or continuing the story on another page. Publisher will add the continued notices, or **jump lines**, to guide readers through the story.

Recall that the F9 **function key** toggles between the current page view and 100% magnification. **Toggle** means the same key will alternate views, or turn a feature on and off. Editing text is much easier if you view the text box at 100% magnification or even larger. Page editing techniques, such as moving graphics, inserting new boxes, and aligning objects, more easily are performed in **whole page view**. Toggling back and forth with the F9 function key works well. You also may choose different magnifications and views by clicking the Zoom box arrow on the Standard toolbar.

Importing Text for the Secondary Story

The next step is to edit the secondary story headline and import the text for the story in the lower portion of page 1 of the newsletter as explained in the steps below.

To Import More Text

1 **Scroll to display the lower portion of page 1 and then click the Secondary Story Headline placeholder text to select it.**

2 **Type** Mountain Biking **to replace the selected headline.**

3 **Click the secondary story to select it.**

4 **Click Insert on the menu bar and then click Text File.**

5 **If not already selected, click 3½ Floppy (A:) in the Look in list.**

6 **Double-click the Mountain Biking file name.**

The story is imported as shown in Figure 2-20. Your screen may differ slightly, depending on the fonts your computer uses.

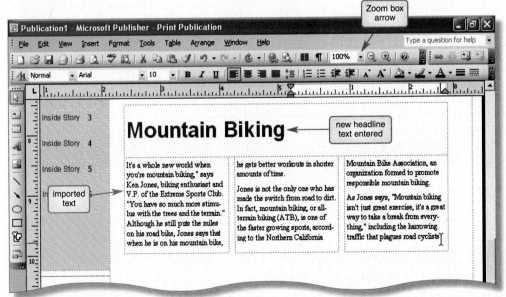

FIGURE 2-20

Importing Text on the Back Page

The final steps to finish the imported stories in the newsletter involve importing text for the back page story, as described in the following steps.

To Import the Back Page Story

1 **Click the Page 2 icon on the Page Navigation Control.**

2 **Click the Back Page Story Headline placeholder text.**

3 **Type** Up for Gravity Games? **to replace the selected text.**

4 **Click the back page story text below the headline to select it.**

5 **Click Insert on the menu bar and then click Text File.**

6 **If not already selected, click 3½ Floppy (A:) in the Look in list.**

7 **Double-click the Gravity Games file name.**

The imported story and headline are shown in Figure 2-21.

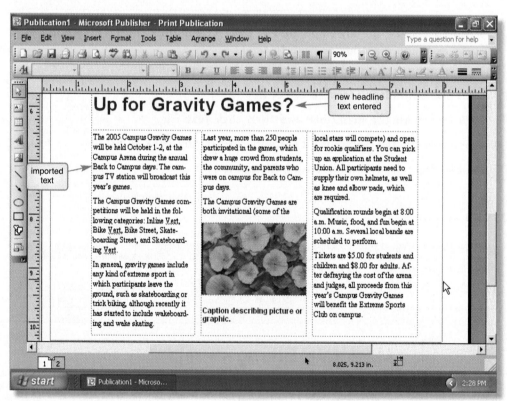

FIGURE 2-21

All the stories for the newsletter now are complete. Importing the stories instead of typing them saves time and adds the convenience of using word processing. Publisher accepts most file formats from popular word processing programs and text editors.

Saving an Intermediate Copy of the Newsletter

A good practice is to save intermediate copies of your work. That way, if your computer loses power or you make a serious mistake, you always can retrieve the latest copy from disk. Use the Save button on the Standard toolbar often, because you can save time later if the unexpected happens.

With the masthead and story headlines edited, and the text files imported, it now is a good time to save the entire newsletter before continuing. For the following steps, it is assumed you have a floppy disk in drive A.

To Save an Intermediate Copy of the Newsletter

1 Click the Save button on the Standard toolbar.

2 Type Extreme Newsletter in the File name text box. If necessary, click 3½ Floppy (A:) in the Save in list.

3 Click the Save button in the Save As dialog box.

Publisher saves the publication on a floppy disk in drive A using the file name, Extreme Newsletter (Figure 2-22). The new file name displays on the Publisher title bar and the Publisher button on the taskbar.

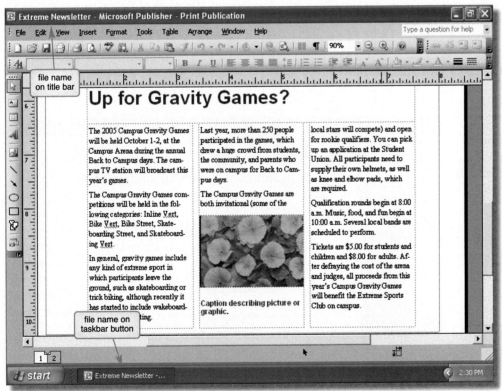

FIGURE 2-22

More About

**Personal
Information Sets**

Publisher maintains four personal information sets: Primary Business, Secondary Business, Other Organization, and Home/Family. Every new publication has the Primary Business personal information set selected by default. You can apply a different personal information set to the publication, however. Simply click Personal Information on the Edit menu and then click the appropriate set.

Working with Personal Information Sets

Publisher permits you to store four unique sets of personal information for use at work and home. The name of the organization, the address, the telephone number, and other pieces of information such as tag lines and logos are stored in personal information sets. In **personal information sets**, Publisher can keep track of data about you, your business, an organization affiliation, or other personal information that you might use to create publications. In this newsletter, you will edit the text box for the organization name, address lines, phone, fax, and e-mail. You will learn more about permanently changing personal information components in a future project.

Editing the Personal Information Components

Both pages of the newsletter contain an Organization Name Text Box. Editing one of these text boxes automatically changes the other. Additionally, after typing the name of your organization, Publisher can reuse the text in other publications, if it is saved as a personal information component. A **personal information component** is a text box or logo that contains information about the organization from the Personal Information Set. This information can carry over from one publication to the next. For example, the name of the company might be displayed at the top of the newsletter, on the business cards, and on the letterhead stationery.

The following steps show how to edit personal information components for this publication only.

To Edit Personal Information Components

1

• **With page 2 still displayed, scroll if necessary, and drag through the placeholder text in the Organization Name Text Box in the upper-left corner.**

Your Personal Information Set may display a different organization name in the text box (Figure 2-23).

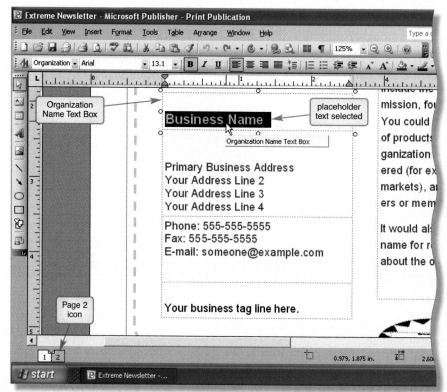

FIGURE 2-23

2

• **Type** Extreme Sports Club **to replace the text in the text box.**

The text, Extreme Sports Club, replaces the selected text (Figure 2-24). Because it is part of the personal information set, Publisher changed the Organization Name Text Box on both pages of the publication.

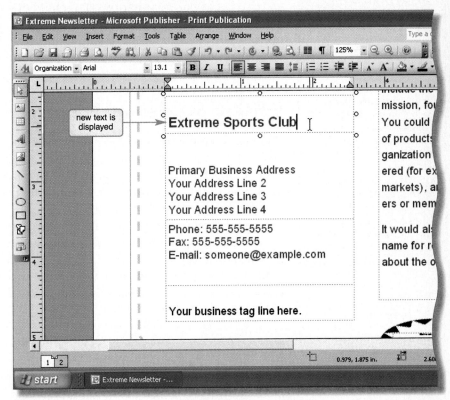

FIGURE 2-24

3

• **Repeat Step 2 to edit the text boxes for the address lines, phone, fax, and e-mail, and the Tag Line Text Box, as shown in Figure 2-25.**

• **As you type, press the ENTER key for new lines of text inside the text boxes when necessary.**

The edited personal information components are displayed in the newsletter (Figure 2-25).

FIGURE 2-25

Q: Which should I use for creating my text, Publisher or Word?

A: Microsoft recommends using the best tool for the job. For desktop publishing, Publisher offers more features and buttons related to the many kinds of objects desktop publishers need and use than does Word. For straight typing tasks, such as term papers and letters that need little or no graphics or advanced page layout and design, Word is a better tool.

Each personal information component has its own preset font, font size, and text alignment. If desired, you can make changes to the formatting for individual publications. If you want to keep Publisher from synchronizing, or repeating, the changed component on other pages, click Undo on the Edit menu.

Editing Stories in Microsoft Word

You have seen that you can edit text directly in Microsoft Publisher or import text from a previously stored file. A third way to edit text is to use Microsoft Word as your editor. Publisher provides an easy link between the two applications.

If you need to edit only a few words, it is faster to stay in Publisher. If you need to edit a longer story that appears on different pages in a publication or one that has not been stored previously, it might be easier to edit the story in Word. Many users are accustomed to working in Word and want to take advantage of available Word features, such as grammar checking and revision tracking. It sometimes is easier to drag and drop paragraphs in a Word window rather than performing the same task in a Publisher window, especially when it involves moving across pages in a larger Publisher publication.

Editing a Story Using Word

In the *Extreme News* newsletter, the back page contains a text box to display more information about the organization. The club's informational text has not been stored previously in a file for importing, so it must be typed.

Microsoft Word version 6.0 or later must be installed on your computer for this procedure to work. Occasionally, if you have many applications running, such as virus protection and other memory-taxing programs, Publisher may warn you that you are low on computer memory. In that case, close the other applications, and try editing the story in Word again.

The following steps illustrate how to use Microsoft Word in conjunction with Publisher to create the text.

To Edit a Story Using Word

1

• **If necessary, click the Page 2 icon on the Page Navigation Control. Scroll to display the text box in the upper-right portion of the page.**

• **Click any text in the text box and then press CTRL+A to select all of the text.**

The text is selected in the text box (Figure 2-26).

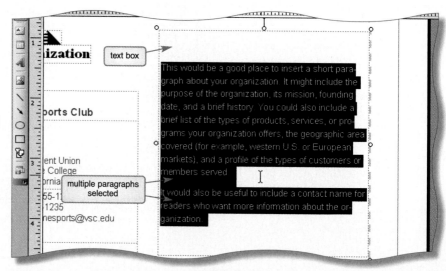

FIGURE 2-26

2

• **Press the DELETE key to delete the current story.**

• **Click Edit on the menu bar.**

Publisher displays the Edit menu (Figure 2-27).

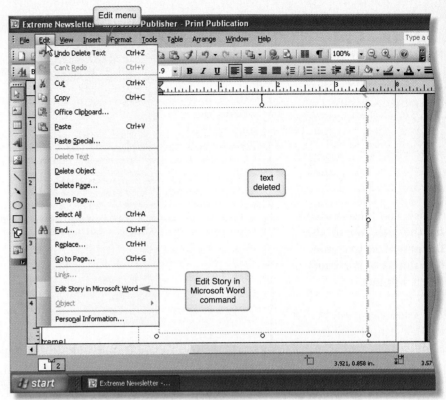

FIGURE 2-27

3

• **Click Edit Story in Microsoft Word.**

Microsoft Word starts in a new window (Figure 2-28).

FIGURE 2-28

FIGURE 2-29

4

• **Type the story as shown in Figure 2-29.**

The text displays the same formatting as the previously deleted text in Publisher. Your display may differ depending on available fonts.

5

• **Click the Close button on the title bar of the Document in Extreme Newsletter – Microsoft Word window.**

The edited story is displayed in the Publisher text box (see Figure 2-30 on the next page).

Other Ways

1. Right-click article, point to Change Text, click Edit Story in Microsoft Word

More About

Text Columns

Publisher provides two ways to create text in columns: connected text boxes and columns. The Newsletter template creates separate text boxes and connects them as frames. You also can use multiple columns within one text box. Either way, the text will flow automatically, and jump lines will guide the reader. If you want separate stories in adjacent columns on the same page, or if you want your story to have unequal column widths, use separate text boxes.

While you are working on a story in Word, you cannot edit the corresponding text box in Publisher. Editing your stories in Word allows you to manipulate the text using the full capabilities of a word processing program.

Displaying Overflow Text

Below the text box in Figure 2-30 is a **Text in Overflow indicator**, which means that there is more text than can fit in the current text box. The **overflow area** is an invisible storage location within your publication to hold extra text — similar to a clipboard, but saved with the publication. The overflow area is not electricity-dependent. You can move your text out of overflow and back into your publication by one of several means: fitting text automatically using the Best Fit option, enlarging the text font size, changing the text size, changing the margins within the text box, or deleting some of the text in the text box.

The following steps resize the text box to accommodate overflow text.

To Display Overflow Text

1

• **Point to the middle-right handle of the text box as shown in Figure 2-30.**

The mouse pointer changes to a double-headed arrow.

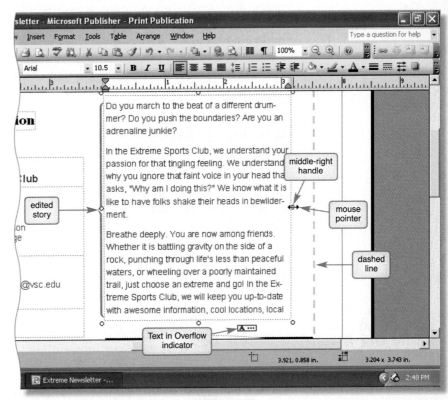

FIGURE 2-30

2

• **Drag the handle to the right until it aligns with the dashed line.**

• **Release the mouse button.**

The text box is resized (Figure 2-31). All of the text now fits inside the text box, and the Text in Overflow indicator no longer is displayed.

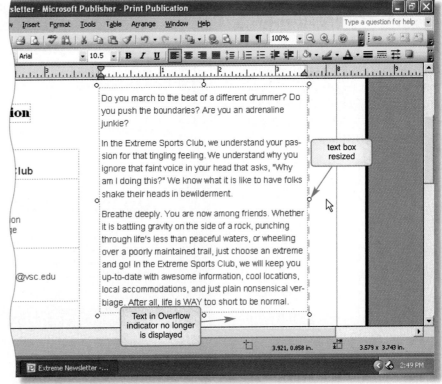

FIGURE 2-31

Other Ways

1. Right-click text, point to Change Text, point to AutoFit Text, click Shrink Text On Overflow
2. Select text, enter smaller number in Font Size box
3. Double-click status bar, increase Width and Height numbers

Microsoft Office
Publisher 2003

Editing the Design Set

Page 2 of the newsletter contains several objects that are part of the newsletter publication design set. A design set is specific to the type of publication and chosen template. Recall that an object in Publisher is any text box, shape, border, image, or table inserted in the publication. The Banded Newsletter design contains a logo and an attention getter on the back page, among other objects. In the following sections, you will learn how to change the design of the attention getter, format the text with a new style, and then delete the logo.

Editing an Attention Getter

Attention getters are eye-catching graphics and text that draw attention to a location on the page. They contain graphic boxes, text frames, geometric designs, and colors intended to draw attention to your publication. Publisher displays a small, nonprinting button just below attention getters that you can click to change their options and design.

The Banded Newsletter uses a starburst cutout attention getter which groups a starburst shape and a text box. You will change the design of the attention getter on the back page. It is located just above the Gravity Games story. The following steps illustrate how to change the design.

To Edit the Attention Getter Design

1

• **If necessary, scroll to display the attention getter above the Gravity Games headline on page 2 of the newsletter. Click the attention getter to select it.**

The attention getter is a starburst with a text box inside it (Figure 2-32). Publisher also displays an Options button. If the AutoFit text feature has been turned on, your attention getter may display more text.

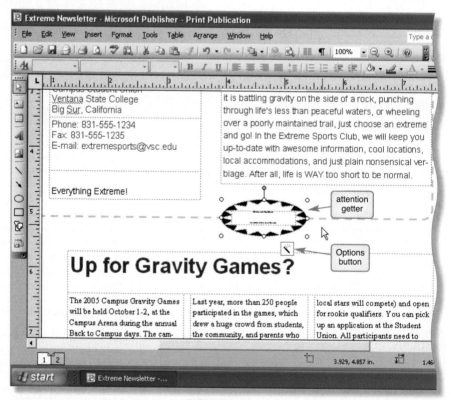

FIGURE 2-32

2

• **Click the Options button.**

• **When the Attention Getter Designs task pane appears, click the Side Curves Attention Getter preview.**

The Attention Getter Designs task pane displays a gallery of attention getters in the Apply a design area (Figure 2-33).

FIGURE 2-33

3

• **Click the Close button in the Attention Getter Designs task pane.**

• **Drag the middle-right handle of the attention getter to the right, until it aligns with the dashed line.**

The attention getter is resized (Figure 2-34).

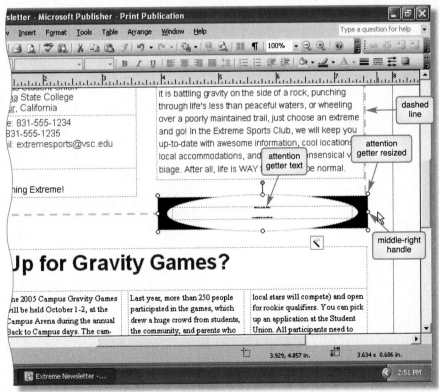

FIGURE 2-34

The next step is to make the attention getter text legible, by changing the font style.

Using Styles

A **style** is a combination of formatting characteristics, such as font, font size, and indentation that are named and stored as a set. When you apply a style, all of the formatting instructions in that style are applied at one time. To apply a style, you simply select the text and then select the style from the **Style list** on the Formatting toolbar.

The following steps edit the font style of the attention getter.

To Edit the Style

1

• **Click the text inside the attention getter's text box.**

• **Click the Style box arrow on the Formatting toolbar.**

The styles associated with the newsletter display (Figure 2-35).

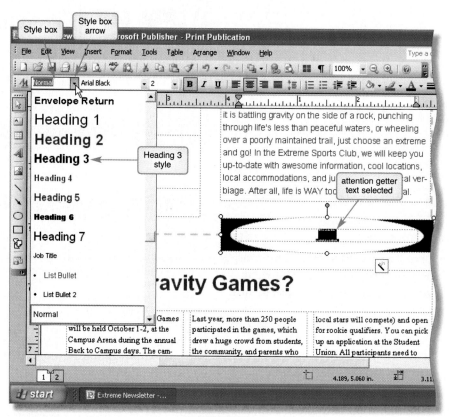

FIGURE 2-35

2

- **Click Heading 3 in the Style list.**
- **With the text still selected, type** Mondays, Student Center, 7 p.m.

The font style changes in the attention getter, and the style name displays in the Style box (Figure 2-36). The newly entered text is displayed with the new formatting.

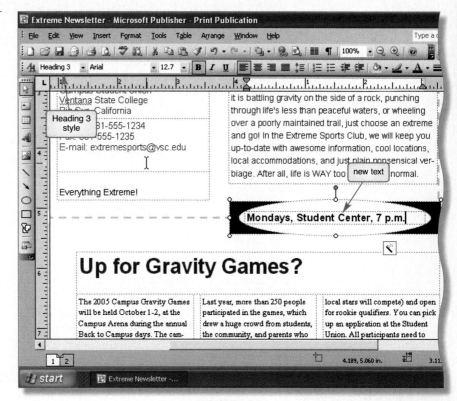

FIGURE 2-36

You can edit the text, text color, fill color, borders, and shadows of attention getters. Publisher's Design Gallery also has other styles and shapes from which you may choose.

Deleting the Logo

The Banded Newsletter design set displays an organization logo on the back page. A **logo** is a personal information component usually containing some combination of small graphics and words that identify or represent a company in a visual way. Publisher-supplied logos vary with each personal information set. Because the Extreme Sports Club has no logo, the following steps show how to delete the logo.

To Delete the Logo

1 Scroll to the top and left of page 2 in the Newsletter to display the logo as shown in Figure 2-37 on the next page.

2 Right-click the logo.

3 Click Delete Object on the shortcut menu.

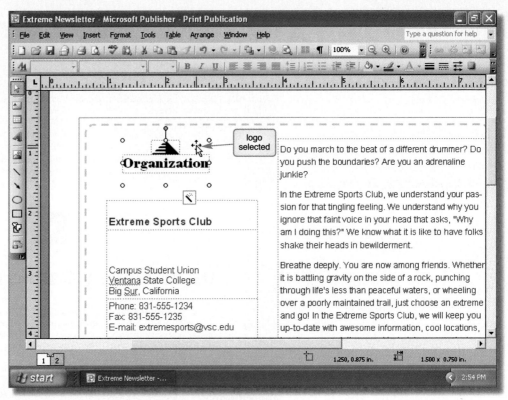

FIGURE 2-37

If you delete an object by accident, click the Undo button on the Standard toolbar. The Edit menu also contains a Delete Object and an Undo command.

WordArt

WordArt is a program that works with Publisher to create fancy text effects. A WordArt object actually is a graphic and not text at all. Publication designers typically use WordArt to create eye-catching headlines and banners. WordArt uses its own toolbar to add effects to the graphic.

Inserting a WordArt Object

The *Extreme News* newsletter will use a WordArt object as a heading in the upper-left corner of the back page. A heading can be text, formatted to draw attention, but using WordArt increases the number of special effect possibilities and options.

The following steps explain how to add a WordArt object as the headline for the back page of the newsletter.

To Insert a WordArt Object in the Newsletter

1

• **If necessary, scroll to the top and left of the back page of the newsletter.**

• **Click the Insert WordArt button on the Objects toolbar. When the WordArt Gallery dialog box is displayed, locate an appropriate style.**

The WordArt Gallery dialog box is displayed (Figure 2-38).

FIGURE 2-38

2

• **Double-click the style.**

Publisher displays the Edit WordArt Text dialog box (Figure 2-39).

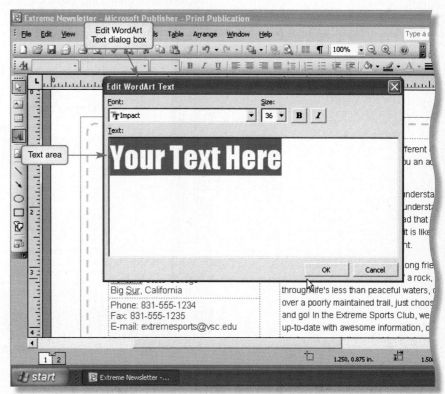

FIGURE 2-39

3

• **Type** Extreme **as the new text.**

The new text is displayed in the Text area (Figure 2-40).

FIGURE 2-40

4

• **Click the OK button.**

Publisher displays the WordArt object and the WordArt toolbar (Figure 2-41).

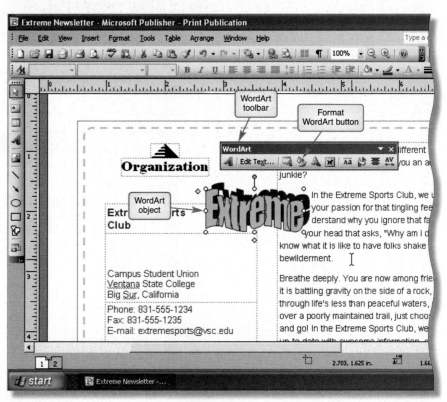

FIGURE 2-41

5

- **Click the Format WordArt button on the WordArt toolbar.**

- **When the Format WordArt dialog box is displayed, if necessary, click the Colors and Lines tab, and then click the Color box arrow in the Fill area.**

Publisher displays the Format WordArt dialog box (Figure 2-42). The Cranberry font scheme colors display in the color palette. Your colors may vary.

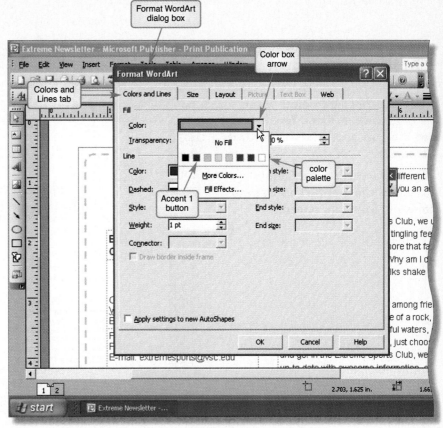

FIGURE 2-42

6

- **Click the Accent 1 button in the color palette.**

The new color is displayed in the Color box in the Fill area (Figure 2-43).

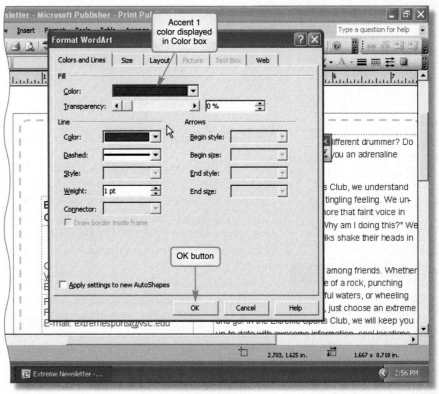

FIGURE 2-43

7

• **Click the OK button in the Format WordArt dialog box.**

• **Drag the WordArt object above the Organization Name Text Box so that it aligns approximately with its left border.**

• **If necessary, click the Close button on the WordArt toolbar to remove it from the screen.**

The WordArt Object, with its new color, is displayed in the newsletter (Figure 2-44).

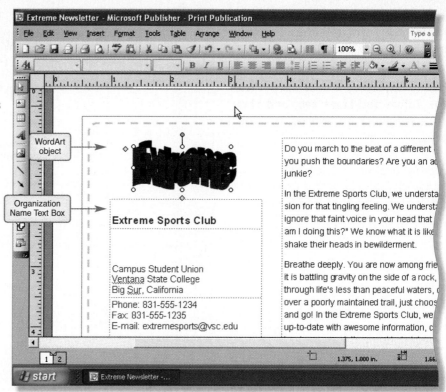

FIGURE 2-44

Microsoft Office
Publisher 2003

Other Ways

1. Click Insert WordArt button on the WordArt toolbar

WordArt includes options for spacing, rotating, shadows, and borders, as well as many of the same features Publisher provides on its Formatting toolbar, such as alignment, bold, italics, underline, and fonts.

Using Graphics in a Newsletter

Most graphic designers employ an easy technique for deciding how many graphics are too many. They hold the publication at arm's length and glance at it. Then, closing their eyes, they count the number of things they remember. Remembering more than five graphics indicates too many, two or fewer indicates too few. Without question, graphics can make or break a publication. The world has come to expect them. Used correctly, graphics enhance the text, attract the eye, and brighten the look of the publication.

You can use Publisher's clip art images in any publication you create, including newsletters. Publisher also accepts graphics and pictures created by other programs, as well as scanned photographs and electronic images. You can import graphics into publications in the same way that you imported stories. In newsletters, you should use photographs when you desire true-to-life representations, such as pictures of employees and products. Graphics, on the other hand, can explain, draw, instruct, entertain, or represent images for which you have no picture. The careful use of graphics can add flair and distinction to your publication.

More About

Clip Art

For samples of shareware clip art available on Web sites, visit the Publisher 2003 More About Web page (scsite.com/pub2003/more) and click Discovering Clip Art.

Graphics do not have to be images and pictures. They also can include tables, charts, shapes, lines, boxes, borders, pull quotes, and sidebars. A **sidebar** is a small piece of text, set off with a box or graphic, and placed beside an article. It contains text that is not vital to understanding the main text; it usually adds interest or additional information. Tables of contents and bulleted points of interest are examples of sidebars. A **pull quote** is an excerpt from the main article to highlight the ideas or to attract readers. As with other graphics, it adds interest to the page. Pull quotes, like sidebars, can be set off with a box or graphic.

The following sections illustrate how to import graphics from the Data Disk, edit the captions and sidebar text, delete a sidebar, and insert a pull quote.

More About

Graphics

For tips on using graphics effectively in a publication, visit the Publisher 2003 More About Web page (scsite.com/pub2003/more) and click Discovering Presentation.

Importing Graphics

Graphics can be imported from previously stored files, just as stories can. The following steps show how to import graphics from the Data Disk associated with this textbook.

To Import Graphics and Edit the Caption

1

• **On the back page of the newsletter, scroll to the Gravity Games article in the lower part of the page.**

• **Right-click the flower graphic. When the shortcut menu is displayed, point to Change Picture and then point to From File on the Change Picture submenu.**

Publisher displays the shortcut menu and the Change Picture submenu (Figure 2-45).

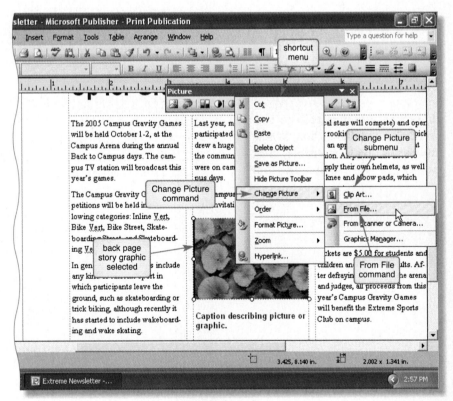

FIGURE 2-45

Microsoft Office
Publisher 2003

2

• **Click From File. When the Insert Picture dialog box is displayed, click the Look in box arrow, and then click 3½ Floppy (A:) in the Look in list.**

• **Click the Skateboarding picture.**

Publisher displays the graphics contained on the floppy disk in drive A (Figure 2-46).

FIGURE 2-46

3

• **Click the Insert button in the Insert Picture dialog box. When the publication again is visible, click the text in the caption text box.**

The picture is inserted as the new graphic for the back page story (Figure 2-47). The text in the caption is selected.

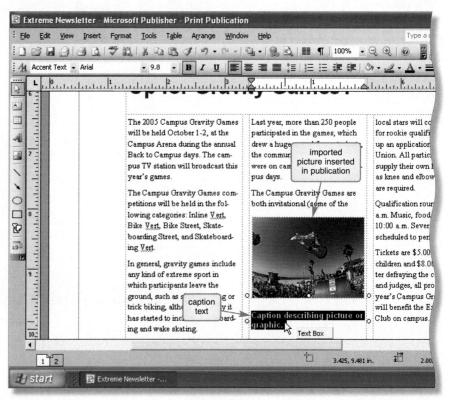

FIGURE 2-47

4

• **Type** Skateboarding tricks thrill the audience at last year's event. **to replace the selected placeholder text.**

Publisher displays the new caption (Figure 2-48).

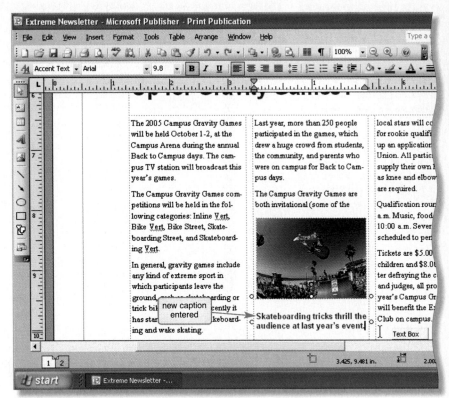

FIGURE 2-48

If necessary, imported graphics may be resized to better complement the stories. Publisher automatically wraps the text around the graphic regardless of its size.

The next step is to import a graphic for the lead story.

To Import a Graphic on Page 1

1 Click the Page 1 icon on the Page Navigation Control.

2 Right-click the graphic in the Surfing Championship Tour story. When the shortcut menu is displayed, point to Change Picture and then click From File on the Change Picture submenu.

3 When the Insert Picture dialog box is displayed, click the Look in box arrow, and then click 3½ Floppy (A:) in the Look in list. Click the Surfing picture (Figure 2-46).

4 Click the Insert button in the Insert Picture dialog box.

5 When the publication again is visible, click the text in the caption text box. **Type** Nate the Great, at it again! **to replace the selected placeholder text.**

Publisher displays the new graphic and caption (Figure 2-49 on the next page).

More About

**Portrait
and Landscape
Orientation**

The terms portrait and
landscape are used to refer
to more than just graphic orientation. Portrait also refers
to printing a document so the
short edge of the paper is the
top of the page. Landscape
printing assumes the long
edge to be the top of the
page.

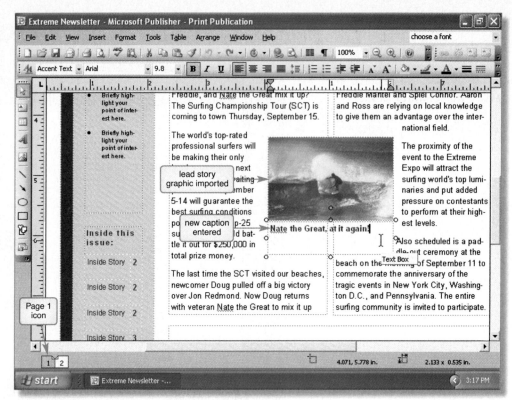

FIGURE 2-49

If you choose to include Publisher-supplied graphics, remember that graphics in the Clip Art Gallery are not all the same size. Some of the images and clip art will be displayed in **portrait** orientation, which means they are taller than they are wide. The opposite graphic orientation is **landscape**. When you change graphics, your choice may alter both the way the columns look and where the columns break. You may want to experiment with dragging the picture in small increments to make the columns symmetrical. The text automatically wraps around the graphic in the newsletter. The column breaks do not have to match the project newsletter exactly.

Graphics in the Clip Art Gallery are proportional, which means the height and width have been set in relation to each other, so as not to distort the picture. If you resize the graphic, be sure to hold down the SHIFT key while dragging a corner sizing handle as described in Project 1. Shift-dragging maintains the graphic's proportional height and width.

Editing a Sidebar

The Banded Newsletter template included two sidebars in the newsletter. The first is a bulleted list of special points of interest. The following steps edit that bulleted list.

More About

Sidebars

This More About box is an
example of a sidebar. The
Shelly Cashman Series textbooks use sidebars to offer
more information about sub-
jects in the text, as well as to
direct readers to Web pages
about the topic. The Other
Ways feature in the book also
is a sidebar.

To Edit a Sidebar

1

- **Scroll to display the Special points of interest sidebar in the upper-left part of page 1.**
- **Click the text of the bulleted list.**

Publisher highlights the entire bulleted list (Figure 2-50).

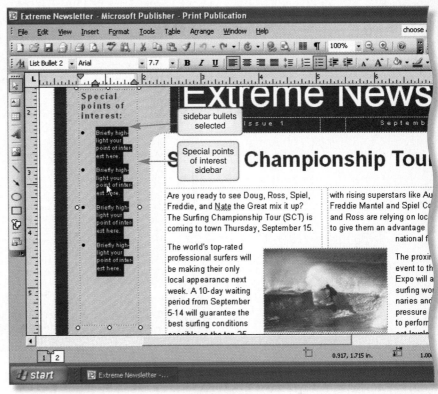

FIGURE 2-50

2

- **Type** Surfing Championship Tour, September 15 **as the first bullet.**

Publisher maintains the bulleted formatting and displays the new text (Figure 2-51).

FIGURE 2-51

3

• **Press the ENTER key. Type**
X-Meeting Mondays, 7:00 p.m.
Student Center **and then press
the ENTER key.**

• **Type** Gravity Games at Back
to Campus Days, October 1-2
to finish the bullets.

The new bullets are entered (Figure 2-52).

FIGURE 2-52

Recall that you can turn off bullets by clicking the Bullets button on the Formatting toolbar. You also can change the format of bullets by clicking Bullets and Numbering on the Format menu.

Deleting a Sidebar

The other sidebar in the Banded Newsletter is a table of contents. Because the newsletter now has only two pages, a table of contents is not necessary. The following steps delete the sidebar.

To Delete the Sidebar

1 Scroll to display the Inside this issue sidebar as shown in Figure 2-53.

2 Right-click the sidebar text.

3 Click Delete Object on the shortcut menu.

4 If a shaded background rectangle still is displayed, repeat Steps 2 and 3 to delete it also.

FIGURE 2-53

This table was an index used to locate articles in longer newsletters. Many newsletters have a table of contents, not only to reference and locate, but also to break up a long text page and attract readers to inside pages. Tables can be used for purposes other than displaying contents and page numbers. You will learn more about tables in a later project.

Inserting a Pull Quote

People often make reading decisions based on the size of the text. Using a pull quote brings a small portion of the text to their attention and invites readership. Pull quotes are especially useful for breaking the monotony of long columns of text. Desktop publishers also use pull quotes to add visual interest. Finally, pull quotes and sidebars are good multiple entry devices, offering readers many ways to digest information. Layout specialists stress that story titles and pull quotes should summarize the intended message.

The final step to complete page 1 of the newsletter is to create a pull quote using Publisher's Design Gallery. The **Design Gallery** is a group of objects that you can place in your publications, including sidebars, pull quotes, mastheads, and other individual objects not readily available on the Objects toolbar.

The pull quote graphic in this newsletter will contain a quote from the Mountain Biking story and should be placed appropriately on the page to draw the reader's attention. As you cut and paste text for the pull quote, Publisher will offer you the choice of keeping the source or original, formatting, or simply copying the text to the new formatting. The **Paste Options button** is displayed after a paste operation to allow you to make this choice. The Paste Options button is one of a series of smart tags contained in Publisher and other Microsoft Office applications. A **Smart Tag** is a button that automatically appears on the screen when Publisher performs a certain action, such as identifying a misspelled word. When the button displays, you may click it to display a menu of actions associated with the button. Table 2-3 summarizes the Smart Tags available in Publisher.

Table 2-3 Smart Tags in Publisher

SMART TAG BUTTON		MENU FUNCTION
	AutoCorrect Options	Undoes an automatic correction, stops future automatic corrections of this type, or displays the AutoCorrect Options dialog box
	Paste Options	Specifies how moved or pasted items should display, e.g., with original formatting, without formatting, or with different formatting
	Smart Tag Actions	Displays a menu of actions related to names, dates, addresses, or places associated with Microsoft Outlook
	• Person's name	Adds this name to Outlook Contacts folder or schedules a meeting in Outlook Calendar with this person
	• Date or time	Schedules a meeting in Outlook Calendar at this date or time
	• Address	Adds this address to Outlook Contacts folder
	• Place	Adds this place to Outlook Contacts folder or schedules a meeting in Outlook Calendar at this location

More About

Typing with Smart Tags

Publisher tries to help you as you type. This AutoCorrect feature, similar to the same feature in word processing applications, will format text and correct some misspellings for you as you type. For instance if you type 2nd, Publisher will convert it to 2nd. If you type teh and then press the SPACEBAR key, Publisher will convert it to the word, the. If you wish to undo an AutoCorrect, point to the smart tag below the word. When it changes to the AutoCorrect Options button, click it, and then click Undo Automatic Corrections.

With the Autocorrect Options button and the Smart Tag Actions button, Publisher notifies you that the smart tag is available by displaying a **Smart Tag indicator** on the screen. The smart tag indicator for AutoCorrect Options is a small blue box. The smart tag indicator for Smart Tag Actions is a purple dotted line. If you want to display the Smart Tag button, point to the Smart Tag indicator.

Clicking a Smart Tag Button displays a menu that contains commands relative to the action performed at the location of the smart tag. For example, if you want to add a name in your Publisher document to the Outlook Contacts folder, point to the purple dotted line below the name to display the Smart Tag Actions button. Then, click the Smart Tag Actions button to display the Smart Tag Actions menu. Finally, click Add to Contacts on the Smart Tag Actions menu to display the Contacts dialog box in Outlook.

A Paste Options button will be displayed in the following steps to add a pull quote to the publication and insert text.

To Add a Pull Quote

1

• **With the lower part of page 1 still displayed, click the Design Gallery Object button on the Objects toolbar. If necessary, click the Objects by Category tab.**

Publisher displays the Design Gallery dialog box (Figure 2-54).

FIGURE 2-54

2

• **Click Pull Quotes in the Categories pane. Scroll to and then click the Punctuation Pull Quote preview shown in Figure 2-55.**

The previews display in alphabetical order in the Pull Quotes pane (Figure 2-55). The Punctuation Pull Quote is selected.

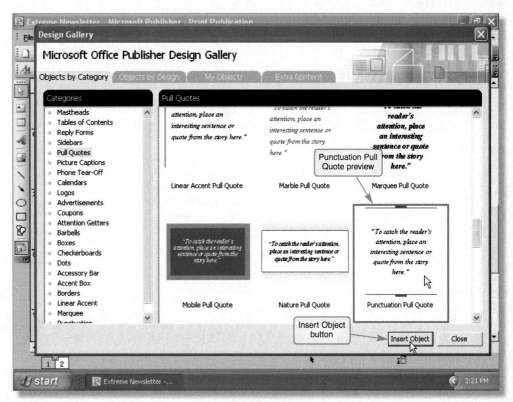

FIGURE 2-55

3

• **Click the Insert Object button.**

The pull quote is inserted in the publication (Figure 2-56).

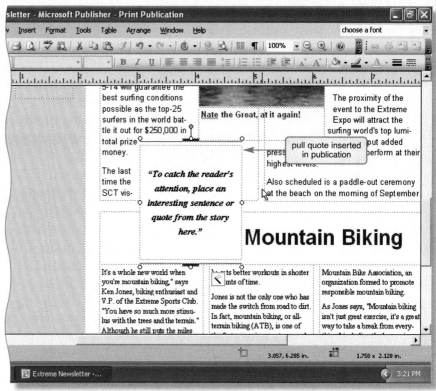

FIGURE 2-56

4

• **Drag the pull quote to the left margin below the Special points of interest sidebar and to the left of the Mountain Biking story.**

The pull quote is dragged to the left of the story (Figure 2-57).

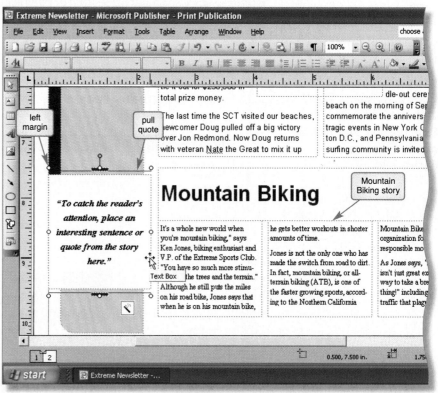

FIGURE 2-57

5

• **In the third column of the Mountain Biking story, select the quotation text as shown in Figure 2-58.**

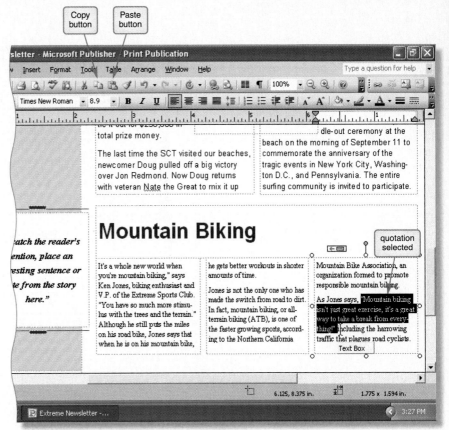

FIGURE 2-58

6

• **Click the Copy button on the Standard toolbar.**

• **Click the placeholder text in the pull quote to select it.**

• **Click the Paste button on the Standard toolbar.**

The new text replaces the placeholder text in the pull quote (Figure 2-59). The Paste Options button also is displayed.

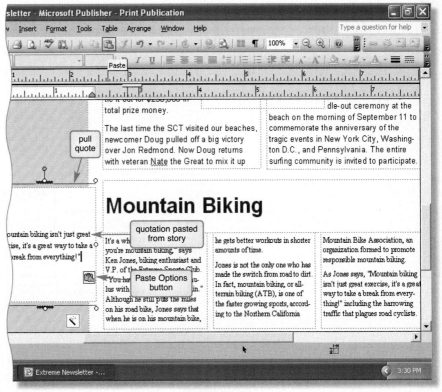

FIGURE 2-59

7

• **Click the Paste Options button.**

The Paste Options menu is displayed (Figure 2-60). The menu includes options to keep the source, or original, formatting, or to keep the text only and let the destination format preside.

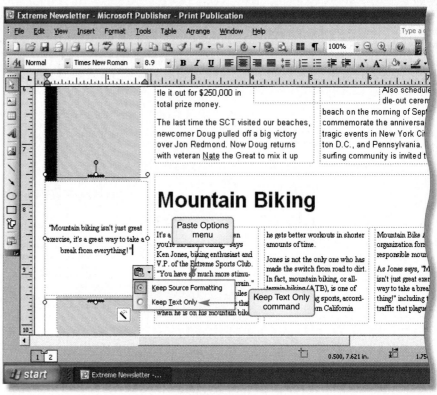

FIGURE 2-60

8

• **Click Keep Text Only.**

The font changes to match the pull quote's original, or source, formatting (Figure 2-61).

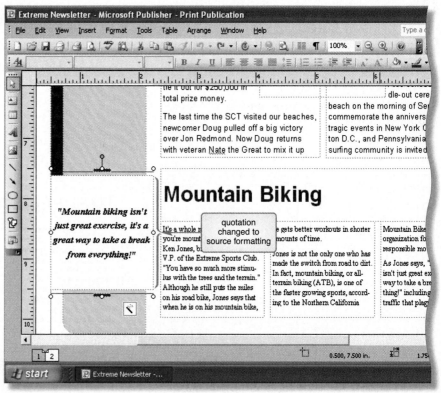

FIGURE 2-61

The Paste Options button, which enables you to specify the formatting of pasted text, appears at the bottom corner of your text as you paste it. You can choose not to display the Paste Options button by clicking Tools on the menu bar, clicking Options, and then clicking Edit.

Adding Page Numbers to the Master Page

Page numbering on a two-page newsletter probably is not as important as it is for longer publications. Many readers, however, reference articles and points by page numbers. Part of the design process is to provide a consistent look and feel to the layout, so page numbers can furnish a reference for the organization in designing future, perhaps longer, newsletters. Additionally, certain features always may appear on specific pages. Placing page numbers in prominent locations, or using fancy fonts and colors, can make page numbers a design element in and of themselves.

The next steps in this project describe how to add page numbers in the lower-left corner of each page of the newsletter by inserting a page number on the publication's master page. The **master page** is a blank sheet located behind your publication where you place objects that will display on every page, such as headers and footers, page numbers, and logos. Most publication objects, such as text and graphics, actually lie in front of the master page, allowing the format to display from behind. You can insert and edit these recurring objects in two ways. If you want an object to display on every page, you can move it to the master page, or you can go to master page view and create the object there.

Inserting Page Numbers on the Master Page

The following steps show how to display the master page and then insert the automatic page number so it will be displayed on all pages.

To Display the Master Page and Insert Automatic Page Numbering

More About

Objects on the Background

Page numbers and headers/footers are not the only objects that display in the background on the master page. A watermark is a lightly shaded object displaying behind everything else on the page. For example, you can place a light gray graphic or a gray WordArt object such as the word, Confidential, on the master page of a publication. It then faintly displays behind text on the foreground.

1

• **Click View on the menu bar.**

Publisher displays the View menu (Figure 2-62).

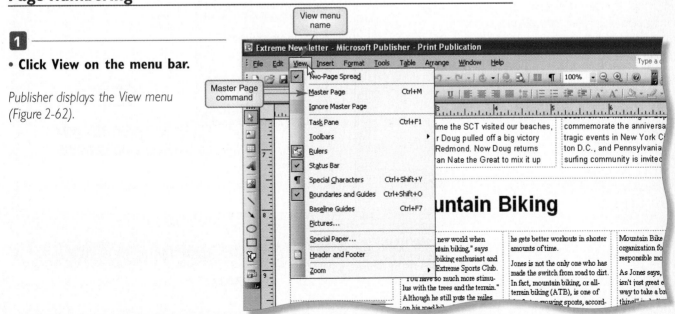

FIGURE 2-62

2

• **Click Master Page.**

• **When the master page is displayed, click Insert on the menu bar.**

The master page displays as a blank page on which you may insert objects that will appear on all pages of the publication (Figure 2-63). Publisher also displays the Edit Master Pages toolbar.

FIGURE 2-63

3

• **Click Page Numbers on the Insert menu. When the Page Numbers dialog box is displayed, click the Position box arrow and then click Bottom of page (Footer) in the list.**

The Page Numbers dialog box offers choices for Position, Alignment, and whether or not to show the page number on the first page (Figure 2-64).

FIGURE 2-64

4

- **Click the OK button in the Page Numbers dialog box.**
- **Click the Close Master View button in the Edit Master Pages toolbar.**

The page number is placed in the publication (Figure 2-65). Publisher automatically reflects the current page number. The Apply Master Page task pane is displayed as well, which allows you to specify a range of pages or change master pages for facing pages.

5

- **Click the Close button in the Apply Master Page task pane.**

FIGURE 2-65

Other Ways

1. Click Insert Page Numbers button on Header and Footer toolbar

Logical choices for objects on a master page might include personal information, dates, times, headers and footers, and page numbers. Options on the Insert menu allow you to insert dates and times derived from the operating system that will update automatically when the publication is edited or printed.

Many newsletters have a master page texture or pattern on each page. As with watermarks, a master page pattern can provide additional interest and contrast. By creating a text box on the master page, you can use fill colors or gradient patterns from the color scheme to add interest and individuality to your newsletter.

If an object does not display when you insert it on the master page, it does not mean that it is gone; rather, it may be behind another object in the foreground. Typically, items in the foreground, or in the front, which partially cover an item in the master page, need to be transparent. The combination keystrokes of CTRL+T will convert selected objects into transparent ones. Should you change your mind, CTRL+T is a toggle; press it again to turn off transparency and make the object opaque again.

More About

Backgrounds on the Master Page

If you want the master page background not to display on a given page, such as a page number text box on page 1, click Ignore Master Page on the View menu.

Checking a Newsletter for Errors

The final phase of the design process is a synthesis involving editing, proofreading, and publishing. Publisher offers several methods to check for errors in your newsletter. None of these methods is a replacement for careful reading and proofreading. Similar to the spell checking programs in word processing applications, Publisher looks for misspelled words, grammatically incorrect sentences, punctuation problems, and mechanical errors in text boxes.

More About

Spelling Options

On the Tools menu, the Spelling command allows you to access Spelling Options for use in checking the spelling of the publication. Included in the Spelling Options dialog box are check boxes for checking the spelling as you type, flagging repeated words, and ignoring words in uppercase, among other options.

Spelling and Grammar Errors

As you type text in a text box, Publisher checks your typing for possible spelling and grammar errors. Recall that if a typed word is not in the dictionary, a red wavy underline is displayed below it. Likewise, if typed text contains possible grammar errors, a green wavy underline is displayed below the text. You can check the entire newsletter for spelling and grammar errors at once or as you are typing.

When a word is flagged with a red wavy underline, it is not in Publisher's dictionary. A flagged word is not necessarily misspelled, as many names, abbreviations, and specialized terms are not in Publisher's main dictionary. In these cases, instruct Publisher to ignore the flagged word. To display a list of suggested corrections for a flagged word, right-click it, and then click a replacement word on the shortcut menu.

When using imported text, as in the newsletter, it may be easier to check all the spelling at once. Publisher's check spelling feature looks through the selected text box for errors. Once errors are found, Publisher offers suggestions and provides the choice of correcting or ignoring the flagged word. If you are creating this project on a personal computer, your text boxes may contain different misspelled words, depending on the accuracy of your typing.

Checking the Newsletter for Spelling and Grammar Errors

The Spelling command is accessed through the Tools menu. The following steps illustrate how to check your newsletter for spelling and grammar errors. You may encounter spelling mistakes you have made while typing. Choose to correct those errors as necessary. The following steps check the newsletter for spelling and grammar errors.

To Check the Newsletter for Spelling and Grammar Errors

1

• **With page 1 of the Extreme Newsletter still displayed, click the Championship Surfing story text box. Click the Spelling button on the Standard toolbar.**

The Check Spelling dialog box is displayed (Figure 2-66). Publisher flags the name, Nate. Because this is a personal name and spelled correctly, you will ignore this flag.

FIGURE 2-66

2

• **Click the Ignore button. Publisher continues to check the story. If you have other errors, correct them using the Check Spelling dialog box.**

Publisher did not find any more errors in the book review article. It displays a dialog box that asks if you want to check the rest of the publication (Figure 2-67).

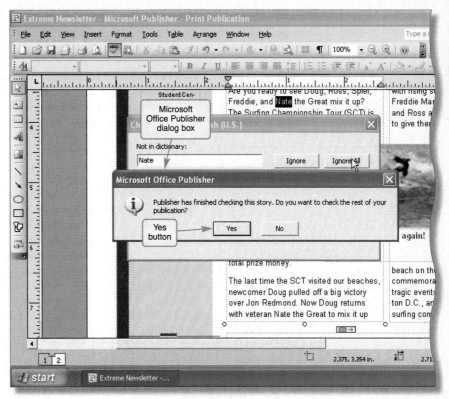

FIGURE 2-67

3

• **Click the Yes button. As Publisher displays more personal names, choose to ignore them. If you have other errors, choose the appropriate measure to fix or ignore them. When the check spelling process is complete, a dialog box will be displayed.**

Publisher displays a dialog box informing you that the process is complete (Figure 2-68).

4

• **Click the OK button.**

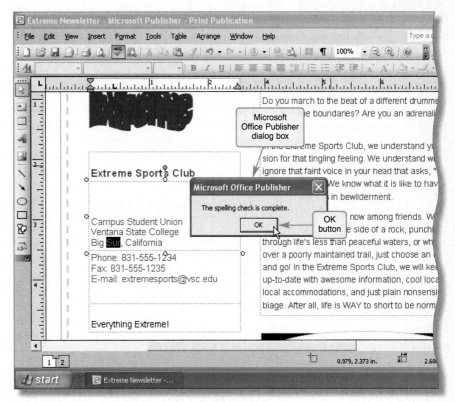

FIGURE 2-68

Even if text is checked for spelling before it is imported, Publisher flags words, phrases, and punctuation not found in its dictionary. The process is worth the time it takes, but again, there is no substitute for proofreading the text yourself.

Checking the Newsletter for Design Errors

Table 2-4   Design Checker Errors
DESIGN CHECKER ERRORS
Empty frames
Covered objects
Text in overflow area
Objects in nonprinting region
Disproportional pictures
Spacing between sentences

You now are ready to check the newsletter for design errors as you did in Project 1. The Design Checker can check single pages or entire publications for a specific type of error or all types of errors. The Design Checker looks for errors related to design issues and object interaction, providing comments and correction choices. Design errors are the most common type of problem when submitting a publication to a professional printer. In a later project, you will learn that, in addition to the interactive Design Checker, Publisher's Pack and Go Wizard checks for errors related to embedded fonts and graphics. Table 2-4 lists errors detected by the Design Checker.

The following steps show how to have Publisher check for all kinds of design errors throughout the newsletter.

To Check the Newsletter for Design Errors

1 Click Tools on the menu bar and then click Design Checker.

2 Click the OK button.

3 If the Design Checker finds errors, choose to fix or ignore them as necessary. When the Design Checker terminates, click the OK button.

If you have made errors in placing graphics or WordArt objects, you may have to accept or ignore other Design Checker recommendations.

If you resized any graphic in the newsletter, Publisher's Design Checker will warn you that the graphic may not be proportionally correct. At that time, you may choose to resize the graphic or ignore the change.

The newsletter is complete and should be saved again before printing. The following step saves the newsletter using the same file name.

To Save an Existing Newsletter Using the Same File Name

1 With your floppy disk in drive A, click the Save button on the Standard toolbar.

Publisher saves the publication using the same file name, Extreme Newsletter, on the floppy disk in drive A.

More About

Hyphenation

You can change the number of hyphens that are added automatically to the text to achieve a more even right edge, to reduce white gaps in the text, or the number of hyphens and short syllables. On the Tools menu, point to Language, and then click Hyphenation. To achieve a different effect, change the number in the Hyphenation zone in one of the following ways: for a more even right edge and fewer white gaps in the text, reduce the number; or for fewer hyphens and fewer short syllables before or after hyphens, increase the number.

Printing a Two-Sided Page

Printing the two pages of the newsletter back to back is a process that is highly dependent upon the printer. Some printers can perform duplex printing, which prints both sides before ejecting the paper, while other printers require the user to reload the paper manually. If you are attached to a single-user printer, you must check the printer's documentation to see if it supports double-sided printing. If you are connected to a network printer, you probably will need to feed the paper through a second time manually.

The following steps illustrate how to print the first page and then manually feed the page through a second time. Adjust the steps as necessary for your printer.

To Print a Two-Sided Page

1

• **If necessary, click the Page 1 icon on the Page Navigation Control. Ready the printer according to the printer instructions. Click File on the menu bar and then click Print. When the Print dialog box displays, click Current page in the Print range area.**

The Print dialog box is displayed (Figure 2-69). Your dialog box may differ.

2

• **Click the OK button. When printing is complete, retrieve the printout.**

The printed newsletter is shown in Figures 2-1a and 2-1b on page PUB 67. Publications with many graphics and fonts take longer to print than plain text documents.

3

• **After retrieving the printout, wait a few seconds for it to dry. Reinsert the printout in the manual tray of the printer; usually blank side down, top first. Click the Page 2 icon on the Page Navigation Control. Click File on the menu bar and then click Print. When the Print dialog box is displayed, repeat Steps 1 and 2 to print page 2 of the newsletter.**

Retrieve the printout from the printer.

FIGURE 2-69

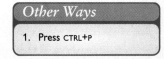

Other Ways

1. Press CTRL+P

More About

Network Printing

If your network printer seems to lock up or prints only part of the page, it may not have enough memory to store the large print files that Publisher creates. Consider one of the following solutions: wait until other print jobs are complete; print in black and white instead of color; print lower-resolution graphics; or finally, print the text only and then send the paper through a second time for the graphics. The memory setting on your printer driver influences your printer's ability to reproduce your publication. If your printer driver's memory setting is too low, the publication may not appear complete when printed.

If you have an Options button, a Properties button, or an Advanced Print Settings button in your Print dialog box (Figure 2-69 on the previous page), you may be able to duplex print. Check your printer documentation, or click the button for more information.

If you are unsure how to load the paper, you can run a test page through the printer. Mark an X in the upper-right corner of a blank sheet and then insert the sheet into the printer, noting where the X is. If your printer has a Manual Feed button or Paper Source list, be sure to click Manual. Print the first page. Note where the X is in relation to the printed page and turn the paper over to print the other side accordingly. In a later project, you will learn more about types of paper best suited for printing on both sides, as well as how to prepare a publication for a printing service.

The newsletter is now complete. The following step quits Publisher.

To Quit Publisher

1 **Click the Close button on Publisher's title bar.**

Publisher closes, and the Windows desktop is displayed.

Project Summary

Project 2 introduced you to the design process and the newsletter medium. Using the Banded Newsletter template, you learned how to edit a masthead, import text from other sources, and add appropriate graphics. You also learned how to insert and delete pages in a newsletter and incorporate personal information components. With WordArt, you inserted a fancy headline with special text effects. You imported graphics and edited captions. Using the Design Gallery, you inserted an attention getter. After you added page numbers to the master page, you used the check spelling feature and the Design Checker to identify spelling, grammar, and design errors. Finally, you printed the newsletter double-sided and saved it on a floppy disk.

Q: Can I convert my newsletter print publication to a newsletter Web publication?

A: Yes, use the same techniques as you did in Project 1; however, when Publisher displays the Add a Navigation Bar step in the conversion process (page PUB 51), click Yes. The pages in your newsletter will be converted to a Web site of pages. You will learn more about converting to a Web site in the special feature later in the book.

Q: How can I save ink, print faster, or decrease printer overrun errors?

A: Print a draft. Click File on the menu bar, click Print. Then, depending on your printer, click the Options button or the Properties button. Select the Draft option. Printing a draft copy in black and white will save color ink.

More About

Folders

You can store publications in any folder on your hard disk, floppy disk, or on a network, but it is a good practice to store them together in a folder that you can find easily. The preset storage location for publications on a new installation of Publisher is in a folder named My Documents. My Documents can serve as a place to store the publications you use frequently. If you work with many different types of documents, you can organize them in subfolders within My Documents.

What You Should Know

Having completed this project, you now should be able to perform the tasks below. The tasks are listed in the same order they were presented in this project. For a list of the buttons, menus, toolbars, and commands introduced in this project, see the Quick Reference Summary at the back of this book and refer to the Page Number column.

1. Start Publisher   (PUB 68)
2. Choose a Newsletter Template and Change Options   (PUB 70)
3. Change and Delete Pages in a Newsletter (PUB 73)
4. Edit the Masthead   (PUB 76)
5. Edit a Headline and Import a Text File (PUB 78)
6. Import More Text   (PUB 81)
7. Import the Back Page Story   (PUB 82)
8. Save an Intermediate Copy of the Newsletter (PUB 83)
9. Edit Personal Information Components (PUB 84)
10. Edit a Story Using Word   (PUB 86)
11. Display Overflow Text   (PUB 89)
12. Edit the Attention Getter Design   (PUB 90)
13. Edit the Style   (PUB 92)
14. Delete the Logo   (PUB 93)
15. Insert a WordArt Object in the Newsletter (PUB 95)
16. Import Graphics and Edit the Caption   (PUB 99)
17. Import a Graphic on Page 1   (PUB 101)
18. Edit a Sidebar   (PUB 103)
19. Delete the Sidebar   (PUB 104)
20. Add a Pull Quote   (PUB 107)
21. Display the Master Page and Insert Automatic Page Numbering   (PUB 111)
22. Check the Newsletter for Spelling and Grammar Errors   (PUB 114)
23. Check the Newsletter for Design Errors (PUB 116)
24. Save an Existing Newsletter Using the Same File Name   (PUB 116)
25. Print a Two-Sided Page   (PUB 117)
26. Quit Publisher   (PUB 118)

Learn It Online

Instructions: To complete the Learn It Online exercises, start your browser, click the Address bar, and then enter the Web address scsite.com/pub2003/learn. When the Publisher 2003 Learn It Online page is displayed, follow the instructions in the exercises below. Each exercise has instructions for printing your results, either for your own records or for submission to your instructor.

1 Project Reinforcement TF, MC, and SA

Below Publisher Project 2, click the Project Reinforcement link. Print the quiz by clicking Print on the File menu for each page. Answer each question.

2 Flash Cards

Below Publisher Project 2, click the Flash Cards link and read the instructions. Type 20 (or a number specified by your instructor) in the Number of playing cards text box, type your name in the Enter your Name text box, and then click the Flip Card button. When the flash card is displayed, read the question and then click the ANSWER box arrow to select an answer. Flip through Flash Cards. If your score is 15 (75%) correct or greater, click Print on the File menu to print your results. If your score is less than 15 (75%) correct, then redo this exercise by clicking the Replay button.

3 Practice Test

Below Publisher Project 2, click the Practice Test link. Answer each question, enter your first and last name at the bottom of the page, and then click the Grade Test button. When the graded practice test is displayed on your screen, click Print on the File menu to print a hard copy. Continue to take practice tests until you score 80% or better.

4 Who Wants To Be a Computer Genius?

Below Publisher Project 2, click the Computer Genius link. Read the instructions, enter your first and last name at the bottom of the page, and then click the PLAY button. When your score is displayed, click the PRINT RESULTS link to print a hard copy.

5 Wheel of Terms

Below Publisher Project 2, click the Wheel of Terms link. Read the instructions, and then enter your first and last name and your school name. Click the PLAY button. When your score is displayed, right-click the score and then click Print on the shortcut menu to print a hard copy.

6 Crossword Puzzle Challenge

Below Publisher Project 2, click the Crossword Puzzle Challenge link. Read the instructions, and then enter your first and last name. Click the SUBMIT button. Work the crossword puzzle. When you are finished, click the Submit button. When the crossword puzzle is redisplayed, click the Print Puzzle button to print a hard copy.

7 Tips and Tricks

Below Publisher Project 2, click the Tips and Tricks link. Click a topic that pertains to Project 2. Right-click the information and then click Print on the shortcut menu. Construct a brief example of what the information relates to in Publisher to confirm you understand how to use the tip or trick.

8 Newsgroups

Below Publisher Project 2, click the Newsgroups link. Click a topic that pertains to Project 2. Print three comments.

9 Expanding Your Horizons

Below Publisher Project 2, click the Articles for Microsoft Word link. Click a topic that pertains to Project 2. Print the information. Construct a brief example of what the information relates to in Publisher to confirm you understand the contents of the article.

10 Search Sleuth

Below Publisher Project 2, click the Search Sleuth link. To search for a term that pertains to this project, select a term below the Project 2 title and then use the Google search engine at google.com (or any major search engine) to display and print two Web pages that present information on the term.

11 Publisher Online Training

Below Publisher Project 2, click the Publisher Online Training link. When your browser displays the Microsoft Office Online Web page, click the Publisher link. Click one of the Publisher courses that covers one or more of the objectives listed at the beginning of the project on page PUB 66. Print the first page of the course before stepping through it.

12 Office Marketplace

Below Publisher Project 2, click the Office Marketplace link. When your browser displays the Microsoft Office Online Web page, click the Office Marketplace link. Click a topic that relates to Publisher. Print the first page.

Apply Your Knowledge

1 Editing a School Newsletter

Instructions: Start Publisher. Open the publication, Apply 2-1 School Newsletter, on the Data Disk. See the inside back cover of this book for instruction for downloading the Data Disk or see your instructor for information about accessing files required in this book.

The publication on the Data Disk is a newsletter from Jefferson Metro College, home of the Patriots. The newsletter contains some template text, a graphic that needs to be replaced, and sidebars that need to be edited. You are to change the following on page 1 of the newsletter: replace the template text, change the newsletter title, edit and move the graphic, delete a sidebar, and insert a pull quote. On page 2, you are to change the attention getter text, and edit the back page story and headline.

The edited page 1 is displayed in Figure 2-70.

FIGURE 2-70

(continued)

Apply Your Knowledge

Editing a School Newsletter *(continued)*

Perform the following tasks.

1. On page 1, highlight the text The Weekly Patriot in the masthead. Type `The Patriot Journal` to replace the text. In the upper-right corner of Page 1, replace the Newsletter Date placeholder text with your current date.
2. In the lower-left of the page, right-click the sidebar titled, Inside this Issue. Click Delete Object on the shortcut menu.
3. Click the Design Gallery Object button on the Objects toolbar and then click Pull Quotes in the Categories list. Insert the Straight Edge Pull Quote. Drag it to the empty space left by the deleted sidebar. With the pull quote still selected, press CTRL+T to make it transparent.
4. Select and copy the next to the last sentence of the article titled, Where to Live? Next, click the pull quote text to select it. Paste the sentence into the pull quote. When the Smart Tag displays, click the Paste Options button and then click Keep Text Only on the Paste Options menu.
5. Delete the picture of the student. Use the Clip Art task pane to find a different picture of students. Drag the picture to the end of the article.
6. Drag a corner handle to resize the picture proportionally until it fits in the third column.
7. Click the Organization Name Text Box located below the masthead. Replace the business name with the name of your school or business.
8. Edit the Special Points of Interest bullets to match those in Figure 2-70 on the previous page.
9. Click page 2 in the Page Navigation Control. Use the Edit menu to delete pages 2 and 3.
10. On the back page, click the attention getter text box at the top of the page. Zoom as necessary. Use your school or business Web page address (URL) in the attention getter.
11. Click the back page story in the lower part of page 2. On the Edit menu, click Edit Story in Microsoft Word. In the Word window, type a few paragraphs describing your first day at school in the current term or your first day on the job. When you are done, close the Word window. In Publisher, change the back page story headline to match your story.
12. Check your publication for spelling errors. Correct any errors.
13. Click File on the menu bar and then click Save As. Save the publication using Apply 2-1 School Newsletter Revised as the file name. Print the revised newsletter using double-sided printing.

1 Creating a Masthead

Problem: The human resources department of Nutshell and Associates has asked you to create a masthead for its newsletter. Mr. Nutshell wants you to incorporate the company logo and colors in the masthead.

Instructions: Perform the following tasks to create the masthead shown in Figure 2-71.

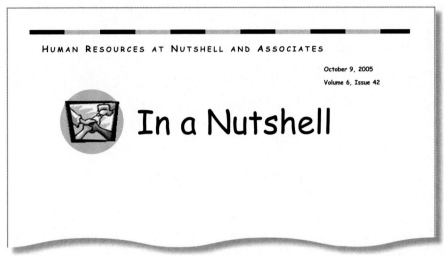

HUMAN RESOURCES AT NUTSHELL AND ASSOCIATES

October 9, 2005

Volume 6, Issue 42

In a Nutshell

FIGURE 2-71

1. Start Publisher. From the New Publication task pane, click Blank Print Publication. Close the Publication Designs task pane.
2. Click the Design Gallery Object button on the Objects toolbar. When the Design Gallery dialog box is displayed, click the Voyage Masthead and then click the Insert Object button.
3. When the masthead is inserted in the page layout, drag it to the top of the blank page.
4. Edit the text boxes to match Figure 2-71.
5. Double-click the star graphic to the left of the title. Using the Clip Art task pane, find a clip related to teamwork. Do not close the Clip Art task pane.
6. On the task pane title bar, click the Other Task Panes button and click Color Schemes in the list. Click Sagebrush in the Apply a Color Scheme list. Click Font Schemes in the task pane and then click Casual in the Apply a Font Scheme list.
7. Use the Design Checker to correct any errors in the publication.
8. Save the publication on your floppy disk using the file name, Lab 2-1 Nutshell Masthead.
9. Print a copy of the masthead.

In the Lab

2 Creating a Special-Purpose Newsletter

Problem: You are leader of a scout group for elementary school children. You thought the scouts and their parents might find a monthly newsletter interesting and informative. The scouts could write the articles concerning happenings in the troop, and you could include dates of future events and projects (Figure 2-72a). In addition, you would like to include a monthly feature called "Caught Being Good," a list of scouts who have gone out of their way to do something good and caring (Figure 2-72b). Using Publisher's Kid Stuff Newsletter template, create a two-page, double-sided newsletter with columns.

The articles for the two front page stories are included on the Data Disk that accompanies this book.

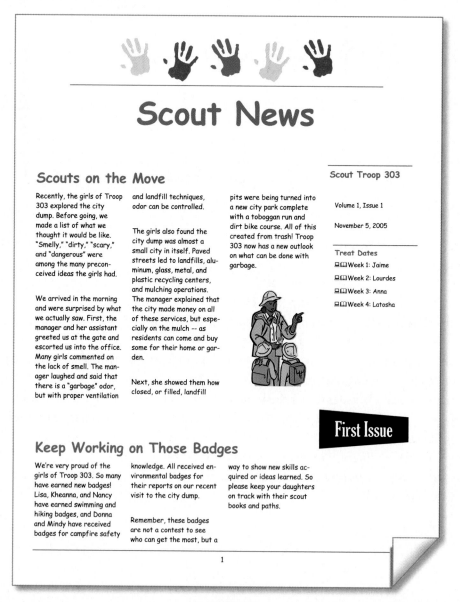

FIGURE 2-72a

In the Lab

Scout Troop 303

Primary Business Address
Your Address Line 2
Your Address Line 3
Your Address Line 4

Phone: 555-555-5555
Fax: 555-555-5555
E-mail: someone@example.com

Your business tag line here.

We're on the Web
www.scoutnews.org

Caught Being Good

Dara Arslanian

Marsha Louks

Katie Marie

Hannah Murphy

Johna Raikes

Rebecca Witte

Popcorn is Coming

This story can fit 175-225 words.

If your newsletter is folded and mailed, this story will appear on the back. So, it's a good idea to make it easy to read at a glance.

A question and answer session is a good way to quickly capture the attention of readers. You can either compile questions that you've received since the last edition or you can summarize some generic questions that are frequently asked about your organization.

A listing of names and titles of managers in your organization is a good way to give your newsletter a personal touch. If your organization is small, you may want to list the names of all employees.

If you have any prices of standard products or services, you can include a listing of those here. You may want to refer your readers to any other forms of communication that you've created for your organization.

You can also use this space to remind readers to mark their calendars for a regular event, such as a breakfast meeting for vendors every third Tuesday of the month, or a biannual charity auction.

If space is available, this is a good place to insert a clip art image or some other graphic.

POP CORN

Caption describing picture or graphic.

2

FIGURE 2-72b

Instructions: Perform the following tasks.

1. Start Publisher. In the New Publication task pane, click Publications for Print.
2. Click Newsletters in the list. Select the Kid Stuff Newsletter. Choose an appropriate color and font scheme in the task pane.
3. Make the following changes on page 1:
   a. Change the newsletter title to Scout News.
   b. Change the Lead Story Headline to Scouts on the Move.
   c. Change the Secondary Story Headline to Keep Working on Those Badges!
   d. Change the Organization name to Scout Troop 303.
   e. Change the date to your current date.

(continued)

Creating a Special-Purpose Newsletter *(continued)*

    f. In the bulleted list sidebar, change the title to `Treat Dates` and then in the list, type the following: `Week 1: Jaime, Week 2: Lourdes, Week 3: Anna, Week 4: Latosha,` pressing the ENTER key after each name so that each entry has a separate bullet.

    g. Delete the Inside this Issue sidebar and insert an attention getter in its place. In the attention getter text box, type `First Issue` as the entry.

4. Select the text in the lead story on page 1. From the Data Disk, import the story, Scouts on the Move. Import the story, Keep Working on Those Badges, for the secondary story on page 1.

5. Replace the graphic with a graphic about children. Delete the caption.

6. Use the Page Navigation Control to move to page 2. Delete pages 2 and 3.

7. Make the following changes to the back page:

    a. Change the back page story headline to, Popcorn is Coming.

    b. Use a keyword to locate and insert a graphic in the back page story about popcorn.

    c. Delete the logo on the back page.

    d. Click the text box in the upper-right corner. With the text still selected, type the following names: `Dara Arslanian, Marsha Louks, Katie Marie, Hannah Murphy, Johna Raikes, Rebecca Witte,` pressing the ENTER key after each to place each name on a separate line. Right-click the text box. On the shortcut menu, point to Change Text. On the Change Text submenu, point to AutoFit Text and then click Best Fit on the AutoFit Text submenu.

    e. Add a WordArt shape with the text, Caught Being Good, positioned above the list.

8. View the master page and insert a page number in the lower center of each page.

9. Spell check and design check the newsletter.

10. Save the newsletter on a floppy disk using the file name, Lab 2-2 Scout Newsletter, and print a copy.

3 Looking at Publisher's Newsletter Choices

Problem: You work in the public relations department of an advertising firm. Your supervisor wants to publish a weekly newsletter for customers and potential clients, but would like to see some samples first. You decide to use Publisher's newsletter templates to give him a variety from which he may choose.

Instructions: Using the techniques presented in this project, access the New Publication task pane, and choose five different newsletter templates. Choose templates you have not used before. Below are some general guidelines for each template.

1. Select the template and choose font and color schemes for each. Make a note of each scheme you choose.

2. Print page 1 of each newsletter. Write on the back the schemes you chose.

3. Identify the parts of the newsletter on the printout. Label things such as the masthead, design set, color scheme, personal information components, and all objects.

4. Pick your favorite of the five newsletters. For that one, print all the pages and identify any different components or objects. If possible, print double-sided.

5. Convert your favorite to a Web publication and print it. Note the differences between the print publication and the Web publication.

6. Let your instructor look at all the printouts.

Cases and Places

The difficulty of these case studies varies:
■ are the least difficult and ■■ are more difficult. The last exercise is a group exercise.

1 ■ Use the Newsletter template titled Bubbles Newsletter to create a letterhead for your personal use. Delete all the pages except page 1. Delete all the objects on page 1 except the masthead and the line graphic across the bottom. Put your name in the Newsletter Title and your address and telephone number in the volume and date text boxes.

2 ■ Use the Newsletter Template titled Voyage Newsletter, to create a two-page newsletter for the Seniors Abroad Club. This local club of senior citizens gets together to take group trips. For the newsletter title, type We're on the Road, and place today's date in the masthead. Include an article headline for the lead story, which concerns the club's most recent trip to Ontario (you may use the default text), and a secondary article headline that tells how to pack light for Europe. Add a list of dates for upcoming trips to Orlando, Paris, and Tokyo in the Special Points of Interest sidebar. Replace the graphics with suitable pictures from Publisher's clip art.

3 ■ Using Table 2-2 on page PUB 69 as an example, make a chart describing the newsletter created in Project 2. Describe the purpose, audience, how you gathered data, the plan for printing, layout, and synthesis.

4 ■■ Ask a local civic group for a sample of its newsletter. Try to recreate its style and format using a blank publication page in Publisher. Use Publisher's Design Gallery and personal information sets to customize the newsletter. Print your final product and compare the two.

5 ■■ Offer to create a newsletter for a department on campus or for a department within your company. Ask others to supply the content for the stories in a word processing file. Try to obtain pictures and graphics from the department. Choose colors and fonts that match the style of the office. Ask the department if they already have a logo. If so, try to obtain an electronic copy of the logo and use it in the newsletter. Use at least one example of a pull quote, WordArt, and an attention getter.

6 ■■ Create a blank print publication with a large text box that fills the page. Using the Edit Story in Microsoft Word feature, type an assignment, such as an essay or short report, for one of your classes. Print a copy. On the back, write three things you found easier to do in Publisher and three things you found easier to do in Word.

Cases and Places

7 ■■ **Working Together**   Many clubs and organizations publish their newsletters on the Web. Browse the Web and look for examples of newsletters. Note how many pages, graphics, and articles they use. Look at their mastheads and logos. Choose a newsletter that you think displays good desktop publishing practices. Print the newsletter or copy its Web address to distribute to each team member. Discuss the newsletters and note which parts were most effective. Each member then independently should use the most effective newsletter ideas, together with the techniques presented in this project, to create a newsletter that would be likely to catch a reader's eye. Use a Publisher Newsletter template to create a newsletter for a club or organization with which you are affiliated. Include at least three articles, one sidebar or pull quote, a masthead, and several graphics. Be sure to check the spelling and run the Design Checker. As a group, critique each newsletter and have each member redesign his or her newsletter based on the group's recommendations. Hand in printouts of each team member's original and final newsletter.

Publishing a Tri-Fold Brochure

PROJECT

3

CASE PERSPECTIVE

The College Computer Club at Oak Park College (OPC) was formed in the early 1980s by a few students from the math and science departments. Now it boasts the largest membership on campus with 80 members from all departments. As both an educational and service organization, the club's objectives include providing an opportunity for its members and the OPC community to learn more about the use of computers and the Web; providing service to the community; and enhancing the image of OPC. The club sponsors and maintains Web pages for organizations and individuals desiring to publish pages on its server. It is the club's intent to provide service primarily to students, faculty, other organizations, and members of the OPC community, thus providing a wider opportunity to have a Web presence or obtain Web publishing experience.

The College Computer Club is sponsoring a fund-raiser for its scholarship fund. Club members voted to sell holiday wrapping paper and trim, contracting with a local supply company. To keep costs down and showcase the desktop publishing skills of some of its members, the club membership has decided to create its own brochures. As a member of the fund-raising committee, you have volunteered to design the brochure. The president of the club would like to see a sample at the first fall meeting.

The brochure should contain images and text that describe the gift wrap and trim items, information about the club, and an order form. You use a tri-fold brochure template in Publisher and customize it with your club's contact information and logo.

As you read through this project, you will learn how to use Publisher to create, save, and print a brochure that includes text, graphics, personal information, a logo, and an order form.

Publishing a Tri-Fold Brochure

Objectives

You will have mastered the material in this project when you can:

- Discuss advantages of the brochure medium
- Use the Brochure Options task pane
- Create a custom color scheme
- Edit placeholder text and personal information components
- Format fonts and paragraphs
- Describe the use of photographs versus images
- Insert a photograph from a file
- Create a logo from scratch using AutoShapes
- Create a composite object in the scratch area
- Group and ungroup objects
- Choose appropriate printing services, paper, and color libraries
- Prepare a publication for outside printing
- Use the Pack and Go Wizard

Introduction

Whether you want to advertise a service, event, or product, or merely want to inform the public about a current topic of interest, brochures are a popular type of promotional publication. A brochure, or pamphlet, usually is a high-quality document with lots of color and graphics, created for advertising purposes. Businesses that may not be able to reach potential clientele effectively through traditional advertising, such as newspapers and radio, can create a long-lasting advertisement with a well-designed brochure.

Brochures come in all shapes and sizes. Colleges and universities produce brochures about their programs. The travel industry uses brochures to entice tourists. Service industries and manufacturers display their products using this visual, hands-on medium.

Project Three — The Holiday Trim Brochure

Project 3 uses Publisher to illustrate the production of the two-page, tri-fold brochure shown in Figure 3-1. The brochure informs the public about a fund-raiser sponsored by a computer club at the local college. Each side of the brochure has three panels. Page 1 (Figure 3-1a) contains the front and back panels, as well as the inside fold. Page 2 (Figure 3-1b) contains a three-panel display that, when opened completely, provides the reader with more details about the items for sale and an order form.

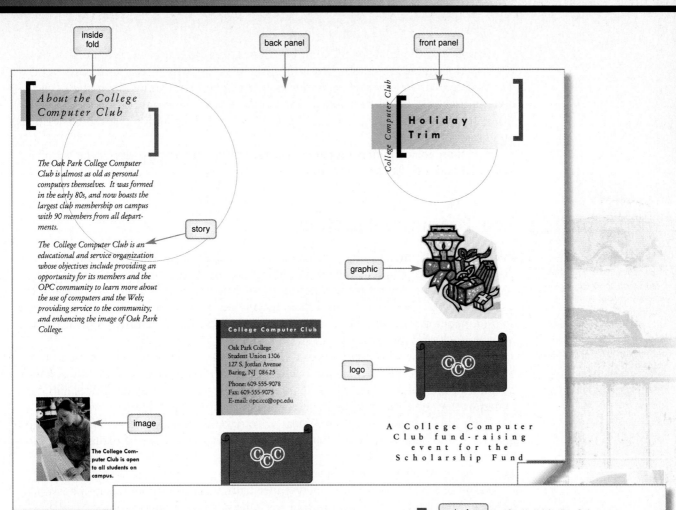

inside fold

back panel

front panel

About the College Computer Club

College Computer Club

Holiday Trim

The Oak Park College Computer Club is almost as old as personal computers themselves. It was formed in the early 80s, and now boasts the largest club membership on campus with 90 members from all departments.

story

The College Computer Club is an educational and service organization whose objectives include providing an opportunity for its members and the OPC community to learn more about the use of computers and the Web; providing service to the community; and enhancing the image of Oak Park College.

graphic

logo

College Computer Club

Oak Park College
Student Union 1306
127 S. Jordan Avenue
Baring, NJ 08625

Phone: 609-555-9078
Fax: 609-555-9075
E-mail: opc.ccc@opc.edu

A College Computer Club fund-raising event for the Scholarship Fund

image

The College Computer Club is open to all students on campus.

(a) Page 1 of Tri-Fold Brochure

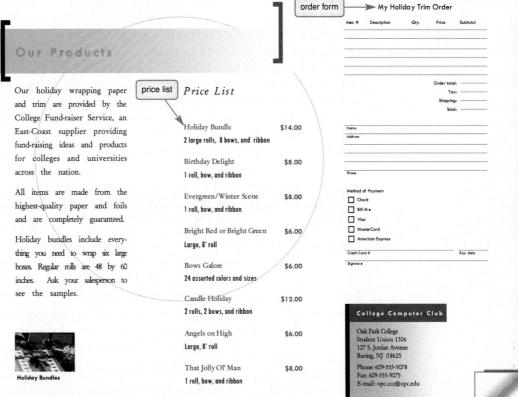

order form → My Holiday Trim Order

Our Products

Item #	Description	Qty.	Price	Subtotal

Our holiday wrapping paper and trim are provided by the College Fund-raiser Service, an East-Coast supplier providing fund-raising ideas and products for colleges and universities across the nation.

All items are made from the highest-quality paper and foils and are completely guaranteed.

Holiday bundles include everything you need to wrap six large boxes. Regular rolls are 48 by 60 inches. Ask your salesperson to see the samples.

price list

Price List

Holiday Bundle	$14.00
2 large rolls, 8 bows, and ribbon	
Birthday Delight	$8.00
1 roll, bow, and ribbon	
Evergreen/Winter Scene	$8.00
1 roll, bow, and ribbon	
Bright Red or Bright Green	$6.00
Large, 8' roll	
Bows Galore	$6.00
24 assorted colors and sizes	
Candle Holiday	$12.00
2 rolls, 2 bows, and ribbon	
Angels on High	$6.00
Large, 8' roll	
That Jolly Ol' Man	$8.00
1 roll, bow, and ribbon	

Order total:
Tax:
Shipping:
Total:

Name
Address

Phone

Method of Payment
☐ Check
☐ Bill Me
☐ Visa
☐ MasterCard
☐ American Express

Credit Card #   Exp. date
Signature

College Computer Club

Oak Park College
Student Union 1306
127 S. Jordan Avenue
Baring, NJ 08625

Phone: 609-555-9078
Fax: 609-555-9075
E-mail: opc.ccc@opc.edu

Holiday Bundles

(b) Page 2 of Tri-Fold Brochure

FIGURE 3-1

On page 1, the front panel contains shapes, text boxes, and a graphic designed to draw the reader's attention and inform the reader of the intent of the brochure. The back panel, which displays in the middle of page 1, contains the name of the club and school, the address, telephone numbers, and the organization logo. The inside fold, on the left, contains an article about the club, with a colored background and graphic.

The three inside panels on page 2 contain more information about the supplier, a price list, and a form the reader may use to place an order.

More About

Brochures

Many brochures are published regularly on the Web. To look at some samples and for information on brochure content, visit the Publisher 2003 More About Web page (scsite.com/pub2003/more) and then click Brochures.

The Brochure Medium

Brochures are professionally printed on special paper to provide long-lasting documents and to enhance the graphics. The brochure medium is intentionally tactile. Brochures are meant to be touched, carried home, passed along, and looked at, again and again. Newspapers and fliers usually are produced for short-term readership on paper that soon will be thrown away or recycled. Brochures frequently use a heavier stock of paper so they can stand better in a display rack.

The content of a brochure needs to last longer, too. On occasion, the intent of a brochure is to educate, such as a brochure on health issues in a doctor's office. More commonly, though, the intent is to market a product or sell a service. Prices and dated materials that are subject to frequent change affect the usable life of a brochure.

Typically, brochures use a great deal of color, and they include actual photographs instead of drawings or graphic images. Photographs give a sense of realism to a publication and should be used to show people, places, or objects that are real, whereas images or drawings more appropriately are used to convey concepts or ideas.

Many brochures incorporate newspaper features such as columns and a masthead, and the added eye appeal of logos, sidebars, shapes, and graphics. Small brochures are separated into panels and folded. Larger brochures resemble small magazines, with multiple pages and a stapled binding.

Brochures, designed to be in circulation for longer periods as a type of advertising, ordinarily are published in greater quantities and on more expensive paper than newsletters and are, therefore, more costly. The cost, however, is less prohibitive when produced **in-house** using desktop publishing rather than hiring an outside service. The cost per copy sometimes is less than a newsletter, because brochures are produced in mass quantities.

Table 3-1 lists some benefits and advantages of using the brochure medium.

Table 3-1 Benefits and Advantages of Using the Brochure Medium	
AREA	**BENEFITS AND ADVANTAGES**
Exposure	An attention getter in displays
	A take-along document encouraging second looks
	A long-lasting publication due to paper and content
	An easily distributed publication — mass mailings, advertising sites
Information	Give readers an in-depth look at a product or service
	An opportunity to inform in a nonrestrictive environment
	An opportunity for focused feedback using tear-offs and forms
Audience	Interested clientele and retailers
Communication	An effective medium to highlight products and services
	A source of free information to build credibility
	An easier method to disseminate information than a magazine

Besides the intent and content of the brochure, you must consider the shape and size of the page when designing this type of publication. Publisher can incorporate a variety of paper sizes from the standard 8½-by-11-inch to 8½-by-24-inch. You also can design smaller brochures, such as those used as liner notes for CD jewel cases or inserts for videotapes. In addition, you need to think about how the brochure or pamphlet will be folded. Publisher's brochure templates can create three or four panels. Using the page setup options, you may create special folds, such as book or card folds.

Starting Publisher

To start Publisher, Windows must be running. The following steps explain how to start Publisher.

To Start Publisher

1 Click the Start button on the Windows taskbar, point to All Programs on the Start menu, point to Microsoft Office on the All Programs submenu, and then click Microsoft Office Publisher 2003 on the Microsoft Office submenu.

2 If the Publisher window is not maximized, double-click its title bar to maximize it.

3 If Publisher does not display the New Publication task pane, click View on the menu bar and then click Task Pane. If the Publication Designs task pane is displayed, click the Other Task Panes button in the task pane title bar, and then click New Publication.

4 If the Language bar displays, click its Minimize button.

You now are ready to use Publisher's New Publication task pane to create a tri-fold brochure.

More About

Starting Publisher

Microsoft Windows provides many ways to start Publisher. You have been using the All Programs submenu on the Start menu. If you have installed the Office toolbar, you may have a button on your desktop for Publisher. You can right-click the desktop, point to New on the shortcut menu, and then click Microsoft Office Publisher Document. Finally, you can open any Publisher file by double-clicking its icon.

Creating a Tri-Fold Brochure

Publisher-supplied templates use proven design strategies and combinations of objects, which are placed to attract attention and disseminate information effectively. The options for brochures differ from other publications in that they allow you to choose from page sizes, special kinds of forms, and panel/page layout options.

Making Choices in the Brochure Options Task Pane

For the Holiday Trim brochure, you will use the Axis Price List Brochure as a template, making changes to its page size, customer address, sign-up form, color scheme, and font scheme. **Page size** refers to the number of panels in the brochure. The **Customer address** selection offers choices to include or not to include the customer's address in the brochure. **Form** options, which display on page 2 of the brochure, include None, Order form, Response form, and Sign-up form. The **Order form** displays fields for the description of items ordered as well as types of payment information, including blank fields for entering items, quantities, and prices. The **Response form** displays check box choices and fields for comments, and blanks for up to four multiple-choice questions and a comment section. The **Sign-up form** displays check box choices, fields for time and price, as well as payment information.

All three forms are meant to be detached and mailed in as turnaround documents. Each form contains blanks for the name and address of prospective customers or clients. The company not only verifies the marketing power of its brochure, but also is able to create a customer database with the information.

Table 3-2 displays the task pane selections you will make in the following steps.

Table 3-2 Task Pane Selections	
BROCHURE OPTIONS TASK PANE	**SELECTION**
Page size (Panels)	3-panel (default value for Price List Brochures)
Customer address	None
Form	Order form
Color Scheme	Custom
Font Scheme	Modern

To Choose Brochure Options

1

• **Click Publication for Print in the New Publication task pane. Click Brochures in the list, then click Price List. If necessary, click the down scroll arrow in the previews pane until the Axis Price List Brochure preview is visible.**

Publisher displays the New Publication task pane on the left and the previews on the right in the Publisher window (Figure 3-2). The list of previews may display differently on your computer.

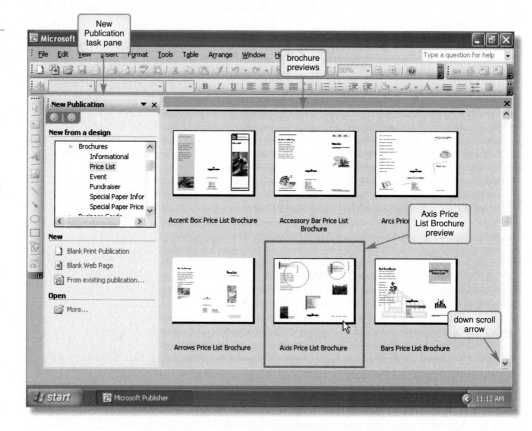

FIGURE 3-2

2

• **Click the Axis Price List Brochure preview. If Publisher displays the Personal Information dialog box, click its Close button.**

Publisher displays page one of the tri-fold brochure (Figure 3-3). The Brochure Options task pane replaces the New Publication task pane.

FIGURE 3-3

3

• **In the Brochure Options task pane, if necessary, click None in the Customer address area. In the Form area, click Order form.**

The selected brochure options for page size, customer address, and sign-up form are displayed (Figure 3-4). Publisher automatically moves to page 2 in the publication in order to display the Order form.

FIGURE 3-4

4

• **Click Page 1 in the Page Navigation control on the status bar. In the task pane, click Font Schemes. Scroll to and then click Modern in the Apply a font scheme list.**

The Modern font scheme includes the Tw Cen MT Bold major font and the Garamond minor font (Figure 3-5).

FIGURE 3-5

Q&A

Q: Can I create a multi-colored font?

A: The color scheme you create will apply to fonts as well as graphics, but only one color per font. Fonts themselves have no color. Software can cause text to display on screen or print out in certain colors, but the fonts themselves have no color. When you see multi-colored fonts displayed in a publication on the Web, such as red, white, and blue lettering, it usually is a graphic image created in a software program. You can apply two color fill effects to shapes.

The changes you make in the Brochure Options task pane change how the publication looks in the workspace. To specifically look at the order form or other changes on page 2, click the Page 2 icon in the Page Navigation control on the Publisher status bar.

Custom Color Schemes

Recall that a color scheme is a predefined set of harmonized colors that you can apply to text and objects. Text and objects with an applied color scheme will change automatically when you switch to a new color scheme or modify the current color scheme. Publisher provides an option for users to create their own color schemes, rather then using one of the predefined sets. Creating a **custom color scheme** means choosing your own colors to use in a publication. You may choose one main color, five accent colors, a hyperlink color, and a followed hyperlink color. The **main color** commonly is used for text in major eye-catching areas of the publication. The first accent color is used for graphical lines, boxes, and separators. The second accent color typically is used as fill color in prominent publication shapes. Subsequent accent colors may be used in several ways, including shading, text effects, and alternate font color. The hyperlink color is used as the font color for hyperlink text. After a hyperlink is clicked, the color changes to show the user what path, or trail, they have clicked previously.

Custom color schemes can be given a name that will appear in the Apply a color scheme list in the Color Schemes task pane. The chosen colors also appear on the Fill Color, Line Color, and Font Color button menus.

Creating a Custom Color Scheme

The Holiday Trim brochure will use holiday accent colors of red and green, as well as a basic black main color for text. Publisher displays an option to create a custom color scheme on the Color Schemes task pane. Publisher then allows users to choose the various colors and name the scheme.

The following steps explain how to create a custom color scheme.

To Create a Custom Color Scheme

1

• **With the Font Schemes task pane still displayed, click Color Schemes.**

Publisher displays the Color Schemes task pane (Figure 3-6).

FIGURE 3-6

2

• **Click Custom color scheme in the lower portion of the Color Schemes task pane.**

• **When Publisher displays the Color Schemes dialog box, if necessary, click the Custom tab.**

The Color Schemes dialog box displays the Custom sheet (Figure 3-7).

FIGURE 3-7

3

• **In the Scheme colors area, click the second New box arrow that corresponds to the Accent 1 color. When the color palette is displayed, point to Red.**

The color palette is displayed (Figure 3-8).

FIGURE 3-8

4

• **Click Red.**

• **Click the Accent 2, New box arrow. When the color palette is displayed, point to Lime.**

Publisher displays the color palette for Accent 2 (Figure 3-9).

FIGURE 3-9

5

• **Click Lime.**

• **Click the Accent 3, New box arrow. When the color palette is displayed, point to Green.**

Publisher displays the color palette for Accent 3 (Figure 3-10).

FIGURE 3-10

6

• **Click Green.**

• **Click the Save Scheme button.**

• **When Publisher displays the Save Scheme dialog box, type** Holiday **in the text box.**

The Save Scheme dialog box allows users to type a name for their custom color scheme (Figure 3-11).

FIGURE 3-11

7

• **Click the OK button in the Save Scheme dialog box.**

• **Click the OK button in the Color Schemes dialog box.**

Publisher now displays the Holiday color scheme in the Apply a color scheme list (Figure 3-12). The selected color scheme is applied to the publication.

8

• **Click the Color Schemes task pane Close button.**

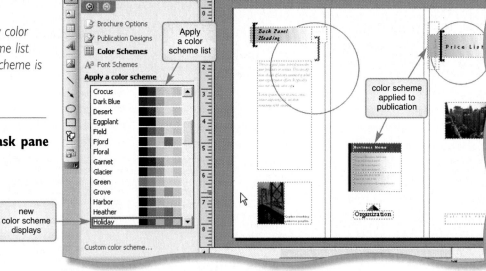

FIGURE 3-12

Other Ways

1. On Format menu click Color Schemes, click Color custom scheme

The scheme colors automatically apply to the standard publication objects in the brochure. Any objects, such as the default logo, that are filled with non-scheme colors, remain the same when you change the color scheme.

Now that several important options have been chosen, it is a good practice to save the publication. The following steps describe how to save the publication with the file name, Holiday Trim Brochure.

To Save the Publication

1 **Click the Save button on the Standard toolbar.**

2 **Type** `Holiday Trim Brochure` **in the File name text box. If necessary, click 3½ Floppy (A:) in the Save in list.**

3 **Click the Save button in the Save As dialog box. If Publisher asks if you want to save the new logo to a personal information set, click the No button.**

Publisher saves the publication on a floppy disk in drive A using the file name, Holiday Trim Brochure.

Replacing Text

Recall that editing text in the brochure involves selecting the current text and replacing it with new, appropriate text in one of two ways: edit text directly in Publisher or use Word to facilitate editing. If you need to edit only a few words, it is faster to use a Publisher text box with the accompanying Publisher tools. If you need to edit a long story, however, perhaps one that appears on different pages in a publication, it might be easier to edit the story in Word.

Publisher inserts placeholder text on page 1 of its supplied templates, which may be selected by a single click. Alternately, personal information components, designed to be changed or personalized for a company, are best edited by dragging through the text. When you change a personal information component, all matching components in the publication change due to synchronization.

Table 3-3 displays the text that needs to be replaced on page 1 of the brochure.

More About

Automatic Saving

Publisher can save your publication at regular intervals for you. On the Tools menu, click Options, and then click the Save tab. Select the Save AutoRecover info every check box. In the minutes box, specify how often you want Publisher to save files. Do not use AutoRecover as a substitute for regularly saving your work.

Table 3-3   Page 1 Text

LOCATION	PUBLISHER-SUPPLIED TEXT AND TEXT BOXES	NEW TEXT
Right Panel	Pice List	Holiday Trim
Middle Panel	Address Text Box	Oak Park College Student Union 1306 127 S. Jordan Avenue Baring, NJ 08625
	Phone/Fax/E-mail Text Box	Phone: 609-555-9078 Fax: 609-555-9075 E-mail: opc.ccc@opc.edu
Left Panel	Back Panel Heading	About the College Computer Club
	Back Panel Story	The Oak Park College Computer Club is almost as old as personal computers themselves. It was formed in the early 80s, and now boasts the largest club membership on campus with 90 members from all departments. The College Computer Club is an educational and service organization whose objectives include providing an opportunity for its members and the OPC community to learn more about the use of computers and the Web; providing service to the community; and enhancing the image of the Oak Park College.
	Caption	The College Computer Club is open to all students on campus.

The following steps edit both placeholder and personal information text on page 1 of the brochure.

To Edit Text in the Brochure

1

• **Click the Price List heading in the right panel on page 1. Press the F9 key to zoom the placeholder text box.**

The placeholder text is selected with a single click (Figure 3-13). This text is the title of the brochure.

FIGURE 3-13

2

• **Type** Holiday Trim **to replace the title text. Select the text in the Organization Name Text Box to the left of the title by dragging through it.**

The new title text displays (Figure 3-14). The personal information component text is selected by dragging. Your text may differ.

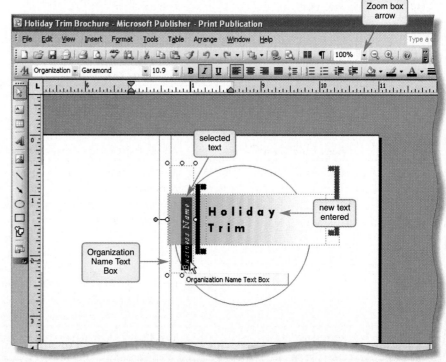

FIGURE 3-14

3

• **Type** College Computer Club **to replace the text.**

Publisher displays the new text (Figure 3-15).

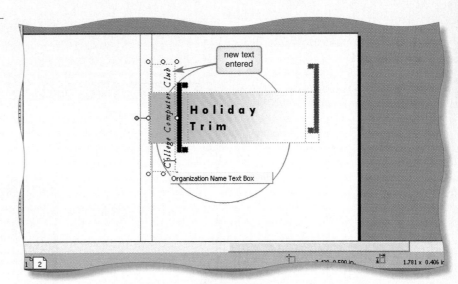

FIGURE 3-15

4

• **Click the Zoom box arrow (Figure 3-14) and then click Whole Page in the Zoom list.**

• **Click the Address Text Box in the middle panel.**

Publisher displays all of page 1 (Figure 3-16). The Address Text Box is selected.

FIGURE 3-16

5

• **Press the F9 key to zoom the text box.**

• **Press CTRL+A to select the text.**

Publisher displays the selected text at 100% magnification (Figure 3-17).

FIGURE 3-17

6

• **Enter the address from Table 3-3 on page PUB 141.**

The new text is displayed (Figure 3-18).

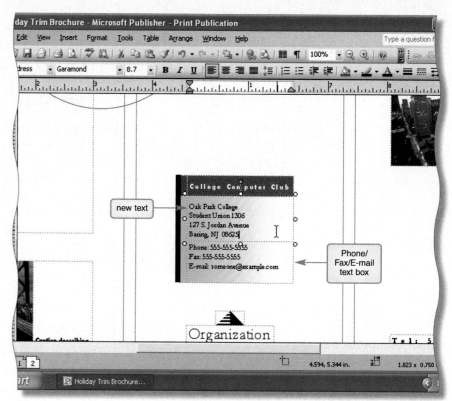

FIGURE 3-18

The following steps describe how to use similar zooming and editing techniques to edit the other text boxes on page 1 of the brochure as listed in Table 3-3 on page PUB 141.

To Edit Other Text Boxes on Page 1

1 Below the Address text box, click the text in the Phone/Fax/E-mail text box, press CTRL+A, and then type the new text from Table 3-3.

2 Scroll to the left panel of page 1 and click the Back Panel Heading located at the top of the panel. Type the new heading from Table 3-3.

3 Click the story below the heading and then type the new text from Table 3-3. Press the ENTER key at the end of each paragraph.

4 Click the caption of the picture in the lower portion of the left panel. Type the new text from Table 3-3.

The headings, placeholder text, personal information, and caption components have been edited.

Deleting Objects on Page 1

In a text box, simply selecting text and then cutting or deleting that text leaves an empty text box on the page. To delete unnecessary text boxes, you select the entire object rather than just the text. One text box in the front panel needs to be deleted, as well as the generic logo in the middle panel of page 1. The following steps describe how to delete each object.

To Delete Objects on Page 1

1 Click the Zoom box arrow and then click Whole Page in the Zoom list.

2 Right-click the telephone text box in the lower portion of the right panel. When the shortcut menu is displayed, click Delete Object.

3 Right-click the logo in the middle panel and then click Delete Object on the shortcut menu.

The two objects are deleted (Figure 3-19). Publisher displays the previously edited text boxes in Whole Page view.

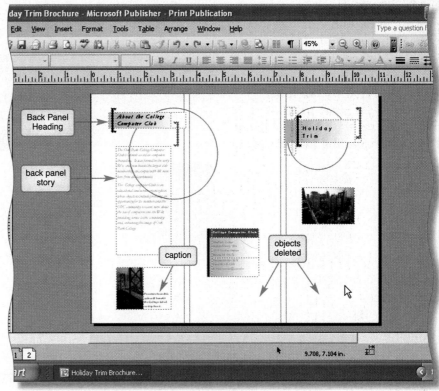

FIGURE 3-19

Font Scheme Styles

Recall that a style is a combination of formatting characteristics, such as font, font size, and formatting that are named and stored as a set. When you selected the Modern font scheme from the Font Schemes task pane, Publisher created styles for title text, headings, accent text, body text, and personal information components using the font scheme. The major font in the Modern font scheme is Tw Cen TM Bold. The minor font is Garamond. Publisher automatically creates more than 25 styles when you select a font scheme, using appropriate fonts, font sizes, font effects, and formatting. The styles include those for Headings, List Bullets, and Normal text, among others.

Applying a Font Scheme Style

When you apply a style, all of the formatting instructions in that style are applied at one time. To apply a style to new text, select the style from the Style list on the Formatting toolbar and then type the text. Alternately, you can select the text first and then select the style.

The steps on the next page create a new text box for the right panel of page 1, apply a Style, and then insert the text itself.

More About

Font Schemes

The Font Scheme Options link in the lower portion of the Font Schemes task pane includes options to update custom text styles in order to match one of the fonts used in the current font scheme. It also allows you to override applied text formatting only which changes the font; it does not affect any other text formatting. A third option allows users to adjust font sizes to maintain the same area covered by the original block of text. This option may cause the font size to increase or decrease from the size set in the style, but it will prevent the text reflowing.

To Insert a Text Box and Apply a Font Scheme Style

1

• **With page 1 of the brochure still displayed, scroll to the lower portion of the right panel. If necessary, type 100% in the Zoom box to increase the magnification.**

Publisher displays the right panel at 100% (Figure 3-20).

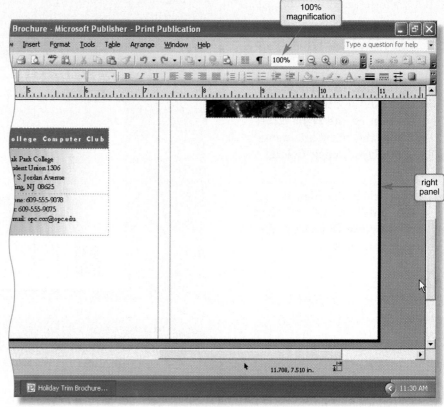

FIGURE 3-20

2

• **Click the Text Box button on the Objects toolbar and then drag a text box approximately 3 inches by 1 inch as shown in Figure 3-21.**

The Object Size box displays the size of the selected object.

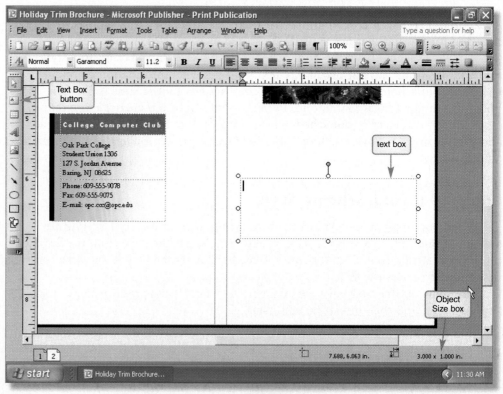

FIGURE 3-21

3

• **Click the Style box arrow on the Formatting toolbar. Scroll to display Heading 4.**

Publisher displays the various Styles created by the choice of the Modern Font Scheme (Figure 3-22).

FIGURE 3-22

4

• **Click Heading 4.**

• **Click the Center button on the Formatting toolbar.**

• **Type** A College Computer Club fund-raising event for the Scholarship Fund **in the text box.**

• **Right-click the text. Point to Change Text on the shortcut menu. When the Change Text submenu is displayed, point to AutoFit Text. Click Best Fit on the AutoFit Text submenu.**

Publisher displays the new text centered in the text box (Figure 3-23).

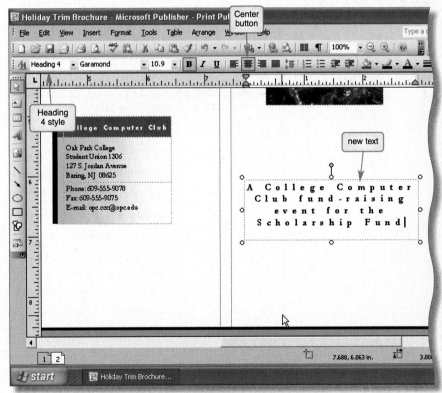

FIGURE 3-23

The text on page 1 is complete. After switching to page 2 of the brochure, the next steps are to format the text, edit the price list, and the order form, as shown in the following steps.

To Switch to Page 2

1 Click the Page 2 icon in the Page Navigation control on the Publisher status bar.

2 Click the Zoom box arrow on the Formatting toolbar and then click Whole Page in the Zoom list.

Formatting Fonts and Paragraphs

Publisher provides many ways to format fonts and paragraphs. Font schemes assist with major and minor fonts. Styles further specify sizes and formatting. Publisher also provides several font effects and line spacing options using menu options and toolbar buttons.

Font Effects

You have learned about font schemes, fonts, font sizes, formatting, and styles. Another way to format fonts is to use an effect. An **effect** is a special font option to add distinction to your text, including such things as outlining, embossing, and shadows.

Table 3-4 lists the font effects available in Publisher. The specific appearance of the font effects are printer- and screen-dependent.

More About

Fonts

You can download free fonts from the Web. For a list of Web addresses, visit the Publisher 2003 More About Web page (scsite.com/pub2003/more) and then click Downloading Fonts.

Table 3-4   Font Effects

FONT EFFECT	DESCRIPTION
All caps	Formats lowercase letters as capitals. All caps formatting does not affect numbers, punctuation, nonalphabetic characters, or uppercase letters.
Emboss	The selected text appears to be raised off the page in relief.
Engrave	The selected text appears to be imprinted or pressed into the page.
Outline	Displays the inner and outer borders of each character.
Shadow	Adds a shadow beneath and to the right of the selected text.
Small caps	Formats selected lowercase text as capital letters and reduces their size. Small caps formatting does not affect numbers, punctuation, nonalphabetic characters, or uppercase letters.
Subscript	Lowers the selected text below the baseline.
Superscript	Raises the selected text above the baseline.

Using a Font Effect

The following steps apply an Outline font effect as new text is entered for the Main Inside Heading of the brochure.

To Apply a Font Effect

1

• **With page 2 displayed, right-click the text, Main Inside Heading.**

• **On the shortcut menu, point to Change Text.**

Publisher displays the shortcut menu and the Change Text submenu (Figure 3-24).

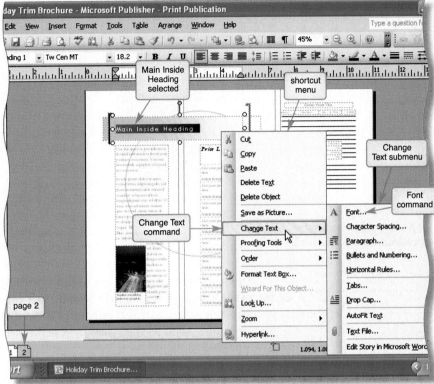

FIGURE 3-24

2

• **Click Font on the Change Text submenu. When the Font dialog box is displayed, click Outline in the Effects area.**

The Font dialog box displays font choices and a Sample preview area (Figure 3-25).

FIGURE 3-25

3

- **Click the OK button.**
- **Type** Our Products **to replace the selected main inside heading text.**

Publisher displays the new text with the Outline font effect (Figure 3-26).

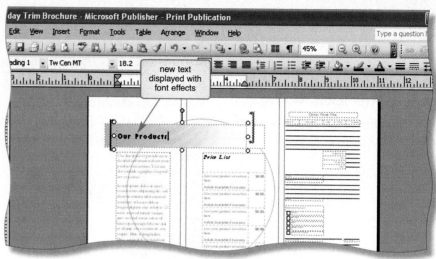

FIGURE 3-26

Two special font effects are superscript and subscript. A **superscript** is a character that appears slightly higher than other text on a line, such as that used in footnotes (reference[1]). A **subscript** describes text that is slightly lower than other text on a line, such as that used in scientific formulas (H_2O).

Formatting Paragraphs

A **paragraph,** in Publisher as well as in most word processing programs, consists of the text you type until you press the ENTER key. Pressing the ENTER key creates a **hard return,** or paragraph, in a text box. Recall that certain kinds of formatting are paragraph-dependent, such as bullets and numbering.

Publisher allows users to change the indentation, alignment, line spacing, baseline guides, and paragraph spacing of paragraphs. **Indentation** determines the distance of the paragraph from either the left or right margins. Within margins, you can increase or decrease the indentation of a paragraph or group of paragraphs. You also can create a negative indent (also known as an exdent), which pulls the paragraph out toward the left margin. You also can create a hanging indent, in which the first line of the paragraph is not indented, but subsequent lines are.

Alignment refers to horizontal appearance and orientation of the edges of the paragraph: left-aligned, right-aligned, centered, or justified. For example, in a left-aligned paragraph (the most common alignment), the left edge of the paragraph is flush with the left margin. **Justified** adjusts the horizontal spacing of text within text boxes, so that all lines, except the last line of the paragraph align evenly along both the left and right margins. Justifying text creates a smooth edge on both sides. Publisher also allows users to create a rarely used **Distribute** alignment, which justifies even the last line of the paragraph.

Line spacing is the amount of space from the bottom of one line of text to the bottom of the next line. Publisher adjusts the line spacing to accommodate the largest font or the tallest graphic in that line. You can use **baseline guides** to align text lines precisely across multiple columns. Publisher also allows you to set when and how lines and paragraphs break across text boxes. For example, you may want to specify that if one line of a paragraph moves to a new column, text box, or page, the entire paragraph Foudh should move.

Paragraph spacing determines the amount of space above or below a paragraph.

Formatting Paragraphs in the Main Inside Story

In the brochure, the main inside story details the specifics about the holiday wrapping paper, as displayed in Table 3-5.

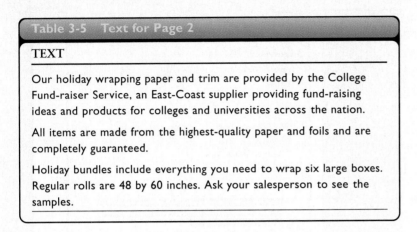

Table 3-5 Text for Page 2
TEXT
Our holiday wrapping paper and trim are provided by the College Fund-raiser Service, an East-Coast supplier providing fund-raising ideas and products for colleges and universities across the nation.
All items are made from the highest-quality paper and foils and are completely guaranteed.
Holiday bundles include everything you need to wrap six large boxes. Regular rolls are 48 by 60 inches. Ask your salesperson to see the samples.

The following steps illustrate how to adjust the alignment of the text to justified, change the line spacing of the paragraphs to 1.5 inches, and then type the text.

To Change the Alignment and Line Spacing

1

• **Right-click the story located below the Our Products heading. On the shortcut menu, point to Change Text and then click Paragraph on the Change Text submenu.**

• **When the Paragraph dialog box is displayed, if necessary, click the Indents and Spacing tab.**

Publisher displays the Paragraph dialog box (Figure 3-27).

FIGURE 3-27

2

• **Click the Alignment box arrow and then click Justified in the list.**

• **In the Line spacing area, select the text in the Between lines box, and then type** 1.5 **to enter the new value.**

Justified alignment and the new value for line spacing between lines are entered (Figure 3-28).

FIGURE 3-28

3

• **Click the OK button.**

• **Press the F9 key to increase the magnification.**

• **Type the text from Table 3-5 on the previous page, pressing the ENTER key after each paragraph.**

Publisher displays the text justified with line spacing of 1.5 (Figure 3-29). Notice the text automatically wraps around the graphic.

FIGURE 3-29

Other Ways

1. On Format menu click Paragraph

The Paragraph dialog box contains a Line and Paragraph Breaks tab where you can set widow and orphan control. A **widow** is the last line of a paragraph printed by itself at the top of a connected text box. An **orphan** is the first line of a paragraph printed by itself at the bottom of a connected text box. Choices include keeping the lines together and starting the paragraph in a new text box.

You can view the paragraph marks by clicking the Special Characters button on the Formatting toolbar. (See Figure 3-27 on page PUB 151.)

Editing the Caption, Price List, and Order Form Heading

To complete the text editing on page 2, the following steps describe how to edit the caption, price list, and order form heading. Table 3-6 displays the text for the price list. As you click and type parts of the price list, the formatting, complete with color and font, will be applied automatically.

Table 3-6 Text for Price List	
ITEM DESCRIPTION	**PRICE**
Holiday Bundle 2 large rolls, 8 bows, and ribbon	$14.00
Birthday Delight 1 roll, bow, and ribbon	$8.00
Evergreen/Winter Scene 1 roll, bow, and ribbon	$8.00
Bright Red or Bright Green Large, 8' roll	$6.00
Bows Galore 24 assorted colors and sizes	$6.00
Candle Holiday 2 rolls, 2 bows, and ribbon	$12.00
Angels on High Large, 8' roll	$6.00
That Jolly Ol' Man 1 roll, bow, and ribbon	$8.00

To Edit the Caption, Price List, and Order Form Heading

1

• **Scroll to display the caption below the graphic in the left panel of page 2. Click the caption to select it.**

• **Type** Holiday Bundles **to replace the selected caption text.**

Publisher replaces the placeholder text with the new caption (Figure 3-30).

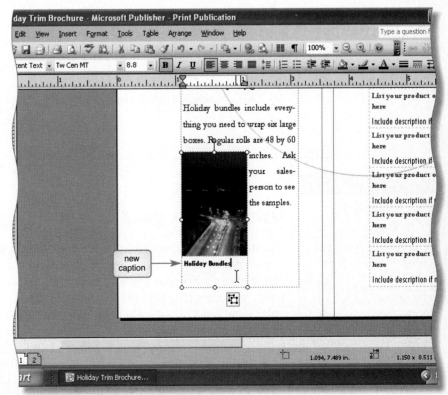

new caption

FIGURE 3-30

2

• Scroll and zoom as necessary to display the price list in the middle panel. One at a time, click each part of the price list and then enter the new text from Table 3-6 on the previous page.

The edited price list is entered (Figure 3-31).

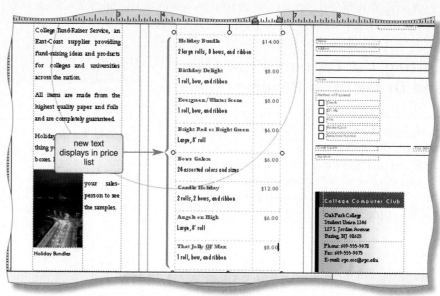

FIGURE 3-31

3

• Scroll to the top of the right panel. Click the text in the Order form heading and then type My Holiday Trim Order to replace the heading.

Publisher replaces the heading (Figure 3-32).

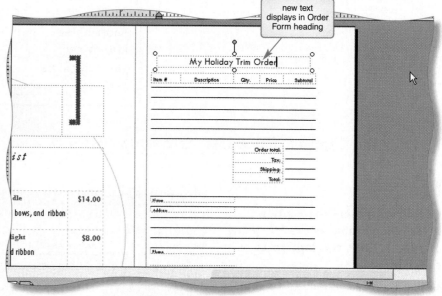

FIGURE 3-32

Using Photographs and Images in a Brochure

The advent of inexpensive photo CDs, along with Web access, has increased exponentially the possibilities for photographic reproduction in publications. Regular cameras using popular types of film now can take pictures that are ultimately digitized, a process that previously required digital cameras. **Digitizing** means converting colors and lines into digital impulses capable of being read by a computer. Digitized photos and downloaded graphics from the Web, combined with high-resolution production from scanners, create endless possibilities. Small businesses now can afford to include photographs in their brochures and other types of publications.

Publisher can accept photographs and images from a variety of input sources. Each graphic you import has a file name, followed by a dot or period, followed by a three-letter extension. Publisher uses **extensions** to recognize individual file formats. Table 3-7 displays some of the graphic formats and their extensions that Publisher can import.

Inserting a Photograph from a File

Publisher can insert a photograph into a publication by accessing the Clip Art task pane, by externally importing from a file, by directly importing an image from a scanner or camera, or by creating a new drawing.

When a Publisher template has grouped a picture with its caption, clicking either will select both. To further select only the picture or only the caption text box, a second click is required.

The next sequence of steps illustrates how to insert a previously scanned photograph from a file into the brochure. The photograph for the brochure is provided on the Data Disk. See the inside back cover of this book for instructions for downloading the Data Disk or see your instructor for information on accessing the files required for this book.

Table 3-7 Supported Graphic Formats
GRAPHIC FORMATS
Compressed Macintosh PICT (.pcz)
Compressed Windows Enhanced Metafile (.emz)
Compressed Windows Metafile (.wmz)
Computer Graphics Metafile (.cgm)
CorelDraw (.cdr)
Encapsulated PostScript (.eps)
Graphics Interchange Format, CompuServe format (.gif or .gfa)
JPEG File Interchange Format (.jpeg, .jpg, .jfif, or .jpe)
Macintosh PICT (.pct or .pict)
Microsoft Windows Bitmap (.bmp)
Portable Network Graphics (.png)
TIFF, Tagged Image File Format (.tif or .tiff)
Windows Enhanced Metafile (.emf)
Windows Metafile (.wmf)
WordPerfect Graphics (.wpg)

To Insert a Photograph from a File

1

• **Insert the Data Disk in drive A. If necessary, click the Page 2 icon in the Page Navigation Control and then click the graphic in the lower portion of the left panel.**

• **Click the picture again to select only the picture from the group.**

• **Right-click the picture and then point to Change Picture on the shortcut menu.**

The Change Picture submenu is displayed (Figure 3-33). Clicking one object in a group a second time selects only that object. The selected object displays a filled handle with an x in it.

FIGURE 3-33

2

- Click From File.
- When the Insert Picture dialog box is displayed, click the Look in box arrow and then click 3½ Floppy (A:) in the list.
- When the folders are displayed, double-click the Project 3 folder and then double-click the file name, paper.

The wrapping paper picture replaces the original picture (Figure 3-34).

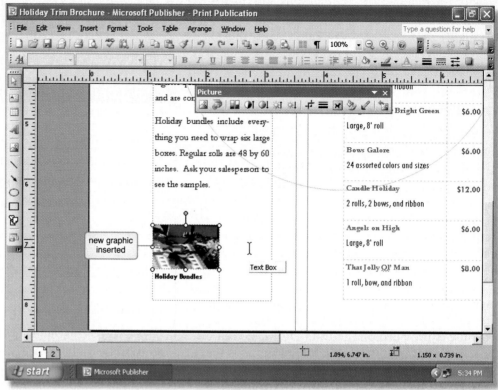

FIGURE 3-34

Another common method of creating new image files, other than scanning, is to use **illustration software.** Designed for artists, illustration software packages such as CorelDRAW! and Adobe Illustrator create graphics to import into desktop publishing software.

FIGURE 3-35

Replacing Graphics on Page 1

The graphics on page 1 come from the clip art included with a full installation of Publisher. The following steps describe how to use the Clip Art task pane to replace the graphics on page 1.

To Replace the Graphics in the Left Panel of Page 1

1 Click the Page 1 icon in the Page Navigation control on the status bar.

2 Zoom as necessary to display the lower portion of the left panel.

3 Click the graphic/caption grouped object in the lower portion of the left panel.

4 Double-click the graphic only. When the Clip Art task pane is displayed, select any text in the Search for text box, type `student` in the Search for text box, and then click the Go button.

5 When the clip art previews are displayed, click a picture similar to the one shown in Figure 3-35.

Publisher displays a graphic of a student sitting at a computer (Figure 3-35).

If the Clip Art task pane does not display as many graphics as you expect, it is possible that the search results may not include all media types. To verify that all media types are being searched, click the Results should be box arrow and confirm that the All media types check box displays a check mark (Figure 3-35).

To Replace the Graphics in the Right Panel of Page 1

1 Zoom as necessary to display the middle portion of the right panel.

2 Double-click the graphic. In the Clip Art task pane, select any text in the Search for text box, type `bows` in the Search for text box, and then click the Go button.

3 When the clip art previews are displayed, click a picture similar to the one shown in Figure 3-36.

4 Click the Close button in the Clip Art task pane.

Publisher displays a holiday graphic (Figure 3-36).

FIGURE 3-36

In addition to the clip art images included in the previews, other sources for clip art include retailers specializing in computer software, the Internet, bulletin board systems, and online information systems. Some popular online information systems are The Microsoft Network, America Online, CompuServe, and Prodigy. A **bulletin board system** is a computer system that allows users to communicate with each other and share files. Microsoft has created a special page on its Web site where you can add new clips to the Clip Organizer.

Creating a Logo from Scratch

Many types of publications use logos to identify and distinguish the page. A **logo** is a recognizable symbol that identifies a person, business, or organization. A logo may be composed of a name, a picture, or a combination of symbols and graphics. In a later project, you will learn how to add a permanent logo to an information set for a company.

Creating a Shape for the Logo

The logo in the Holiday Trim brochure is a combination of a shape and three text boxes with symbols. Created individually in the workspace and then grouped together, the logo easily is positioned and sized to the proper places in the brochure. The logo appears both on the front of the brochure (right panel of page 1) and on the back of the brochure (middle panel of page 1).

Microsoft Office
Publisher 2003

More About

AutoShapes

You can set the fill color, line weight, and line color for new AutoShapes or drawing objects, such as curves, lines and WordArt in the current publication. Right-click an AutoShape or drawing object that has the attributes such as line fill or text color that you want to use as the default. Then, on the shortcut menu, click the Format option. In the dialog box, click the Colors and Lines tab. Finally, select the Apply settings to new AutoShapes check box.

The background of the logo is from the AutoShapes menu. Accessed through the Objects toolbar, the **AutoShapes** menu displays seven categories of shapes you may use as graphics in a publication. These shapes include lines, connectors, basic shapes, block arrows, stars, and banners, among others. AutoShapes differ from WordArt in that they do not contain text; rather, they are graphic designs with a variety of formatting options, such as color, border, size, and shadow.

The workspace, also called the **scratch area**, can serve as a kind of drawing board to create new objects. Without disturbing any object already on the publications page, you can manipulate and edit objects in the workspace and then move them to the desired location. The rulers and status bar display the exact size of the new object. Moving objects off the page and into the workspace is sometimes advantageous as well. Small objects that are difficult to revise on the publication can be moved into the workspace, magnified and edited, and then moved back. As you place new objects in the workspace, more workspace room is allocated.

The following steps illustrate creating the logo in Publisher's workspace to the right of the brochure.

To Create a Shape for the Logo

1

• **If necessary, click the Page 1 icon in the Page Navigation control on the status bar and then increase the magnification to view the whole page. Drag the scroll box to the right, to view more of the workspace.**

The brochure moves left as you scroll right, providing more workspace area (Figure 3-37).

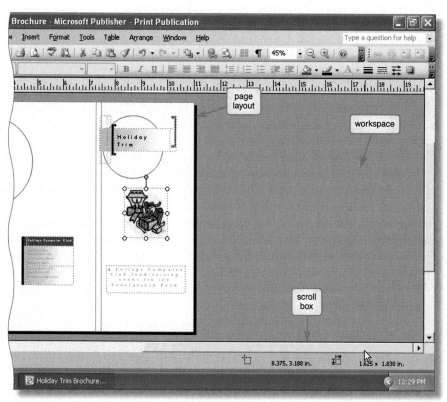

FIGURE 3-37

2

- **Click the AutoShapes button on the Objects toolbar.**
- **Point to Stars and Banners on the AutoShapes menu and then point to Horizontal Scroll.**

The AutoShapes menu is displayed (Figure 3-38).

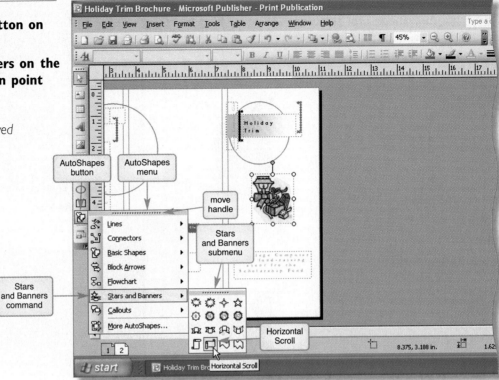

FIGURE 3-38

3

- **Click Horizontal Scroll and then move the mouse pointer to the workspace to the right of the brochure.**
- **Drag down and to the right until the shape is approximately 1.75 × 1.25 inches as displayed in the Object Size box on the status bar. Release the mouse button.**
- **Press the F9 key.**

The workspace displays the horizontal scroll shape for the logo (Figure 3-39). The Object Size box displays the size of the object. The AutoShape displays at 100% magnification.

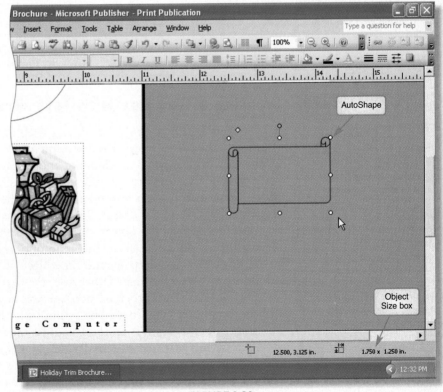

FIGURE 3-39

4

• **With the AutoShape still selected, click the Fill Color button arrow on the Formatting toolbar.**

The Fill Color palette is displayed (Figure 3-40).

FIGURE 3-40

5

• **Click Accent 1 (Red).**

The shape's fill color changes to red to match the brochure's Holiday color scheme (Figure 3-41).

FIGURE 3-41

The AutoShape menu can be changed to a floating toolbar by dragging the move handle at the top of the menu (shown in Figure 3-38 on the previous page).

Creating a Text Box with Text Wrapping

The way that text wraps, or adjusts itself around objects, is not limited to wrapping around graphics. **Text wrapping** in Publisher implies how text wraps whenever it is close to or overlapping another Publisher object. You can choose how you want the text to wrap around an object using one of the following **wrapping styles**. **Square** wraps text around all sides of the selected object. **Tight** wraps text as closely as possible to the object. **Through** wraps text around the perimeter and inside any open portions of the object. **Top and bottom** wraps text above and below the object, but not on either side. The **None** option removes all text-wrapping formatting so that text does not wrap around the object. If the object is transparent, the text behind it will show through. Otherwise, the text will be hidden behind the object.

The Holiday Trim brochure needs a text box to hold a symbol used in the College Computer Club logo. The symbol should fill the text box. Recall that Publisher uses the Best Fit option to adjust the size of text to fill a text box.

Because this text box eventually will be displayed on top of the AutoShape, a transparent text box will allow the color of the AutoShape to show through. Black text on a dark background does not print as well as it displays on the screen. On a color desktop printer, the darker black is applied over the top of the background color, which lends itself to streaking. Therefore, a white symbol will be placed on top of the red AutoShape.

The text box should be formatted with a white font, centered text, with the Best Fit option, and no text wrapping, as described in the following steps.

...

To Create a Text Box with Text Wrapping

1

• **Click the Text Box button on the Objects toolbar. In a blank area of the workspace, near the horizontal scroll AutoShape, drag to create a text box approximately .75 × .75 inches.**

The text box is displayed in the workspace (Figure 3-42).

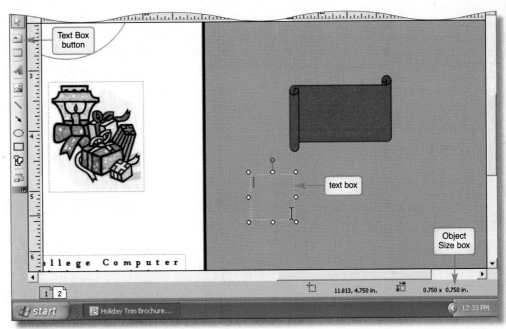

FIGURE 3-42

2

• **Press CTRL+E to center the text inside the text box.**

• **Click the Font Color button arrow on the Formatting toolbar and then click white on the color palette.**

• **With the insertion point still located in the text box, right-click the text box, point to Change Text, point to AutoFit Text on the Change Text Submenu, and then click Best Fit on the AutoFit Text submenu.**

• **Click Arrange on the menu bar. Point to Text Wrapping.**

Publisher displays the Arrange menu and the Text Wrapping submenu (Figure 3-43).

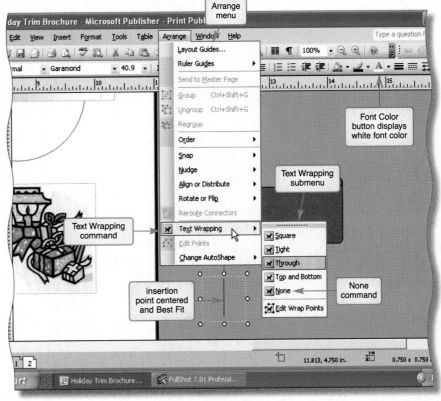

FIGURE 3-43

3

• **Click None on the Text Wrapping submenu.**

The text box will use no text wrapping as it is layered or moved closer to other objects.

More About

Symbols

If you need a character that is not on your keyboard, such as a trademark symbol or a foreign language character, click Insert on the menu bar and then click Symbol. The Symbol dialog box contains a huge selection of characters in a variety of fonts and subsets. Click the character you want, and then click the Insert button.

Inserting a Symbol

The next step is to insert the symbol used for the College Computer Club logo, who is selling the holiday trim paper and bows. A **symbol** is a special character, not typically represented on the keyboard. Foreign language letters, mathematical symbols, and music notation symbols are examples of characters that you may want to use and print, but are not available on most keyboards. Publisher's Symbol command on the Insert menu displays a dialog box containing hundreds of symbols from which you may choose.

The following steps insert a symbol into the previously formatted text box.

To Insert a Symbol

1

• **Click Insert on the menu bar.**

Publisher displays the Insert menu (Figure 3-44).

FIGURE 3-44

2

• **Click Symbol on the Insert menu.**

• **When the Symbol dialog box is displayed, if necessary, click the Symbols tab. Scroll to display the symbol, ©.**

The Symbol dialog box is displayed (Figure 3-45).

FIGURE 3-45

3 ───────────

• **Click the symbol, ©, click the Insert button, and then click the Close button in the Symbol dialog box.**

The symbol is inserted in the text box (Figure 3-46).

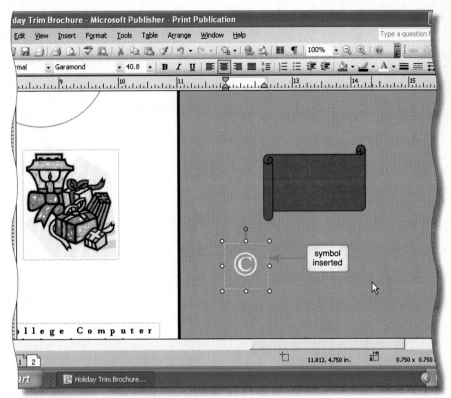

FIGURE 3-46

───────────────

Mixed colors of layered objects create challenges for commercial printing. Professional printers use a technique known as knocking out. **Knocking out** removes the background colors underneath foreground objects or text so the foreground colors print directly on the paper instead of on top of other colors. When colors print on top of each other on a commercial printer, they can mix to create an undesired color. For example, if a blue circle prints on top of a red rectangle, the overlapping colors can mix to create purple.

A cost-saving alternative is to change the color as you did in the previous set of steps. Copy shops, printing services, and media design professionals all recommend white text on darker backgrounds. The white letters stand out and offer an appearance of distinction to the publication.

Copying Text Boxes

Because the Computer College Club logo combines three occurrences of the © symbol, the next task is to create two more identical text boxes, as shown in the step on the next page.

To Copy Text Boxes

1

• **With the symbol text box selected, right-click the text box and then click Copy on the shortcut menu.**

• **Right-click the workspace, away from the text box. Click Paste on the shortcut menu.**

• **Right-click the workspace again, away from the previous text boxes. Click Paste on the shortcut menu.**

The three text boxes are displayed in the workspace (Figure 3-47).

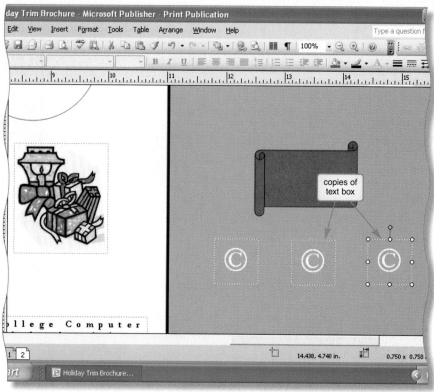

FIGURE 3-47

Aligning and Nudging the Logo Text Boxes

The logo, when complete, is a composite object: three text boxes and a background shape. Repositioning, aligning, and resizing objects independently can be tedious and prone to error. Placing objects on top of other objects, known as **layering**, can cause design errors if you are not careful. Moving the front objects first can cause an **order** error with parts of objects obscured behind others.

Publisher's Arrange menu contains choices for nudging, arranging, aligning, and rotating objects, among others. When you **align** objects, it means to line up or arrange them in relation to one another. For example, you might want to align tall and short graphics along their bottom edges to present a straight line appearance. Table 3-8 lists Publisher's align or distribute commands, available through the Arrange menu.

Table 3-8 Align or Distribute Commands

COMMAND	RESULT
Align Left	Lines up the left borders of the objects
Align Center	Lines up the centers of the objects vertically
Align Right	Lines up the right borders of the objects
Align Top	Lines up the top borders of the objects
Align Middle	Lines up the middles of the objects horizontally
Align Bottom	Lines up the bottom borders of the objects
Distribute Horizontally	Evenly arranges the objects horizontally
Distribute Vertically	Evenly arranges the objects vertically

When you **nudge** an object, it means to move it a set distance each time you press an arrow key (or ALT+ARROW key for text boxes). The default nudge distance is 0.13" (or its equivalent if you are using another measurement unit). You can change the nudge distance, however.

The following steps reposition the symbol text boxes, middle-aligning two of them and nudging the third into place, to create the College Computer Club logo.

To Align and Nudge the Logo Objects

1

• **Point to one of the symbol text boxes. When the mouse pointer changes to a double two-headed arrow, drag the text box to the left center of the AutoShape as shown in Figure 3-48.**

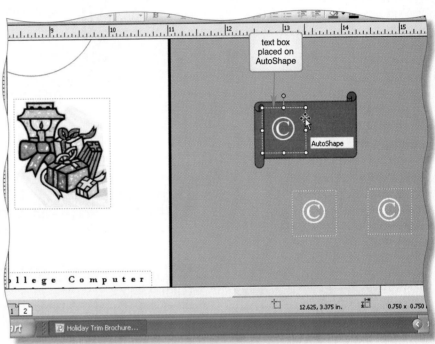

FIGURE 3-48

2

• **Drag another of the symbol text boxes to the right center of the AutoShape.**

The text box displays in front of the shape (Figure 3-49).

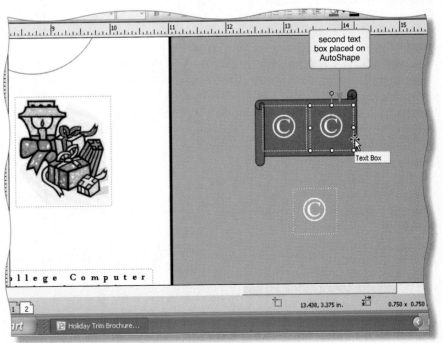

FIGURE 3-49

3

• **With the symbol text box still selected, SHIFT-click the first symbol text box so that both are selected.**

• **Click Arrange on the menu bar and then point to Align or Distribute on the Arrange menu.**

Pressing SHIFT-click selects multiple objects (Figure 3-50). Publisher displays the Align or Distribute submenu.

FIGURE 3-50

4

• **Click Align Middle.**

• **Drag the third symbol text box to the center of the AutoShape, so that it displays between the two other symbol text boxes and slightly lower, as shown in Figure 3-51.**

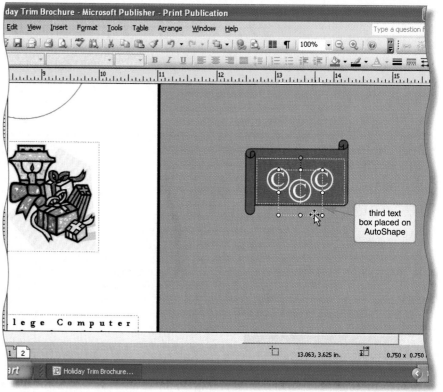

FIGURE 3-51

5

• To place the text box precisely so that the © symbols overlap, with the center text box selected, press and hold the ALT key. Press the UP or DOWN ARROW key as necessary to nudge the text box in the direction that you want it to move.

• As necessary, select and nudge the other two text boxes left or right using the ALT key and the appropriate LEFT or RIGHT ARROW key. Be careful to select the text boxes individually and not the AutoShape.

The three © symbols overlap so that their outside circles touch the inner c of each other (Figure 3-52).

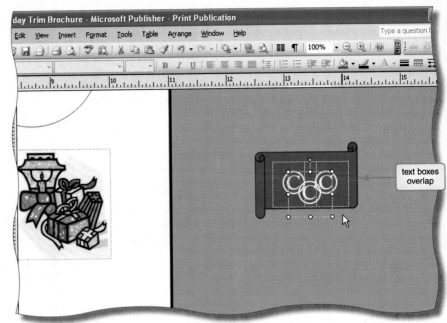

FIGURE 3-52

Grouping Objects

When you **group** objects, you combine them so you can work with them as though they were a single object. You can flip, rotate, resize, or scale all objects in a group as a single unit. You also can change the attributes of all objects in a group at one time — for example, you might change the fill color or add a shadow to all objects in the group.

Objects can be moved, resized, formatted, and copied easily, provided they are grouped and aligned carefully. It is important to adhere to the scheme colors, and pay close attention to layering.

The following steps describe how to group the logo.

To Group Objects

1

• Above and to the left of the AutoShape and text boxes, click and drag the mouse pointer down and to the right to encompass the objects. Do not release the mouse button.

The mouse pointer creates a visual rectangle as it drags through the area (Figure 3-53).

FIGURE 3-53

2

• **Release the mouse button.**

Publisher selects all of the objects and displays the Group Objects button (Figure 3-54). The Group Objects button always is displayed when multiple objects are selected.

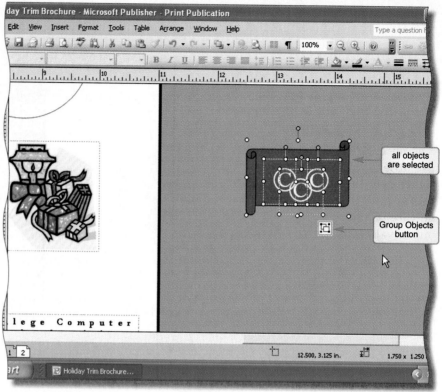

FIGURE 3-54

3

• **Click the Group Objects button.**

The objects display as a grouped object with a single set of handles (Figure 3-55). The Group Objects button becomes the Ungroup Objects button as indicated by the button's changed icon.

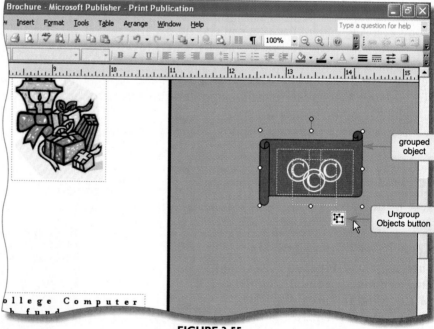

FIGURE 3-55

Other Ways

1. On Arrange menu click Group
2. Press CTRL+SHIFT+G
3. In Voice Command mode, say "Arrange, Group"

Repositioning Objects

The next series of steps repositions the logo in the page layout and then copies and pastes it to a second location in the brochure.

To Reposition the Logo

1

• **Click the Zoom Out button on the Standard toolbar several times until the entire page layout and workspace area is visible.**

Publisher displays the page layout and the logo in the workspace (Figure 3-56).

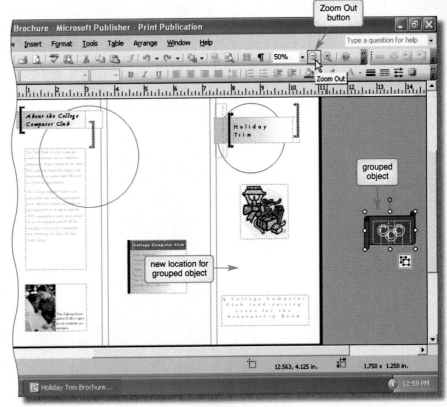

FIGURE 3-56

2

• **Point to the logo. When the mouse pointer changes to a double two-headed arrow, drag the logo to a position below the bows graphic in the right panel of page 1.**

The logo is displayed in the front panel of the brochure (Figure 3-57).

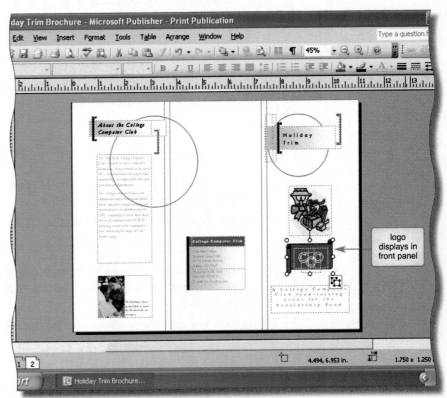

FIGURE 3-57

3

• **Right-click the logo and then click Copy on the shortcut menu.**

• **Right-click the middle panel below the address text box and then click Paste on the shortcut menu.**

The copy of the logo is inserted in the middle panel of the brochure (Figure 3-58). Drag the logo to the location shown, if necessary.

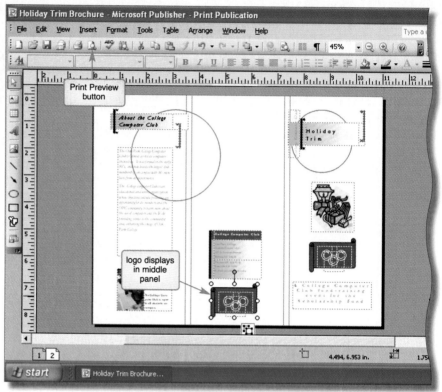

FIGURE 3-58

If the logos are not perfectly aligned horizontally or vertically with other objects in the panel, you can nudge or align them as necessary.

Checking and Saving the Publication

The publication now is complete. You should check for spelling errors in the publication, run the Design Checker, and then save the publication again.

To Check the Publication and Save Again

1 Click the Spelling button on the Standard toolbar. If Publisher flags any words that are misspelled, fix them.

2 When Publisher asks to check the entire document, click the Yes button.

3 Choose to ignore the abbreviated word, OI'. Fix any other errors.

4 Click Tools on the menu bar and then click Design Checker. If the Design Checker identifies any errors, fix them as necessary and then close the Design Checker task pane.

5 Ignore any messages about extra space below the top margin or RGB mode.

6 Click the Save button on the Standard toolbar.

The checked document saves in the same location with the same file name.

More About

Positioning Objects

You can drag objects to new positions or you can press and hold the ALT key while pressing the arrow keys to nudge objects to new positions. If you increase the magnification of the screen, you can resize and reposition objects precisely. For instance, at 400% magnification, you can move an object .003 inch by pressing and holding the ALT key and then pressing an arrow key. The Arrange menu also contains options for nudging and aligning. The Measurements toolbar allows you to enter exact horizontal and vertical positions, as well.

Outside Printing

When they need mass quantities of publications, businesses generally **outsource**, or submit their publications to an outside printer, for duplicating. You must make special considerations when preparing a document for outside printing.

Previewing the Brochure Before Printing

The first step in getting the publication ready for outside printing is to examine what the printed copy will look like from your desktop. The following steps preview the brochure before printing.

To Preview the Brochure Before Printing

1 **Click the Print Preview button on the Standard toolbar (Figure 3-58).**

Page 2 displays without the special characters and guides (Figure 3-59). You also may preview page 1 by clicking the Page 1 icon in the Page Navigation Control on the status bar.

2 **Click the Close button on the Print Preview toolbar.**

3 **Click the Page 2 icon in the Page Navigation Control on the status bar and then again click the Print Preview button on the Standard toolbar to view page 2.**

4 **Click the Close button on the Print Preview toolbar.**

FIGURE 3-59

You also can view two pages of the brochure at once by clicking the Multiple Pages button on the Print Preview toolbar. While viewing two full pages with intensive graphics and text may give you a good overview of the publication, it provides few checking capabilities.

The next sequence of steps recommends publishing this brochure on a high grade of paper to obtain a professional look. A heavier stock paper helps the brochure to stand up better in display racks, although any paper will suffice. If you do use a special paper, be sure to click the Properties or Advanced Settings button in the Print dialog box for your printer and then specify the paper you are using. Following your printer's specifications, print one side of the paper, turn it over, and then print the reverse side. The completed brochure prints as shown in Figure 3-1 on page PUB 131. You then can fold the brochure to display the title panel on the front.

More About

Laser Printers

For details on laser printers, visit the Publisher 2003 More About Web page (scsite.com/pub2003/more) and then click Discovering Laser Printers.

The following steps print a copy of the brochure.

To Print the Brochure

1 Ready the printer according to the printer instructions, and insert paper.

2 With page 1 displaying in the workspace, click File on the menu bar and then click Print. When the Print dialog box is displayed, click Current page. If necessary, click the Properties button to choose a special paper. Click the OK button.

3 When page 1 finishes printing, turn the page over and reinsert it top first (or as your printer requires) into the paper feed mechanism on your printer.

4 Click the Page 2 icon in the Page Navigation Control on the status bar. Click File on the menu bar and then click Print. When the Print dialog box is displayed, again click Current page and then click the OK button.

The brochure prints as shown in Figure 3-1 on page PUB 131.

More About

Printing in Color

Some printers do not have enough memory to print a wide variety of images and color. In these cases, the printer prints up to a certain point on a page and then chokes — resulting in only the top portion of the publication printing. Check with your instructor to see if your printer has enough memory to work with colors.

Printing Considerations

If you start a publication from scratch, it is best to **set up** the publication for the type of printing you want before you place objects on the page. Otherwise, you may be forced to make design changes at the last minute. You also may set up an existing publication for a printing service. In order to provide you with experience in setting up a publication for outside printing, this project takes you through the preparation steps — even if you are submitting this publication only to your instructor.

Printing options, such as whether to use a copy shop or commercial printer, have advantages and limitations. You may have to make some trade-offs before deciding on the best printing option. Table 3-9 shows some of the questions you can ask yourself about printing.

Table 3-9 Picking a Printing Option

CONSIDERATION	QUESTIONS TO ASK	DESKTOP OPTION	PROFESSIONAL OPTIONS
Color	Is the quality of photographs and color a high priority?	Low- to medium-quality	High quality
Convenience	Do I want the easy way?	Very convenient and familiar	Time needed to explore different methods, unfamiliarity
Cost	How much do I want to pay?	Printer supplies and personal time	High-resolution color/high quality is expensive; the more you print, the less expensive the per copy price
Quality	How formal is the purpose of my publication?	Local event; narrow, personal audience	Business, marketing, professional services
Quantity	How many copies do I need?	1 to 10 copies	10 to 500 copies: copy shop 500+ copies: commercial printer
Turnaround	How soon do I need it?	Immediate	Rush outside printing, probably an extra cost

Paper Considerations

Professional brochures are printed on a high grade of paper to enhance the graphics and provide a longer lasting document. Grades of paper are based on weight. Desktop printers commonly use **20 lb. bond paper**, which means they use a lightweight paper intended for writing and printing. A commercial printer might use 60 lb. glossy or linen paper. The finishing options and their costs are important considerations that may take additional time to explore. **Glossy paper** is a coated paper, produced using a heat process with clay and titanium. **Linen paper**, with its mild texture or grain, can support high-quality graphics without the shine and slick feel of glossy paper. Users sometimes pick a special stock of paper such as cover stock, card stock, or text stock. This textbook is printed on 45 lb., blade-coated paper. **Blade-coated paper** is coated and then skimmed and smoothed to create the pages you see here.

These paper and finishing options may sound burdensome, but they are becoming conveniently available to desktop publishers. Local office supply stores have shelf after shelf of special computer paper specifically designed for laser and ink-jet printers. Some of the paper you can purchase has been prescored for special folding.

Color Considerations

When printing colors, desktop printers commonly use a color scheme called **Composite RGB.** RGB stands for the three colors — red, green, and blue — that are used to print the combined colors of your publication. Professional printers, on the other hand, can print your publication using color scheme processes, or **libraries.** These processes include black-and-white, spot-color, and process-color.

In **black-and-white printing**, the printer uses only one color of ink (usually black, but you can choose a different color if you want). You can add accent colors to your publication by using different shades of gray or by printing on colored paper. Your publication can have the same range of subtleties as a black-and-white photograph.

A **spot color** is used to accent a black and white publication. Newspapers, for example, may print their masthead in a bright, eye-catching color on page 1 but print the rest of the publication in black and white. In Publisher, you may apply up to two spot colors with a color matching system called **Pantone. Spot-color printing** uses semitransparent, premixed inks typically chosen from standard color-matching guides, such as Pantone. Choosing colors from a **color-matching library** helps ensure high-quality results, because printing professionals who license the libraries agree to maintain the specifications, control, and quality.

In a spot-color publication, each spot color is **separated** to its own plate and printed on an offset printing press. The use of spot colors has become more creative in the last few years. Printing services use spot colors of metallic or florescent inks, as well as screen tints to get color variations without increasing the number of color separations and cost. If your publication includes a logo with one or two colors, or if you want to use color to emphasize line art or text, then consider using spot-color printing.

Process-color printing means your publication can include color photographs and any color or combination of colors. One of the process-color libraries, called **CMYK**, or **four-color printing**, is named for the four semitransparent process inks — cyan, magenta, yellow, and black. CMYK process-color printing can reproduce a full range of colors on a printed page. The CMYK color model defines color as it is absorbed and reflected on a printed page rather than in its liquid state.

Process-color printing is the most expensive proposition; black-and-white printing is the cheapest. Using color increases the cost and time it takes to process the publication. When using either the spot-color or process-color method, the printer

More About

Spot Color Printing

If you choose black plus one spot color in a publication, Publisher converts all colors except for black to tints of the selected spot color. If you choose black plus two spot colors, Publisher changes only exact matches of the second spot color to 100 percent of the second spot color. All other colors in the publication, other than black, are changed to tints of the first spot color. You then can apply tints of the second spot color to objects in the publication manually.

More About

CMYK Process Colors

When CMYK Process is selected, Publisher converts all colors in text, graphics, and other objects to CMYK values and then creates four plates, regardless of the color scheme originally used to create the publication. Some RGB colors, including some of Publisher's standard colors, cannot be matched exactly to a CMYK color. After setting up for process-color printing, be sure to evaluate the publication for color changes. If a color does not match the color you want, you will have to include the new color library when you pack the publication.

More About

Printing Service Colors

Your printing service may use the initials SWOP, which stand for Standard for Web Offset Printing — a widely accepted set of color standards used in web offset printing. Web offset printing has nothing to do with the World Wide Web. It is merely the name for an offset printing designed to print thousands of pieces in a single run from a giant roll of paper.

More About

**Flipping Objects
to Print on
T-Shirts**

You can use Publisher to create T-shirt designs with pictures, logos, words, or any of
the Publisher objects. You
need thermal T-shirt transfer
paper that is widely available
for most printers. Then create your design in Publisher.
On the File menu, click Page
Setup. On the Printer &
Paper sheet, select Letter.
If your design is a picture,
clip art, or WordArt, flip it
horizontally. If your design
includes text, cut it from the
text box, and insert it into a
WordArt object; then flip it
horizontally.

first must output the publication to film on an **image setter**, which recreates the publication on film or photographic paper. The film then is used to create color **printing plates**. Each printing plate transfers one of the colors in the publication onto paper in an offset process. Publisher can print a preview of these individual sheets showing how the colors will separate before you take your publication to the printer.

A new printing technology called **digital printing** uses toner instead of ink to reproduce a full range of colors. Digital printing does not require separate printing plates. Although not yet widely available, digital printing promises to become cheaper than offset printing without sacrificing any quality.

Publisher supports all three kinds of printing and provides the tools commercial printing services need to print the publication. You should ask your printing service which color-matching system it uses.

Choosing a Commercial Printing Tool

After making the decisions about printing services, paper, and color, you must prepare the brochure for outside printing. The first task is to assign a color library from the commercial printing tools, as illustrated in the following steps.

To Choose a Commercial Printing Tool

1

• **Click Tools on the menu bar. Point to Commercial Printing Tools.**

The Commercial Printing Tools submenu displays (Figure 3-60).

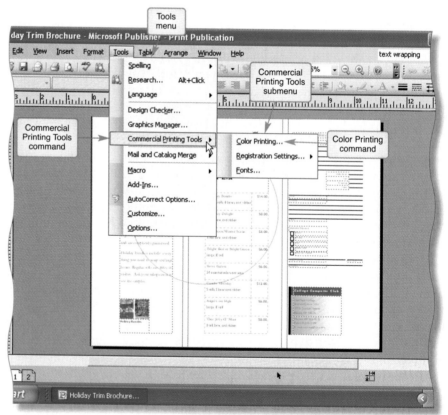

FIGURE 3-60

2

- **Click Color Printing on the Commercial Printing Tools submenu. When the Color Printing dialog box is displayed, click Process colors (CMYK). If a dialog box is displayed, click its OK button.**

Publisher will convert all colors in text, graphics, and other objects to CMYK values and then internally create four plates, regardless of the color model originally used to create the colors (Figure 3-61).

3

- **Click the OK button.**

Depending on your screen colors and resolution, you may or may not see a noticeable difference.

FIGURE 3-61

Other Ways

1. In Voice Command mode, say "Tools, Commercial Printing Tools"

Packaging the Publication for the Printing Service

The publication file can be packaged for the printing service in two ways. The first way is to give the printing service the Publisher file in Publisher format using the Pack and Go Wizard. The second way is to save the file in a format called Encapsulated PostScript. Both of these methods are discussed in the following sections.

Using the Pack and Go Wizard

The **Pack and Go Wizard** guides you through the steps to collect and pack all the files the printing service needs and then compress the files to fit on one or more disks. Publisher checks for and embeds the TrueType fonts used in the publication. **Embedding** ensures that the printing service can display and print the publication with the correct fonts. The Pack and Go Wizard adds a program called **Unpack.exe** to the disk that the printing service can use to unpack the files. At the end of Publisher's packing sequence, you are given the option of printing a composite color printout or color separation printouts on your desktop printer.

You need either sufficient space on a floppy disk or another formatted disk readily available when using the Pack and Go Wizard. Graphic files and fonts require a great deal of disk space. The Pack and Go Wizard also creates on disk a **Readme file** intended for the printing service. In the steps on the next page, if you use a disk other than the one on which you previously saved the brochure, save it again on the new disk before beginning the process.

More About

The Pack and Go Readme File

To look at a sample Pack and Go Readme file, visit the Publisher 2003 More About Web page (scsite.com/ pub2003/more) and then click Pack and Go.

The following steps illustrate using the Pack and Go Wizard to ready the publication for submission to a commercial printing service.

To Use the Pack and Go Wizard

1

• **With a floppy disk in drive A, click File on the menu bar. Point to Pack and Go.**

The File menu and Pack and Go submenu are displayed (Figure 3-62). Publisher also uses a Pack and Go Wizard to transport publications to other computers for printing and viewing purposes only.

FIGURE 3-62

2

• **Click Take to a Commercial Printing Service on the Pack and Go submenu.**

The first Pack and Go Wizard dialog box is displayed (Figure 3-63). This wizard guides you through each step of the packing process. Read each individual screen as you progress through the steps.

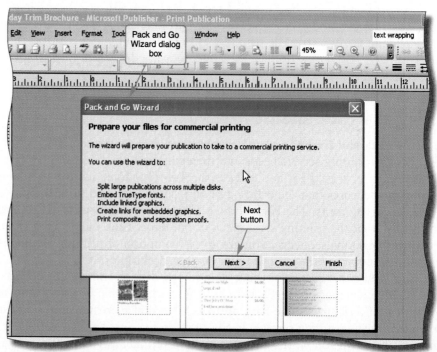

FIGURE 3-63

3

• **Click the Next button for each of the wizard steps, accepting the preset options.**

The last dialog box of the Pack and Go Wizard is displayed (Figure 3-64).

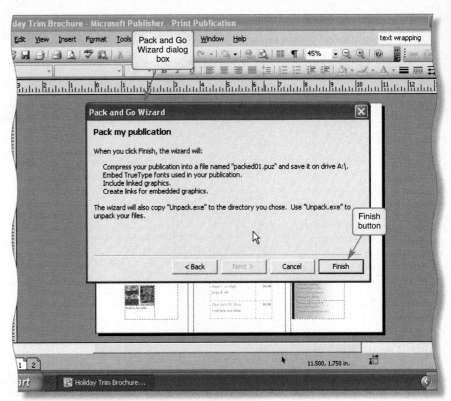

FIGURE 3-64

4

• **Click the Finish button. If you used graphics from an external source, Publisher will ask you to insert the disk. If you used system fonts that cannot be embedded, Publisher will display a dialog box in which you may click the OK button for the purposes of this project.**

After Publisher finishes packing your publication, a confirming dialog box is displayed (Figure 3-65). Both print check boxes are selected.

FIGURE 3-65

5

• **If necessary, click both print check boxes so neither one is selected.**

The check marks are removed from the check boxes (Figure 3-66). You already have printed the brochure and unless you are actually submitting this publication to a printing service, a separation print is unnecessary. If you want to see what the separations look like, you may print them.

6

• **Click the OK button.**

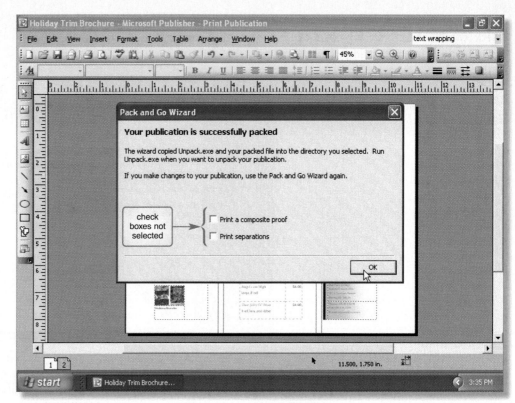

FIGURE 3-66

Other Ways

1. In Voice Command mode, say "File, Pack and Go"

The files are saved on the disk in drive A. Publisher names and numbers the packed files and adds a .puz extension to the files. For example, the first file will be named Packed01.puz, the second file will be named Packed02.puz, and so on. If you make changes to the publication after packing the files, be sure to run the Pack and Go Wizard again so the changes are part of the packed publication.

Using PostScript Files

If your printing service does not accept Publisher files, you can hand off, or submit, your files in PostScript format. **PostScript** is a page definition language that describes the document to be printed in language that the printer can understand. The PostScript printer driver includes a page definition language translator to interpret the instructions and print the document on a printer or a PostScript output device, such as an image setter. Because you cannot open or make changes directly to a PostScript file, everything in the publication must be complete before saving it.

Nearly all printing services can work with some type of PostScript file, either regular PostScript files, known as **PostScript dumps**, or **Encapsulated PostScript** (**EPS**) files, which are graphic pictures of each page. If you hand off a PostScript file, you are responsible for updating graphics, including the necessary fonts, and ensuring that you have all the files your printing service needs. Publisher includes several **PostScript printer drivers** (**PPD**s) and their description files to facilitate printing at the publisher. You must install a PPD before saving in PostScript form. Because the most common installation of Publisher is for a single user in a desktop environment, this project will not take you through the steps involved to install a PostScript printer driver. That process would necessitate using original operating system disks and a more thorough knowledge of PostScript printers. Ask your printing service representative for the correct printer driver, and see your Windows documentation for installing it. Then use the Save As command on the File menu to save the publication in PostScript format.

Another question to ask your printing service is whether it performs the **prepress tasks** or a **preflight check**. You may be responsible for making color corrections, separations, setting the printing options, and other printing tasks.

More About

Submitting PostScript Files

If you decide to hand off a PostScript "dump," or file, to an outside printer or service bureau, include a copy of the original document as well — for backup purposes. Many shops slowly are changing over from Macintosh-based to cross-platform based operations. If something happens, the printer technician can correct the error from the original without another trip by you to the print shop.

Quitting Publisher

The following steps quit Publisher.

To Quit Publisher

1 **Click the Close button on the Publisher title bar.**

2 **If a dialog box displays reminding you to save the document, click its No button.**

The Publisher window closes.

Project Summary

Project 3 introduced you to the brochure medium. You learned how to create custom color schemes, apply font effects, and change paragraph formatting. You learned about the use of photographs versus images, and how to insert a photograph from a file. After entering new text and deleting unwanted objects, you created a logo from scratch using a custom shape and symbols grouped in the workspace. You also learned about design and printing considerations such as overlapping, separations, color libraries, paper types, and costs. In anticipation of taking the brochure to a professional publisher, you previewed and printed your publication and then used the Pack and Go Wizard to create the necessary files.

What You Should Know

Having completed this project, you should be able to perform the tasks below. The tasks are listed in the same order they were presented in this project. For a list of the buttons, menus, toolbars, and commands introduced in this project, see the Quick Reference Summary at the back of this book and refer to the Page Number column.

1. Start Publisher   (PUB 133)
2. Choose Brochure Options   (PUB 134)
3. Create a Custom Color Scheme   (PUB 137)
4. Save the Publication   (PUB 141)
5. Edit Text in the Brochure   (PUB 142)
6. Edit Other Text Boxes on Page 1   (PUB 144)
7. Delete Objects on Page 1   (PUB 145)
8. Insert a Text Box and Apply a Font Scheme Style (PUB 146)
9. Switch to Page 2   (PUB 148)
10. Apply a Font Effect   (PUB 149)
11. Change the Alignment and Line Spacing (PUB 151)
12. Edit the Caption, Price List, and Order Form Heading   (PUB 153)
13. Insert a Photograph from a File   (PUB 155)
14. Replace the Graphics in the Left Panel of Page 1 (PUB 156)

What You Should Know *(continued)*

15. Replace the Graphics in the Right Panel of Page 1 (PUB 157)

16. Create a Shape for the Logo   (PUB 158)

17. Create a Text Box with Text Wrapping (PUB 161)

18. Insert a Symbol   (PUB 162)

19. Copy Text Boxes   (PUB 164)

20. Align and Nudge the Logo Objects   (PUB 165)

21. Group Objects   (PUB 167)

22. Reposition the Logo   (PUB 169)

23. Check the Publication and Save Again (PUB 170)

24. Preview the Brochure Before Printing   (PUB 171)

25. Print the Brochure   (PUB 172)

26. Choose a Commercial Printing Tool   (PUB 174)

27. Use the Pack and Go Wizard   (PUB 176)

28. Quit Publisher   (PUB 179)

More About

The Publisher Help System

The best way to become familiar with the Publisher Help system is to use it. Appendix A includes detailed information on the Publisher Help system and exercises that will help you gain confidence using it.

More About

Quick Reference

For a table that lists how to complete tasks covered in this book using the mouse, menu, shortcut menu, and keyboard, see the Quick Reference summary at the back of this book or visit the Shelly Cashman Series Office XP Web page (scsite.com/offxp/qr), and then click Microsoft Publisher 2003.

Learn It Online

Instructions: To complete the Learn It Online exercises, start your browser, click the Address bar, and then enter the Web address scsite.com/pub2003/learn. When the Publisher 2003 Learn It Online page is displayed, follow the instructions in the exercises below. Each exercise has instructions for printing your results, either for your own records or for submission to your instructor.

1 Project Reinforcement TF, MC, and SA

Below Publisher Project 3, click the Project Reinforcement link. Print the quiz by clicking Print on the File menu for each page. Answer each question.

2 Flash Cards

Below Publisher Project 3, click the Flash Cards link and read the instructions. Type 20 (or a number specified by your instructor) in the Number of playing cards text box, type your name in the Enter your Name text box, and then click the Flip Card button. When the flash card is displayed, read the question and then click the ANSWER box arrow to select an answer. Flip through Flash Cards. If your score is 15 (75%) correct or greater, click Print on the File menu to print your results. If your score is less than 15 (75%) correct, then redo this exercise by clicking the Replay button.

3 Practice Test

Below Publisher Project 3, click the Practice Test link. Answer each question, enter your first and last name at the bottom of the page, and then click the Grade Test button. When the graded practice test is displayed on your screen, click Print on the File menu to print a hard copy. Continue to take practice tests until you score 80% or better.

4 Who Wants To Be a Computer Genius?

Below Publisher Project 3, click the Computer Genius link. Read the instructions, enter your first and last name at the bottom of the page, and then click the PLAY button. When your score is displayed, click the PRINT RESULTS link to print a hard copy.

5 Wheel of Terms

Below Publisher Project 3, click the Wheel of Terms link. Read the instructions, and then enter your first and last name and your school name. Click the PLAY button. When your score is displayed, right-click the score and then click Print on the shortcut menu to print a hard copy.

6 Crossword Puzzle Challenge

Below Publisher Project 3, click the Crossword Puzzle Challenge link. Read the instructions, and then enter your first and last name. Click the SUBMIT button. Work the crossword puzzle. When you are finished, click the Submit button. When the crossword puzzle is redisplayed, click the Print Puzzle button to print a hard copy.

7 Tips and Tricks

Below Publisher Project 3, click the Tips and Tricks link. Click a topic that pertains to Project 3. Right-click the information and then click Print on the shortcut menu. Construct a brief example of what the information relates to in Publisher to confirm you understand how to use the tip or trick.

8 Newsgroups

Below Publisher Project 3, click the Newsgroups link. Click a topic that pertains to Project 3. Print three comments.

9 Expanding Your Horizons

Below Publisher Project 3, click the Articles for Microsoft Publisher link. Click a topic that pertains to Project 3. Print the information. Construct a brief example of what the information relates to in Publisher to confirm you understand the contents of the article.

10 Search Sleuth

Below Publisher Project 3, click the Search Sleuth link. To search for a term that pertains to this project, select a term below the Project 3 title and then use the Google search engine at google.com (or any major search engine) to display and print two Web pages that present information on the term.

11 Publisher Online Training

Below Publisher Project 3, click the Publisher Online Training link. When your browser displays the Microsoft Office Online Web page, click the Publisher link. Click one of the Publisher courses that covers one or more of the objectives listed at the beginning of the project on page PUB 130. Print the first page of the course before stepping through it.

12 Office Marketplace

Below Publisher Project 3, click the Office Marketplace link. When your browser displays the Microsoft Office Online Web page, click the Office Marketplace link. Click a topic that relates to Publisher. Print the first page.

1 Editing a Publication

Instructions: Start Publisher. Open the publication named, Apply-3-1, from the Data Disk. See the inside back cover of this book for instructions for downloading the Data Disk or see your instructor for information on accessing the files required for this book. The edited publication is shown in Figures 3-67a and 3-67b.

Perform the following tasks:

1. With page 1 displayed, click View on the menu bar and then click Task Pane on the View menu. Click the Other Task Panes buttons, and then click Brochure Options. Click Include in the Customer address area and click Response form in the Form area.
2. On page 1, make the following text changes, zooming as necessary:
    a. Click the text, Seminar or Event Title. Type `Music among the Maples` to replace the text.
    b. Drag through the text, Business Name. Type `The Performing Arts Center` to replace the text.
    c. In the lower portion of the right panel of page 1, insert a text box below Performing Arts Center. Click the Font Color button arrow on the Formatting toolbar and then click white on the color palette. Press CTRL+E to center the text. Press F9 to increase the magnification. Type `In conjunction with the Day-ton Symphonic Orchestra` and then press the ENTER key. Type `2005 Fall Concert Series` to complete the entry.
    d. Delete the organization logo if it displays.
3. In the left panel, double-click each of the three graphics, one at a time. Use the keywords, violin, conductor, and entertainment, respectively, to search for pictures similar to Figure 3-67a.
4. Click the Page 2 icon in the Page Navigation control on the status bar. Delete the text box in the center panel by right-clicking the text box and then clicking Delete Object on the shortcut menu. Delete the picture of the graduate and its caption. Drag the instruments picture upward to the center of the panel.
5. SHIFT-drag the red rectangle from the center panel to the left panel and place it to the left of the text.
6. Select all of the story on page 2. Change the line spacing to 1.5 and the alignment to justified.
7. Create a 5-point Star AutoShape button in the workspace. Use the Accent 1 scheme color to fill the star. Create a centered text box using the Best Fit option and a white font color. Insert a musical notation symbol. (*Hint*: the musical notes in Figure 3-67b are found using the Times New Roman Font in the Symbol dialog box.) Drag the text box on top of the star and group. Drag the grouped object to the center panel.
8. Check spelling and run the Design Checker. Correct errors if necessary.
9. Click File on the menu bar and then click Save As. Use the file name, Concert Series Brochure.
10. Click Tools on the menu bar, point to Commercial Printing Tools, and then click Color Printing on the Commercial Printing Tools submenu. When the Color Printing dialog box is displayed, click Process colors (CMYK) and then click the OK button.
11. With a floppy disk in drive A, click File on the menu bar. Point to Pack and Go and then click Take to a Commercial Printing Service on the Pack and Go submenu. Click the Next button in each progressive dialog box. When the final dialog box is displayed, click the Finish button.
12. When the wizard completes the packing process, if necessary click the Print a composite check box to select it. The brochure will print on two pages.

Apply Your Knowledge

(a)

2005 Fall Concert Series

This year's Fall Concert Series promises to be the best yet. The Performing Arts Center has brought in some of the more gifted and talented conductors from across the United States. Whether you want to hear the latest Broadway medley or Straus's "Also Sprach Zarathustra" used in 2001: A Space Odyssey, the 2005 Fall Concert Series will entertain and delight you.

Robert Stewart
Director of the Dayton Symphonic Orchestra for the last five years

Amy Hayes
The first woman conductor of the Ohio Pops Orchestra

Our Own Jazz
The newest member of the series

The Performing Arts Center
2003 Fall Concert Series
1728 Nottingham Drive
Dayton, OH 45402

Music Among the Maples

The Performing Arts Center

In conjunction with the
Dayton Symphonic Orchestra
2005 Fall Concert Series

(b)

The Concerts

The Classical Series: Performed by the Dayton Symphonic Orchestra, the Classical Series has been the mainstay of the summer repertoire since the series' inception in 1987. This 80-piece orchestra, made up of professional and semiprofessional musicians, has performed all over the northeast. This year's theme is music of the late nineteenth and twentieth centuries

The Broadway Series: The Ohio Pops Orchestra is back by popular demand playing, show tunes by famous duos. Performances of music by Rogers & Hammerstein and Lerner & Lowe highlight this family-oriented series.

The Jazz Series: The group, Our Own Jazz brings its unique interpretation of jazz greats, Duke Ellington and Count Basie to the Fall Concert Series. Don't miss this newest addition.

Friday and Saturday evening concerts begin at 8:00 p.m.; Sunday Matinees at 2:00 p.m.

For more information, visit our web site at
www.arts.dayton.oh.org.

Order Fall Concert Series Tickets

Enter the number of tickets you wish to purchase in the boxes. All orders are filled using best seating available.

Classical Series
- September 19
- September 28
- October 4

Broadway Series
- September 20
- September 26
- October 5

Jazz Series
- September 21
- September 27
- October 3

Season Tickets
- Friday Series
- Saturday Series
- Sunday Matinee Series

Name
Address

Telephone

Method of Payment
- Check
- Bill Me
- Visa
- MasterCard
- American Express

Credit Card #   Exp. date
Signature

The Performing Arts Center
Ticket Hotline: 802-555-8484
2005 Fall Concert Series
1728 Nottingham Drive
Dayton, OH 45402

FIGURE 3-67

1 Creating a Brochure Layout with One Spot Color

Problem: A large marketing firm is planning a seminar for salesmen in the oil industry. They would like you to create a sample publication, advertising the event. Their theme is "Reach Your Goal." They would like a tri-fold brochure with a graphic related to the oil industry and a large blue arrow with white diagonal lettering, spelling the word, GOAL. On the inside of the brochure, the marketing firm would like a response form to gain some knowledge of the participants' backgrounds. If they like the sample, the firm then will submit text for the other text boxes.

Instructions: Start Publisher and perform the following tasks to create the one spot color brochure shown in Figures 3-68a and 3-68b.

1. From the New Publication task pane, choose the Accent Box Informational Brochure. Choose to display the customer address and a response form.
2. Edit the text frames in the right panel as shown in Figure 3-68a. Delete the logo in the middle panel.
3. Double-click the graphic in the front panel. Insert a clip using the keyword, oil.
4. Click the AutoShapes button on the Objects toolbar. Point to Block Arrows and then click the arrow shape that points right. In the workspace, SHIFT-drag to create an arrow approximately two inches square. Use the Fill Color button to choose Accent 1 (Medium Blue).
5. Drag to create a text frame in the workspace approximately .35 inch square. Use the Fill Color button to choose Accent 1 (Medium Blue). Use the Font Color button to choose Accent 5 (White). Type G in the text frame. On the Format menu, point to AutoFit Text and then click Best Fit. Choose no text wrapping.
6. Copy the text frame three times. Drag each copy away from the original. Replace the text in each copy with the letters O, A, and L, respectively.
7. Drag the text frames on top of the large arrow so they display diagonally across the arrow as shown in Figure 3-68a. Click the G text frame and then SHIFT-click each of the other letters. SHIFT-click the large arrow itself, away from the letters. Group the objects to create a composite logo. Drag the logo to the empty space above the picture.
8. Click the Response form (page 2). Make the text changes as indicated in Figure 3-68b.
9. Click Tools on the menu bar and then point to Commercial Printing Tools. Click Color Printing. When the Color Printing dialog box is displayed, click Spot colors. Click the OK button.
10. Save the publication using the file name, Lab 3-1 GOAL Brochure. Print a copy.

In the Lab

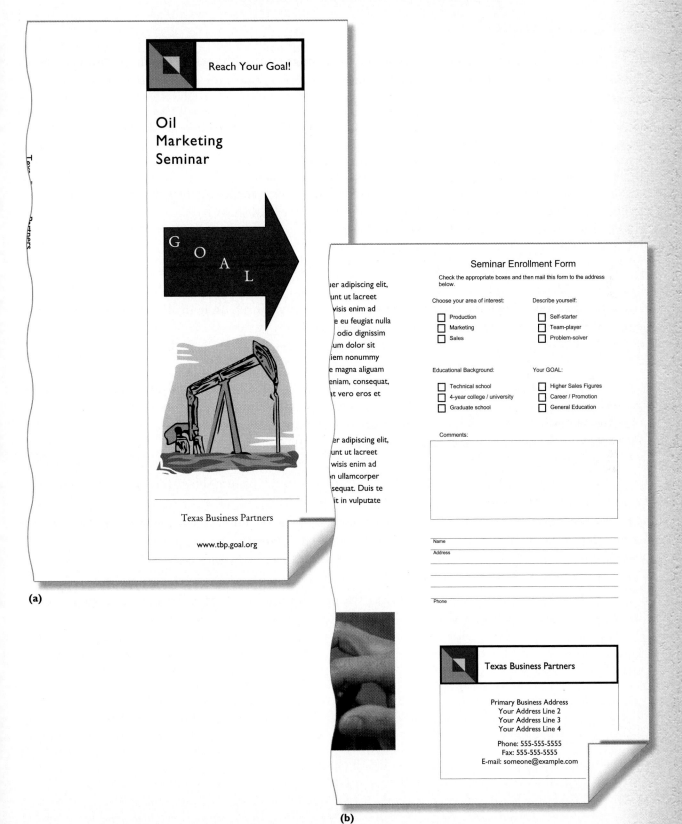

(a)

Reach Your Goal!

Oil Marketing Seminar

G O A L

er adipiscing elit,
unt ut lacreet
visis enim ad
e eu feugiat nulla
odio dignissim
um dolor sit
iem nonummy
e magna aliguam
eniam, consequat,
t vero eros et

er adipiscing elit,
unt ut lacreet
visis enim ad
n ullamcorper
sequat. Duis te
it in vulputate

Texas Business Partners

www.tbp.goal.org

Seminar Enrollment Form

Check the appropriate boxes and then mail this form to the address below.

Choose your area of interest:

☐ Production
☐ Marketing
☐ Sales

Describe yourself:

☐ Self-starter
☐ Team-player
☐ Problem-solver

Educational Background:

☐ Technical school
☐ 4-year college / university
☐ Graduate school

Your GOAL:

☐ Higher Sales Figures
☐ Career / Promotion
☐ General Education

Comments:

Name
Address

Phone

Texas Business Partners

Primary Business Address
Your Address Line 2
Your Address Line 3
Your Address Line 4

Phone: 555-555-5555
Fax: 555-555-5555
E-mail: someone@example.com

(b)

FIGURE 3-68

2 Creating a CD Liner

Problem: Your friend has recorded a new CD of his original guitar music. Knowing of your interest in desktop publishing, he has asked you to create the CD liner. You decide to create a publication with four pages, using Publisher's CD liner template.

Instructions: Perform the following tasks to create the two-panel, two-sided CD liner as shown in Figures 3-69a and 3-69b.

1. Start Publisher.
2. In the New Publication task pane, click Publications for Print, click Labels, and then click CD/DVD Labels. When Publisher displays the previews, click CD/DVD Case Insert Booklet.
3. Choose the Glacier color scheme and the Modern font scheme.
4. Edit the text in both panels as shown in Figure 3-69a.
5. Select the large rectangle border in the right panel. Press CTRL+T to make the rectangle transparent, in preparation for the watermark.
6. Replace the picture in the right panel using the Clip Art task pane. Search using the keyword, guitar.
7. Copy the graphic using the Copy button on the Standard toolbar.
8. On the Insert menu, click Page to insert a new blank page to follow page 1. Click the Page 2 icon in the Page Navigation control, if necessary.
9. Paste the picture from page 1. Drag it to the left panel and SHIFT-drag a corner handle, resizing so it fills the entire panel.
10. Use the Clip Art task pane to search for an appropriate line drawing graphic, similar to the one in Figure 3-69b, for a watermark effect using the keyword, music.
11. Drag the music graphic to the right panel and SHIFT-drag a corner handle, resizing so it fills the entire panel.
12. Create a large text frame in the left panel. Make it transparent so the picture shows through. Use a white font color. Type the text as shown in Figure 3-69b.
13. Using the Design Gallery Object button, insert a Voyage style table of contents. Use the Size and Position dialog box to place it exactly as follows: Width: 3.4; Height: 4.5; Horizontal: 5.4; and Vertical .1 in the right panel. Make it transparent. Edit the table of contents as shown in Figure 3-69b.
14. Save the publication on a floppy disk using the file name, Lab 3-2 Guitar CD Liner.
15. Print a copy of the CD liner, using duplex printing. The default settings will print the liner in the middle of an 8½-by-11-inch piece of paper, with crop marks. Trim the printout.

In the Lab

(a)

Manufactured in the United States by Starks Recording Corporation. Printed in the United States. All Rights Reserved.

<u>Warning:</u> unauthorized reproduction of this recording is prohibited by federal law and subject to criminal prosecution.

© Starks Recording Corporation

137 East 25th Street
New York, New York 10001

Visit the artist's home page at
www.starks.net\gobert

Jonathan Gobert

MUSIC OF MY LIFE

Jonathan Gobert

(b)

Jon Gobert's style of guitar crosses the boundaries among classical, rock, and blues. His unique style of fingering and his use of percussive wood sounds mark him as one of the up and coming artists of the twenty-first century.

Jon studied at the New England Conservatory of Music and has performed with the Greater New York Chamber Guitar Society.

He tours regularly on college campuses and performs at night clubs and coffee houses. Hon also plays studio guitar and has performed with artists such as singer David J. Taylor and blues great Billie Davis.

Music of My Life

All I Have	1
Your Love	2
The City	3
Street Musician	4
Classical, But Not a Gas	5
Forever Bach	6
Winter Blues	7

FIGURE 3-69

In the Lab

3 Creating a Travel Brochure

Problem: Alpha Zeta Mu fraternity is planning a ski trip to Sunset Mountain, Colorado during spring break. They have asked you to design a brochure that advertises the trip. They would like a full-color tri-fold brochure on glossy paper that includes pictures of Sunset Mountain, a sign-up form, and the Alpha Omega logo. The fraternity plans to use mailing labels as they distribute the brochures.

Instructions: Perform the following tasks to create the two-panel, two-sided CD liner as shown in Figures 3-70a and 3-70b.

1. From the New Publication task pane, choose the Straight Edge Informational Brochure. Choose a 3-panel display, choose to include the customer address, and select the Sign-up form.
2. Choose the Clay color scheme and the Modern Font Scheme.
3. On Page 1, in the right panel, edit the brochure title as shown in Figure 3-70a. Delete the tag line and telephone number text boxes in the lower portion of the right panel. Delete the address text box in the center of the middle panel.
4. Table 3-10 displays the text for the left panel. Enter the text. Press CTRL+A to select all of the text. On the Format menu, click Paragraph. Choose justified alignment and type 2 in the line spacing text box. Close the Paragraph dialog box. With the text still selected, click the Font Color button and select white in the color palette.

Table 3-10 Text for Page 1	
LOCATION	**TEXT**
Left Panel Heading	Sunset Mountain
Left Panel	Located in the beautiful Colorado Rockies, Sunset Mountain's extreme elevation allows it to boast the latest ski season in Colorado and one of the longest ski runs at more than a mile! Sunset Mountain is off the beaten path, so lifts are not crowded. Four double chair lifts accommodate 1,000 people per hour, so you never have a long wait to begin your skiing adventure. Whether you are into "bunny" slopes or telemark skiing, you will love Sunset Mountain.
Left Panel Caption	Sunset Mountaintop
Middle Panel	University Spring Break Alpha Zeta Mu 1050 Greek Row P.O. Box 1050-3211 Kansas City, MO 64118
Right Panel	University Spring Break March 7-10, 2005

5. Click the Page 2 icon in the Page Navigation Control.
6. Table 3-11 on page PUB 190 displays the text for the three stories on Page 2. Enter the text and headings as shown in Figure 3-70b.
7. Using the Clip Art task pane, search for graphics, similar to the ones shown in Figure 3-70, that are related to lodge, mountain, fireplace, and skiing. Replace the placeholder graphics in the brochure.

In the Lab

Sunset Mountain

Located in the beautiful Colorado Rockies, Sunset Mountain's extreme elevation allows it to boast the latest ski season in Colorado and one of the longest ski runs at more than a mile!

Sunset Mountain is off the beaten path, so lifts are not crowded. Four double chair lifts accommodate 1,000 people per hour, so you never have a long wait to begin your skiing adventure. Whether you are into "bunny" slopes or telemark skiing, you will love Sunset Mountain.

Sunset Mountaintop

University Spring Break

Alpha Zeta Mu
1050 Greek Row
P.O. Box 1050-3211
Kansas City, MO 64118

University Spring Break
March 7-10, 2005

*Spring Break
Ski Trip*

(a)

*Winter Sports:
Skiing and
Beyond*

Sunset Mountain offers a wide variety of winter sports, including downhill and cross-country skiing, as well as snowboarding, tubing, and bobsledding runs. Downhill slopes for beginner, intermediate, and advanced skiers are groomed daily. Experienced ski instructors conduct small group lessons.

Ski rental available

If skiing isn't your "thing," think variety! Sunset Mountain is offering an advanced tubing course this season, with banked turns and jumps to make your trip down the mountain more exciting.

Alpha Zeta Mu Ski Trip

Alpha Zeta Mu Sorority is sponsoring a 4-day, 3-night ski trip to Colorado. Sorority members and their guests will fly from Kansas City International to Denver on JLM Airlines and then board a free shuttle to Sunset Mountain. All package option prices are based on Alpha Zeta Mu's ability to book at least 20 people, two to a room, with a maximum of 40. You may mix and match any of the options. You will receive a confirmation postcard in the mail.

Lodging

Sunset Mountain Lodge is the only bed and breakfast among the seven lodging experiences on Sunset Mountain. Nestled among the tall lodge pole pines, the lodge offers modern rooms with full baths. An optional dinner package is available at a modest cost. Other amenities include a game room, hot tub, meeting room, and of course the grand hearth — where the fireplace always is lit and the hot cinnamon cocoa always is ready!

**Visit the lodge at:
www.skicolorado.com**

Alpha Zeta Mu Ski Trip March 7-10

Sign up for:	Price
☐ Round-trip KCI/Denver/KCI	$300.00
☐ 4 days, 3 nights w/breakfast	$325.00
☐ 3 days ski rental and lift tickets	$125.00
☐ 2-hour ski lesson	$ 50.00
☐ 3 dinner option	$ 50.00
☐ Single-day lift ticket	$ 40.00

Subtotal: _____
Tax: _____
Total: _____

Name _____
Address _____
_____
_____

Phone _____

Method of Payment
☐ Check
☐ Bill Me
☐ Visa
☐ MasterCard
☐ American Express

Credit Card # _____ Exp. date _____
Signature _____

*University Spring Break
March 7-10, 2005*

Alpha Zeta Mu
1050 Greek Row
P.O. Box 1050-3211
Kansas City, MO 64118
Phone: 816-555-1217
Fax: 816-555-1218
Email: greekao@midland.edu

(a)

FIGURE 3-70

(continued)

Creating a Travel Brochure *(continued)*

Table 3-11 Text for Page 2	
HEADING	TEXT
Winter Sports: Skiing and Beyond	Sunset Mountain offers a wide variety of winter sports, including downhill and cross-country skiing, as well as snowboarding, tubing, and bobsledding runs. Downhill slopes for beginner, intermediate, and advanced skiers are groomed daily. Experienced ski instructors conduct small group lessons.
	If skiing isn't your "thing," think variety! Sunset Mountain is offering an advanced tubing course this season, with banked turns and jumps to make your trip down the mountain more exciting.
Left Panel caption	Ski rental available
Alpha Zeta Mu Ski Trip	Alpha Zeta Mu Fraternity is sponsoring a 4-day, 3-night ski trip to Colorado. Fraternity members and their guests will fly from Kansas City International to Denver on JLM Airlines and then board a free shuttle to Sunset Mountain. All package option prices are based on Alpha Zeta Mu's ability to book at least 20 people, two to a room, with a maximum of 40. You may mix and match any of the options. You will receive a confirmation postcard in the mail.
Lodging	Sunset Mountain Lodge is the only bed and breakfast among the seven lodging experiences on Sunset Mountain. Nestled among the tall lodge pole pines, the lodge offers modern rooms with full baths. An optional dinner package is available at a modest cost. Other amenities include a game room, hot tub, meeting room, and of course the grand hearth — where the fireplace always is lit and the hot cinnamon cocoa always is ready!
Middle Panel Caption	Visit the lodge at: www.skicolorado.com
Order Form Detail	Add 6 lines from upper right of Figure 3-70a on the previous page.

8. Click the AutoShapes button on the Objects toolbar, point to Stars and Banners, and then click the Wave shape. Drag a wave shape in the scratch area, approximately 1.6 by 1.2 inches in size. Use the Fill Color button to fill the shape with Accent 1 (Dark Red).

9. Create a text box in the scratch area, approximately .5 by 5. inches. Change the text box to Best Fit with gray text. Copy the text box and paste it twice, creating three boxes. Using the Insert Symbol dialog box, enter the Greek letters Alpha, Zeta, and Mu as shown in Figure 3-70a. Drag each of the text boxes on top of the Wave shape and group them with the shape.

10. Click the Copy button. Drag the grouped shape to the right panel of page 2.

11. Click the Paste button. With the copy of the grouped shape selected, click Arrange on the menu bar and then click Rotate Right. Drag a corner handle to resize the shape to approximately 1 by .75 inches. Drag the shape to the middle panel as shown in Figure 3-70a.

12. Check the publication for Spelling. Run the Design Checker. Fix any errors.

13. Click Tools on the menu bar and then point to Commercial Printing Tools. Click Color Printing. When the Color Printing dialog box is displayed, click Process Colors (CMYK).

14. Save the publication using the file name, Lab 3-3 Ski Trip Brochure.

15. Print the publication two sided. Fold the brochure and submit it to your instructor.

Cases and Places

The difficulty of these case studies varies:
■ are the least difficult and ■■ are more difficult. The last exercise is a group exercise.

1 ■ You recently have joined Success America, Incorporated as the new in-house desktop publisher. You are to design a tri-fold event brochure for their October 2005 training event in Indianapolis. The theme will be "Every American Can Win." Featured speakers will include former U.S. Senator Charles Goolsby, television news anchor Holly Schulke, and prominent businessman Dennis Louks. Your employer wants to mail the brochures to potential attendees. The company logo is a blue triangle with a white Sigma S (Greek S) symbol in the center. Create a rough draft using an Event brochure that includes a sign-up form with a placeholder for the customer address. The technical writer will send you content for the stories at a later date.

2 ■ Use the Blends Information brochure to create a brochure announcing the Youth Baseball League. Pick an appropriate color and font scheme. Type Spring Sign-Up as the brochure title. Type The Youth Baseball League as the Organization name. Type your address and telephone number in the appropriate text boxes. Delete the logo. Replace all graphics with sports-related clip art. Edit the captions to match. The league commissioner will send you content for the stories at a later date. Include a sign-up form on page 2. Edit the sign-up form event check boxes as displayed in Table 3-12.

Table 3-12 Sign-Up Form Check Box Content		
EVENT NAME	**TIME**	**PRICE**
Preschool T-Ball: ages 4 and 5	10:00	$25.00
Pee-Wee T-Ball: ages 6 and 7	11:00	$25.00
Coach Pitched: ages 8 and 9	1:00	$40.00
Intermediate: ages 10 and 11	2:30	$40.00
Advanced: ages 12 and 13	4:00	$40.00
City Team, audition only	6:00	TBA

On a separate piece of paper, make a table similar to Table 3-1 on page PUB 132, listing the type of exposure, kinds of information, audience and purpose of communication. Turn in the table with your printout.

3 ■ Create a new color scheme named, My Favorite Colors. Use the Color Scheme task pane to access the Color Schemes dialog box. Choose colors that complement one another. Using the New Publication task pane, create a blank publication. Insert six different AutoShapes and fill each with a color from your color scheme. Create text box captions for each of the AutoShapes, identifying the name of the shape and the color. Print the publication.

Cases and Places

4 ■■ Using the Blank Print Publications link on the New Publication task pane, recreate as closely as possible your school or company logo on a full-page publication. Use the AutoShapes button, fill and font colors, text boxes, and symbols to match the elements in your logo. You also may use WordArt. Ask your instructor or employer for clip art files, if necessary. Use the workspace scratch area to design portions of the logo and then layer and group them before dragging them onto the publication.

5 ■■ Bob Bert of Bert's Beanery has hired you to "spice up" and modernize the look of the restaurant's menu. You decide to use a menu template to create a full color menu for publication at a local copy shop. Bob wants special attention paid to his famous "Atomic Chili®," which is free if a customer can eat five spoonfuls without reaching for water. You will find the registered trademark symbol in the Symbol dialog box. Bob serves salads, soups, and sandwiches a la carte. He has several family specials, as well as combo meals and a variety of drinks and side dishes.

6 ■■ **Working Together** Individually, visit or call several local copy shops or commercial printers in your area. Ask them the following questions: What kind of paper stock do your customers choose for brochures? What is the most commonly used finish? Do you support all three color processes? Will you accept files saved with Microsoft Publisher Pack and Go, or EPS files? What prepress tasks do you perform? Come back together as a group and create a blank Publisher publication to record your answers. Create a table with the Insert Table button on the Objects toolbar. Insert the questions down the left side. Insert the names of the print shops across the top. Fill in the grid with the answers they provide.

MICROSOFT
Office Publisher 2003

Creating an E-Mail Letter Using Publisher

CASE PERSPECTIVE

Your friend, Burt Carlo, is the president of the Community Action Group that looks at public policy related to the town of Marshall, Missouri. The steering committee members of his group recently have created a listserv of e-mail addresses so they may communicate with members of the community more quickly. Many residents have subscribed to the committee's listserv.

Burt knows of your interest in Microsoft Publisher and wonders if you can create a publication that he can send out via e-mail. Together you look through the available templates in the New Publication task pane and discover an e-mail letter template that will serve Burt's purpose. The Community Action Group wants to invite people to a special zoning meeting where a contractor will present a proposal to build new homes in the area.

Burt wants the e-mail message to catch the recipient's eye with strong colors and fonts so they will not delete it right away. He wants to display his group's motto, Building a better community, at the top of the e-mail. Burt also wants the Marshall County logo, as well as an interesting graphic, to appear in the body of the e-mail message. The text of the e-mail letter should remind people of the purpose, date, and time of the meeting.

In the lower portion of the e-mail message, Burt wants a return e-mail address and telephone number to be displayed. You remind him that listserv e-mails always should provide a way for the recipient to unsubscribe.

Objectives

You will have mastered the material in this project when you can:

- Select and format an e-mail letter template
- Edit text boxes in an e-mail letter
- Choose a logo design
- Insert an e-mail hyperlink
- Preview an e-mail letter
- Send an e-mail message using Publisher

Introduction

E-mail, short for electronic mail, is a popular form of communication to transmit messages and files via a computer network. People use e-mail in ways similar to traditional mail, sending correspondence, business communication, greeting cards, letters, brochures, newsletters, and other type of publications.

You can send any Publisher publication as an attachment to an e-mail message; however, if you use Microsoft Outlook 2003 or Microsoft Outlook Express version 5.0 or later as your e-mail program, you can use Publisher 2003 to create and send just a page of the publication as an e-mail letter or message.

This Special Feature illustrates how to send an e-mail letter using Publisher to create the publication. An **e-mail letter** displays both traditional correspondence-related text and graphics, as well as hyperlinks similar to a Web page. All of the objects in an e-mail letter are displayed in the body of the e-mail message rather than as a separate publication attached to the e-mail message.

Q: Do most people prefer to receive a publication as an e-mail attachment?

A: It is not necessarily better to use attachments. For immediate viewing, such as an announcement, letter, or card, it is better to send a single page in the body of an e-mail. If you do send an attachment, the person receiving your e-mail will have to have Publisher installed on his or her system in order to open and view the publication. Additionally, with a large attachment, you may run the risk of the e-mail being blocked by firewalls and filters at the receiving end.

More About

E-Mail Letter Templates

Microsoft has additional e-mail letter templates that you may download. For a link to the Microsoft Office Publisher download site, visit the Publisher 2003 More About Web page (scsite.com/pub2003/more) and then click Download Templates.

Publisher provides several ways to create an e-mail letter. You can use a template, create an e-mail letter from scratch, or convert a single page of another publication into an e-mail letter, expanding the use of your existing content. Publisher's e-mail letter templates are preformatted to the correct page size. The templates use placeholder text and graphics that download quickly and are suitable for the body of an e-mail message. When sending a page of another publication type as an e-mail message, some adjustments may need to be made to the width of your publication in order for it to fit in an e-mail message.

When you send a single page of a publication as an e-mail message, recipients can read the message using an HTML-enabled e-mail program such as Hotmail, AOL, and Yahoo!, as well as the current versions of Outlook and Outlook Express. Recipients do not need to have Publisher installed to view the message, because the page you send will be displayed as the body of the e-mail message. Sending a one-page publication by e-mail to a group of customers or friends is an efficient and inexpensive way to deliver a message. When you send an entire publication as an e-mail attachment, the recipient must have Microsoft Publisher 2002 or Microsoft Office Publisher 2003 installed to view it. When the recipient opens the attached file, Publisher automatically opens and displays the publication. An attachment is the only way to send a multipage publication in e-mail.

Figure 1 displays an e-mail letter sent to a list of residents interested in community housing and zoning matters. The e-mail letter includes a colorful heading, a logo, a graphic, and directions for obtaining more information.

This E-Mail Feature is for instructional purposes only. You do not have to be connected to the Internet or have an e-mail program on your system in order to create the e-mail letter. You can create and save the e-mail letter on a floppy disk rather than send it via e-mail.

Starting Publisher

To start Publisher, Windows must be running. The following steps explain how to start Publisher.

To Start Publisher

1 Click the Start button on the Windows taskbar, point to All Programs on the Start menu, point to Microsoft Office on the All Programs submenu, and then click Microsoft Office Publisher 2003 on the Microsoft Office submenu.

2 If the Publisher window is not maximized, double-click its title bar to maximize it.

3 If Publisher does not display the New Publication task pane, click View on the menu bar and then click Task Pane. If the Publication Designs task pane is displayed, click the Other Task Panes button on the task pane title bar, and then click New Publication.

4 If the Language bar is displayed, click its Minimize button.

You now are ready to use Publisher's New Publication task pane to create a tri-fold brochure.

FIGURE 1

E-Mail Templates

E-mail can be an efficient and cost-effective way to keep in touch with friends, customers, co-workers, or other interested parties. It is easy to design and send professional-looking e-mail using Publisher. Each of Publisher's design sets features several e-mail publication types, so you can create and send e-mail that is consistent in design with the rest of the business communication and marketing materials that you create using Publisher. Table 1 lists the types of e-mail publications and their purpose.

Table 1	E-mail Template Publications	
E-MAIL TEMPLATE	**PURPOSE**
Newsletter	Informs interested clientele about an organization or business with stories, dates, contact information, and upcoming events
Letter	A more personalized document to correspond with one or more people, including specific information on a single topic
Event/Speaker	A notice of a specific upcoming event that includes a speaker and usually contains pictures, dates, times, and a map
Event/Activity	A notice of a specific upcoming activity or event containing a combination of pictures, dates, times, maps, agenda, and the ability to sign up
Product List	A sales-oriented publication to display products, prices, and special promotions including Web page links for more information
Featured Product	A publication that provides information about a company and a specific product or service, including graphics and Web page links for more information

Creating an E-mail Letter

The following steps describe how to open an e-mail letter template.

FIGURE 2

To Open an E-Mail Letter Template

1 In the New Publication task pane, click Web Sites and E-mail in the New from a design list.

2 When the Web Sites and E-mail list is displayed, click E-mail.

3 When the E-mail list is displayed, click Letter.

4 When the previews are displayed, scroll to the Quadrant Letter E-mail preview.

Publisher displays the New Publication task pane and the Quadrant Letter E-mail preview (Figure 2).

The following steps describe how to select the design set, color scheme, and font scheme for the e-mail letter.

To Select Publication Options

1 Click the Quadrant Letter E-mail preview. If Publisher displays the Personal Information dialog box, click its Cancel button.

2 When the Publication Design task pane is displayed, click Color Schemes and then click Marine in the Apply a color scheme list.

3 Click Font Schemes and then click Modern in the Apply a font scheme list.

4 Click the Close button on the Font Schemes task pane title bar.

5 On the Standard toolbar, click the Zoom box arrow and then click 100% in the Zoom list.

6 Scroll to display the upper portion of the page layout.

Publisher displays the upper portion of the e-mail letter template in the workspace (Figure 3).

FIGURE 3

E-mail letter templates contain text boxes, logos, hyperlinks, and graphics. To customize the e-mail letter, you replace the placeholder text and graphics with your own content, just as you would in any other template publication.

Editing Text

The text boxes in an e-mail letter template include headings, the greeting, the salutation, the body of the letter, the closing, the signature block, and the informational text box at the bottom of the e-mail letter.

Editing the Headings and Greeting

The following steps show how to edit the placeholder text in the various heading and personal information text boxes. Your placeholder text may differ from that shown in the figures.

More About

Business Letters

For more information about the proper formatting and style of business letters, visit the Publisher 2003 More About Web page (scsite.com/pub2003/more) and then click Business Letters.

To Edit the Headings and Greeting

1. **Drag through the text in the Organization Name Text Box to select it. Type** `Community Action Group` **to replace the text.**

2. **Drag through the text in the Tag Line Text Box to select it. Type** `Building a better community` **to replace the text.**

3. **Click the text, Letter, in the text box below the Tag Line Text Box to select it. Type** `Attention Residents` **to replace the text.**

4. **Click the text, Dear Customer, in the salutation text box to select it. Type** `Dear Citizens,` **to replace the text.**

The edited text boxes are displayed in the publication (Figure 4 on the next page).

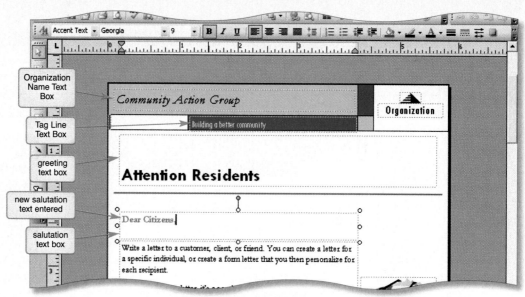

FIGURE 4

Editing the Body of the E-mail Letter

Table 2 displays the text for the body of the e-mail letter.

Table 2   Text for Body of E-Mail Letter
TEXT
The Strategy Corporation is requesting a zoning change in order to build 712 homes in our neighborhood. This large number of homes – virtually a small town in itself – presents a host of problems, including stress on our schools, roads, and utilities, among other concerns.
We need your help and the help of all our neighbors to support the efforts of the Controlled Growth Group. It is extremely important for all of us to attend the special zoning hearing on Monday, November 14, 2005 at 6:30 p.m. We also need as many individual letters and e-mails of protest as possible sent before November 10 to the addresses provided below. Your correspondence and meeting attendance has been instrumental in stemming the tide of this kind of growth. Together, our efforts can make Marshall a better place to live.
Please write to:
Marshall County Commissioners 355 South Washington Street Marshall City, MO 64118
Or e-mail: Local_rep@marshall.county.gov

The placeholder text in the e-mail template formats single-spaced lines within paragraphs, and a double-space, or blank line, between paragraphs. While this is normal for the regular text, you commonly do not double-space each line in an address. Because Publisher creates a new paragraph each time you press the ENTER key, the address would be double-spaced. You can override this spacing between paragraphs by pressing SHIFT+ENTER after the first two lines of the address. Sometimes called a soft return or new line, pressing SHIFT+ENTER creates a new line of text using single spacing.

To facilitate editing with paragraphs, you can click the Special Characters button on the Standard toolbar to display paragraph marks and special characters, such as the space between words.

The following steps show how to enter the text in the body of the e-mail letter.

To Edit the Body of the E-Mail Letter

1 If necessary, click the Special Characters button on the Standard toolbar to display paragraph marks.

2 Click the text in the body of the e-mail letter to select it.

3 Enter the text from Table 2, pressing the ENTER key after each paragraph. Press SHIFT+ENTER after each of the first two lines in the address.

The body of the letter is entered (Figure 5).

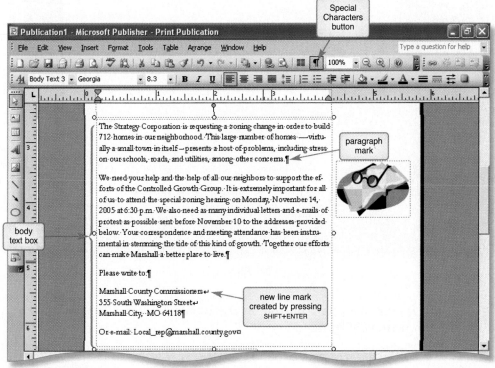

FIGURE 5

Other uses for the SHIFT+ENTER key combination include multiple lines of text within bullets and numbering, as well as short lines in addresses, lists, and titles.

Editing the Closing Text Boxes

To complete the text box editing in the e-mail letter, the steps on the next page describe editing the closing, signature block, and contact information.

More About

Pressing SHIFT+ENTER

When you press SHIFT+ENTER, you create a manual line break. A manual line break ends the current line and continues the text on the next line. For example, suppose your paragraph style includes an extra blank line before each paragraph. To omit this extra space between short lines of text, such as those in an address block or a poem, insert a manual line break after each line instead of pressing the ENTER key. Using a manual line break in a bulleted list will keep the next bullet from displaying as you create a new line. Pressing the ENTER key then will add a new bullet.

To Edit the Closing Text Boxes

1 **Click the text in the signature text box and then type** Burt M. Carlo, President **to replace the text.**

2 **Click the text in the address text box and then type** Community Action Group **to replace the text. Press SHIFT+ENTER and then type** P. O. Box 10050 **as the second line of the address. Press SHIFT+ENTER and then type** Marshall, MO 64118 **to complete the address.**

3 **In the contact text box at the bottom of the page, click the text, someone@example.com. Type** CommunityAction@MarshallCounty.org **to replace the text.**

4 **Click the text, or call 555-555-5555. Type** or call 816 555-9631 **to replace the text.**

The new text is entered (Figure 6).

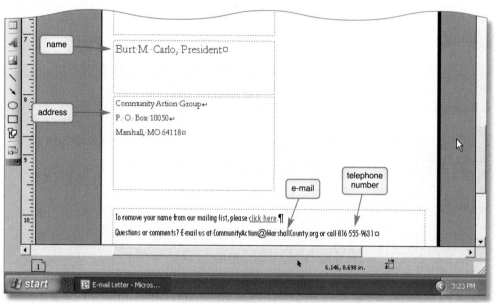

FIGURE 6

5 **Click the Special Characters button on the Standard toolbar to turn off the paragraph mark display.**

Creating a Hyperlink

E-mail letters can contain hyperlinks just as Web pages do. Recall that a hyperlink is a colored and underlined text or a graphic that you click to go to a file, a location in a file, a Web page, or an e-mail address. When you insert a hyperlink, you select the text or object and then click the Insert Hyperlink button on the Standard toolbar. When clicked, hyperlinks can take the viewer to an existing file or Web page, another place in the publication, a new document, or open an e-mail program and create a new message.

Editing the Hyperlink

In the e-mail letter template, the words, click here, display as a hyperlink. The following steps illustrate how to create a clickable link that opens the user's e-mail program and creates a new message.

To Edit the Hyperlink

1 Select the text, click here, in the contact information text box at the bottom of the page.

2 Click the Insert Hyperlink button on the Standard toolbar.

3 When the Insert Hyperlink dialog box is displayed, click E-mail Address in the Link to bar on the left.

4 In the E-mail address text box, type unsubscribe@MarshallCounty.org as the entry.

Publisher automatically adds the mailto: prefix as you type in the E-mail address text box (Figure 7).

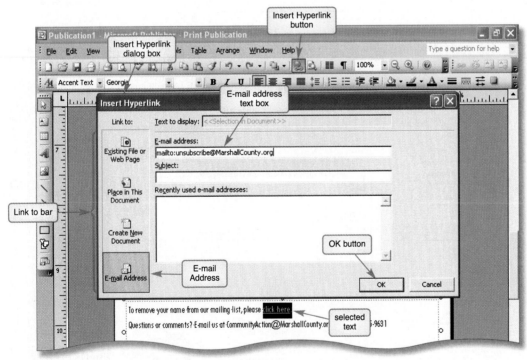

FIGURE 7

5 Click the OK button.

The **mailto:** prefix is added to the e-mail address automatically by Publisher. The prefix is necessary to direct the user's system to start an e-mail program rather than a browser or other application.

E-Mail Logos and Graphics

Most of the e-mail templates contain both logos and graphics that you can edit to suit your publication. In the upper-right corner of the e-mail letter template, Publisher displays one of the predesigned logos from the Design Gallery. Recall that

More About

Logos

For more information about logos and graphics in e-mail letters, visit the Publisher 2003 More About Web page (scsite.com/pub2003/more) and then click E-mail Logos and Graphics.

a logo is a recognizable symbol that identifies a person, business, or organization. A logo may be composed of text, a picture, or a combination of symbols.

Further down in the e-mail letter, Publisher displays a graphic that you can change to reflect the purpose of your publication. You edit e-mail graphics in the same way as you edit graphics in other publications. You can select a clip art clip, insert a graphic from a file, or import a graphic from a scanner or digital camera.

Editing the Logo

A Publisher-provided logo may be formatted in several ways. When selected, a logo displays a small wizard button with a picture of a wand. Clicking this button causes Publisher to display the Logo Designs task pane (Figure 8). In that task pane, you may select an alternate design or click Logo Options to choose a different combination of graphics and text, or even insert your own graphic as a logo.

The following steps show how to select an alternate design and edit the text in the logo.

To Edit the Logo

1

• **Scroll to the upper-right portion of the publication.**

• **Click the logo to select it. When Publisher displays the wizard button, click the button.**

Publisher displays the Logo Designs task pane (Figure 8).

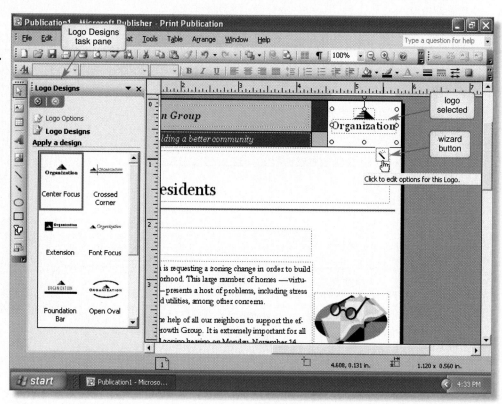

FIGURE 8

2

• **In the Apply a design list, click the Open Oval preview.**

Publisher changes the logo design in the publication (Figure 9).

3

• **Within the logo, double-click the text, Organization, to select it. Type** Marshall County **to replace the text, as shown in Figure 10.**

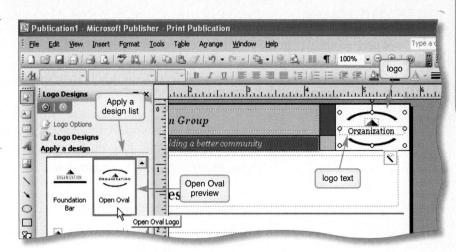

FIGURE 9

Editing the Graphic

Because the purpose of the letter is to inform residents about a housing and zoning meeting of the town council, a graphic representing a home is appropriate. The following steps describe how to edit the graphic.

To Edit the Graphic

1 Double-click the graphic in the e-mail letter.

2 When the Clip Art task pane is displayed, type homes in the Search for text box. If necessary, click the Search in box arrow and then click Everywhere in the list. If necessary, click the Results should be box arrow and then click All media types in the list.

3 Click the Go button (Figure 10).

4 Click a graphic similar to the one shown in the task pane in Figure 10.

FIGURE 10

The publication is now complete. The following steps describe how to check the publication for spelling and design errors.

To Check for Spelling and Design Errors

1 **Click the Spelling button on the Standard toolbar. Correct any errors. Click the Yes button when Publisher asks you to check the rest of the document.**

2 **On the Tools menu, click Design Checker. Correct any problems and then close the Design Checker task pane.**

The following steps illustrate how to save the e-mail letter.

To Save the E-Mail Letter

1 **Click the Save button on the Standard toolbar.**

2 **When the Save As dialog box is displayed, click the Save in box arrow and then click 3½ Floppy (A:) in the Save in list. Type** E-mail Letter **in the File name text box.**

3 **Click the Save button in the Save As dialog box.**

The publication saves on the floppy disk.

Sending an E-Mail Letter

E-mail letters can be sent to one or more people. Many organizations create a **listserv,** which is a list of interested people with e-mail addresses who want to receive news and information e-mails about the organization. A listserv e-mail is one e-mail sent to everyone on the list. Listserv e-mails always should contain a link to allow recipients to remove their name from the list to prevent receiving future e-mails.

Using the Send E-Mail Command

The following steps describe how to preview and then send an e-mail using Publisher's Send E-Mail command. You do not have to send the e-mail, nor do you have to be connected to the Internet to perform the steps.

To Preview and Send a Publication Via E-Mail

1

• **With the publication displayed, click File on the menu bar and then point to Send E-Mail.**

Publisher displays the Send E-Mail submenu (Figure 11).

FIGURE 11

2

• **Click the E-Mail Preview command on the Send E-Mail submenu.**

The browser window displays a preview of the E-mail letter (Figure 12).

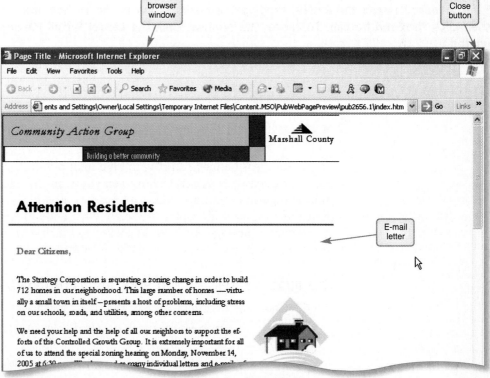

FIGURE 12

3

• Click the **Close** button on the browser's title bar.

• Click the **Send This Page as Message** button on the Standard toolbar (Figure 10 on page 203).

• If your system is connected to an e-mail program, when Publisher displays the Choose Profile dialog box, click the **Profile Name** box arrow and select your system's e-mail profile; then click the **OK** button.

Publisher displays the E-mail toolbar (Figure 13). If your system is not connected to the Internet, Publisher may not display the Send button.

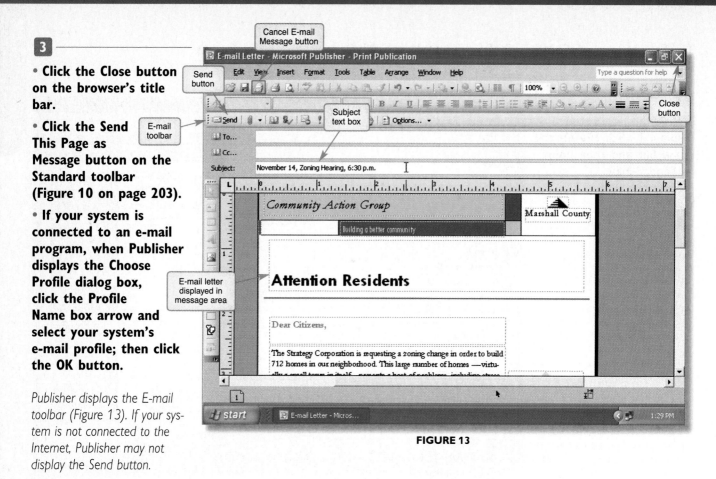

FIGURE 13

4

• If you want to send the e-mail, type your e-mail address in the To box and then click the Send button. To cancel the request, click the Cancel E-Mail Message button.

Sending Print Publications as E-Mail Messages

In general, it is better to start with an e-mail publication template such as the e-mail letter or e-mail newsletter. If, however, you want to send a page of another publication as an e-mail message, you may need to modify the width and margins to ensure that the message will display attractively for e-mail recipients. The typical page size of an e-mail message is 5.8 by 11 inches so that the recipients will not need to scroll horizontally to view the entire width of message.

TO MODIFY THE PAPER SIZE AND MARGINS

1. Click File on the menu bar and then click Page Setup.
2. When the Page Setup dialog box is displayed, if necessary click the Layout tab.
3. Enter the new width and height entries in the Width and Height boxes.
4. Click the OK button.

It is a good idea to send the publication to yourself first to see how it will look before sending it to other recipients.

Occasionally, you may encounter unexpected formatting results when sending a page of a publication as an e-mail message. Some of these problems have easy solutions, while others involve the unavoidable loss of formatting. You can take measures to prevent formatting problems as you add and manipulate text and graphics in your publication.

The final task is to quit Publisher, as described in the following step.

To Quit Publisher

1 **Click the Close button on the Publisher title bar. If Publisher displays a dialog box, click its No button.**

The Publisher window closes.

> **More About**
>
> ### Sending Publications Via E-Mail
>
> You can avoid formatting problems in publications sent via e-mail by using one of the many e-mail templates. For a list of possible problems and solutions when sending other types of publications via e-mail, type `troubleshoot e-mail` in the Type a question for help box on the menu bar.

E-Mail Feature Summary

This E-Mail Feature introduced you to creating an e-mail letter by illustrating how to select and format an e-mail letter template. The feature then showed how to edit both the text boxes and graphics. Next, you learned how to choose a logo design and create an e-mail hyperlink. Finally, the project showed how to preview and send a publication as an e-mail message.

What You Should Know

Having completed this project, you should be able to perform the tasks below. The tasks are listed in the same order they were presented in this project. For a list of the buttons, menus, toolbars, and commands introduced in this project, see the Quick Reference Summary at the back of this book and refer to the Page Number column.

1. Start Publisher   (PUB 194)
2. Open an E-Mail Letter Template   (PUB 196)
3. Select Publication Options   (PUB 196)
4. Edit the Headings and Greeting   (PUB 197)
5. Edit the Body of the E-Mail Letter   (PUB 199)
6. Edit the Closing Text Boxes   (PUB 200)
7. Edit the Hyperlink   (PUB 201)
8. Edit the Logo   (PUB 202)
9. Edit the Graphic   (PUB 203)
10. Check for Spelling and Design Errors (PUB 204)
11. Save the E-Mail Letter   (PUB 204)
12. Preview and Send a Publication Via E-Mail (PUB 205)
13. Modify the Paper Size and Margins   (PUB 206)
14. Quit Publisher   (PUB 207)

In the Lab

1 Creating an E-mail Featured Product List

Problem: Your work for a telecommunications company in the marketing department. Your boss wants you to send an e-mail out to all previous customers advertising the latest cell phone that your company sells. You decide to use a Publisher E-mail Featured Product template to design the e-mail message.

Instructions:

1. Start Publisher and choose the Watermark Featured Product E-mail. Select the Sapphire color scheme and the Foundry font scheme.
2. Think of a name for your telecommunications company and replace it in the heading. Use the phrase, Everything Cellular, as the tag line text.
3. Use the Clip Art task pane to replace the graphic with one picturing a cell phone.
4. Use the Logo Designs task pane to replace the logo.
5. Describe your cell phone or a friend's cell phone and its features in the lower text boxes.
6. Edit the hyperlink at the bottom to reflect your e-mail address.
7. Check the publication for spelling and design errors.
8. Save the publication with the file name, Lab E-1 Cell Phone E-mail. Preview the e-mail.
9. If you have permission, send the publication to your instructor as an e-mail message. Include an appropriate subject line in the Subject text box.

2 Sending a Newsletter as an E-mail Message

Problem: You created the newsletter shown in Figure 2-1 on page PUB 195. You decide to send the first page of the newsletter as an e-mail publication.

Instructions:

1. Open the file you created in Project 2. (If you did not create the publication in Project 2, see your instructor for a copy.)
2. Right-click page 2 in the Page Navigation Control on the status bar, and then click Delete Page on the shortcut menu.
3. Delete the Special Points of Interest sidebar toward the upper-left of the page and then delete the pull quote in the lower portion of the page.
4. Insert a text box toward the bottom of the page that lists your contact information and a link to your e-mail.
5. On the File menu, click Page Setup. In the Page Setup dialog box, if necessary, click the Layout tab. Click Custom in the Publication type list. Type 5.8 in the Width box. Click the OK button. If Publisher asks to adjust your publication for the margins, click the Yes button.
6. Check the publication for spelling and design errors.
7. Save the publication as Lab E-2 Extreme E-mail. Preview the e-mail.
8. If you have permission, send the publication to your instructor as an e-mail message. Include an appropriate subject line in the Subject text box.

Appendix A

Microsoft Publisher Help System

Using the Publisher Help System

This appendix shows you how to use the Microsoft Publisher Help system. At any time while you are using Publisher, you can interact with its Help system and display information on any Publisher topic. It is a complete reference manual at your fingertips.

As shown in Figure A-1, five methods for accessing the Publisher Help system are available:

1. Microsoft Office Publisher Help button on the Standard toolbar
2. Microsoft Office Publisher Help command on the Help menu
3. Function key F1 on the keyboard
4. Type a question for help box on the menu bar
5. Office Assistant

FIGURE A-1 (a) Publisher Help Task Pane   (b) Search Results Task Pane   (c) Microsoft Office Publisher Help Window

All five methods result in the Publisher Help system displaying a task pane on the left side of the Publisher window. The first three methods cause the **Publisher Help task pane** to display (Figure A-1a on the previous page). This task pane includes a Search for text box in which you can enter a word or phrase on which you want help. Once you enter the word or phrase, the Publisher Help system displays the Search Results task pane (Figure A-1b on the previous page). With the Search Results task pane displayed, you can select specific Help topics.

As shown in Figure A-1, methods 4 and 5 bypass the Publisher Help task pane and immediately display the **Search Results task pane** (Figure A-1b) with a list of links that pertain to the selected topic. Thus, the ultimate result of any of the five methods for accessing the Publisher Help system is the Search Results task pane. Once the Publisher Help system displays this task pane, you can choose links that relate to the word or phrase for which you searched. In Figure A-1, for example, border was the search topic. Clicking the Create a custom border link resulted in the Publisher Help system displaying the **Microsoft Office Publisher Help window** with information about creating custom borders (Figure A-1c on the previous page).

Navigating the Publisher Help System

The quickest way to enter the Publisher Help system is through the Type a question for help box on the right side of the menu bar at the top of the screen. Here you can type words, such as format, replace, or file formats; or you can type phrases, such as preview a Web page, or how do I do remove text formatting. The Publisher Help system responds by displaying the Search Results task pane with a list of links.

Here are two tips regarding the words or phrases you enter to initiate a search: (1) check the spelling of the word or phrase; and (2) keep your search specific, with fewer than seven words, to return the most accurate results.

For the following example, assume that you want to remove a bullet from a line of text, and you do not know how to do it. The likely keyword is bullets. The following steps show how to use the Type a question for help box to obtain useful information by entering the keyword, bullets. The steps also show you how to navigate the Publisher Help system.

To Obtain Help Using the Type a Question for Help Box

1

• **Click the Type a question for help box on the right side of the menu bar, type** bullets **and then press the ENTER key.**

The Publisher Help system displays the Search Results task pane on the left side of the window. The Search Results task pane includes eight resulting links (Figure A-2). If you do not find what you are looking for, you can modify or refine the search in the Search area at the bottom of the Search Results task pane. The results returned in your Search Results task pane may be different.

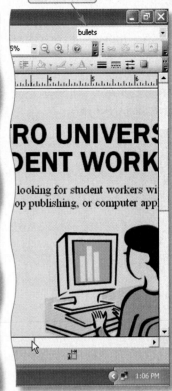

FIGURE A-2

2

• **In the list of links in the Search Results task pane, click the Remove bullets or numbers from a list link.**

• **When the Publisher Help system opens the Microsoft Office Publisher Help window, click its Auto Tile button in the upper-left corner of the window, if necessary, to tile the windows.**

The Publisher Help system opens the Microsoft Office Publisher Help window with the desired information about removing bullets from a list (Figure A-3). Your Help window may be displayed in a different part of the screen. With the Microsoft Office Publisher Help window and Microsoft Publisher window tiled, you can read the information in one window and complete the task in the other window.

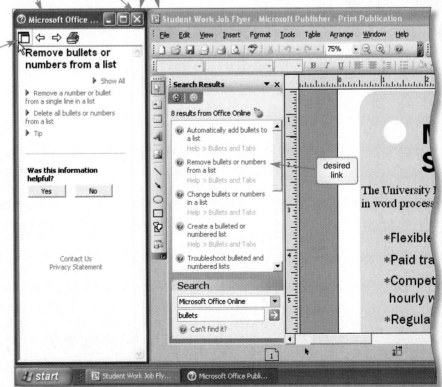

FIGURE A-3

3

• **Double-click the Microsoft Office Publisher Help window title bar.**

• **Click the Show All link in the upper-right corner of the window.**

• **After reviewing the information, click the Hide All link that replaced the Show All link.**

The Microsoft Office Publisher Help window is maximized so it fills the entire screen (Figure A-4). If you are connected to the Internet, you can give Microsoft your opinion as to whether the information was helpful by clicking the Yes or No button at the bottom of the page. The Show All link expands the coverage of information, and the Hide All link condenses the information displayed on the topic in the Publisher Help window.

4

• **Click the Restore Down button on the right side of the Microsoft Office Publisher Help window title bar to return to the tiled state shown in Figure A-3 on the previous page.**

• **Click the Close button on the Microsoft Office Publisher Help window title bar.**

The Microsoft Office Publisher Help window closes, and the Publisher window is active.

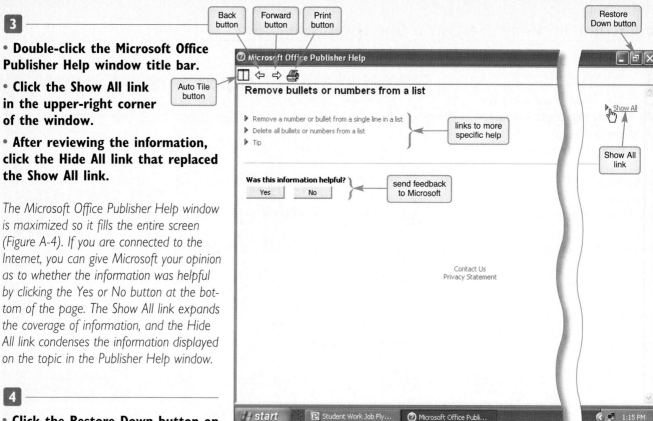

FIGURE A-4

Use the four buttons in the upper-left corner of the Microsoft Office Publisher Help window (Figure A-4) to tile or untile, navigate through the Help system, or print the contents of the window. As you click links in the Search Results task pane, the Publisher Help system displays new pages of information. The Publisher Help system remembers the links you visited and allows you to redisplay the pages visited during a session by clicking the Back and Forward buttons (Figures A-3 and A-4).

If none of the links presents the information you want, you can refine the search by entering another word or phrase in the Search area in the Search Results task pane (Figure A-3). If you have access to the Web, then the scope is global for the initial search. **Global** means all the categories listed in the Search box of the Search area in Figure A-5 are searched. Alternately, you can restrict the scope to **Offline Help**, for example, which results in a search of related links only on your hard disk.

FIGURE A-5

Figure A-5 shows several additional features of the Search Results task pane with which you should be familiar. The buttons immediately below the name of the task pane allow you to navigate between task panes. The Other Task Panes button and the Close button on the Search Results task pane title bar let you change task panes and close the active task pane. You can drag the move handle to reposition the task pane on the screen.

In the lower portion of the Search Results list is a set of links to other places to look for help.

As you enter questions and terms in the Type a question for help box, the Publisher Help system adds them to its list. Thus, if you click the Type a question for help box arrow, a list of previously used words and phrases are displayed (Figure A-6).

FIGURE A-6

The Office Assistant

The **Office Assistant** is an icon (middle of Figure A-7) that Publisher displays in the Publisher window while you work. For the Office Assistant to display, it must be activated by invoking the Show the Office Assistant command on the Help menu. This Help tool has multiple functions. First, when clicked, the Office Assistant will respond in the same way as the Type a question for help box with a list of topics that relate to the entry you make in the text box of the Office Assistant balloon. The entry can be in the form of a word or phrase as if you were talking to a person. For example, if you want to learn more about creating a banner, in the balloon text box, you can type any of the following words or phrases: banner, create a banner, how do I create a banner, or anything similar.

In the example in Figure A-7, the phrase, create a banner, is entered in the Office Assistant balloon. The Office Assistant responds by displaying the Search Results task pane with a list of links from which you can choose. Once you click a link in the Search Results task pane, the Publisher Help system displays the information in the Microsoft Office Publisher Help window (Figure A-7).

FIGURE A-7

Second, during a session, the Office Assistant monitors your work and accumulates tips on how you might increase your productivity and efficiency. The accumulation of tips must be enabled. You enable the accumulation of tips by right-clicking the Office Assistant, clicking Options on the shortcut menu, and then selecting the types of tips you want accumulated. You can view the tips at any time. The accumulated tips display when you activate the Office Assistant balloon. Also, if at anytime you see a lightbulb above the Office Assistant, click it to display the most recent tip. If the Office Assistant is hidden, the lightbulb shows on the Microsoft Publisher Help button on the Standard toolbar.

You hide the Office Assistant by clicking the Hide the Office Assistant command on the Help menu or by right-clicking the Office Assistant and then clicking Hide on the shortcut menu. The Hide the Office Assistant command shows on the Help menu only when the Office Assistant is active in the Publisher window. If the Office Assistant begins showing up on your screen without you instructing it to show, then right-click the Office Assistant, click Options on the shortcut menu, click the Use the Office Assistant check box to remove the check mark, and then click the OK button.

Third, if the Office Assistant is active in the Publisher window, Publisher displays all program and system messages in the Office Assistant balloon.

You may or may not want the Office Assistant to display on the screen at all times. As indicated earlier, you can hide it and then show it later through the Help menu. For more information about the Office Assistant, type `office assistant` in the Type a question for help box and then click the links in the Search Results task pane.

Help Buttons in Dialog Boxes and Subsystem Windows

As you invoke commands that display dialog boxes or other windows and task panes, you will see buttons and links that offer helpful information. Figure A-8 shows the types of Help buttons and links you will see as you work with Publisher.

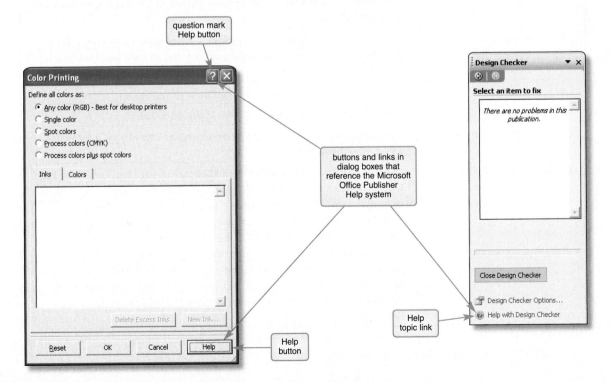

FIGURE A-8

Other Help Commands on the Help Menu

Thus far, this appendix has discussed the first two commands on the Help menu:
(1) the Microsoft Office Publisher Help command (Figure A-1 on page APP 1) and
(2) the Show the Office Assistant command (Figure A-7 on page APP 6). Several
additional commands are available on the Help menu as shown in Figure A-9.
Table A-1 summarizes these commands.

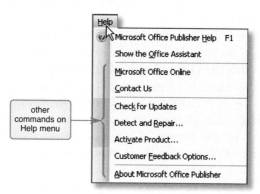

other
commands on
Help menu

Help

Microsoft Office Publisher Help   F1
Show the Office Assistant
Microsoft Office Online
Contact Us
Check for Updates
Detect and Repair...
Activate Product...
Customer Feedback Options...
About Microsoft Office Publisher

FIGURE A-9

Table A-1 Summary of Other Commands on the Help Menu	
COMMAND ON HELP MENU	**FUNCTION**
Microsoft Office Online	Activates your browser, which displays the Microsoft Office Online Home page. The Microsoft Office Online Home page contains links that can improve your Office productivity.
Contact Us	Activates your browser, which displays Microsoft contact information and a list of useful links.
Check for Updates	Activates your browser, which displays a list of updates to Office 2003. These updates can be downloaded and installed to improve the efficiency of Office or to fix an error in one or more of the Office applications.
Detect and Repair	Detects and repairs errors in the Publisher program.
Activate Product	Activates Publisher if it has not been activated already.
Customer Feedback Options	Gives or denies Microsoft permission to collect anonymous information about your hardware.
About Microsoft Office Publisher	Displays the About Microsoft Office Publisher dialog box. The dialog box lists the owner of the software and the product identification. You need to know the product identification if you call Microsoft for assistance. The three buttons below the OK button are the System Info button, the Tech Support button, and the Disabled Items button. The System Info button displays system information, including hardware resources, components, software environment, and applications. The Tech Support button displays technical assistance information. The Disabled Items button displays a list of disabled items that prevent Publisher from functioning properly.

Use Help

1 Using the Type a Question for Help Box

Instructions: Perform the following tasks using the Publisher Help system.

1. Use the Type a question for help box on the menu bar to obtain help on creating tables.
2. Click Create a table in the list of links in the Search Results task pane. Tile the windows, if necessary. Double-click the Microsoft Office Publisher Help window title bar to maximize it. Click the Show All button. Read and print the information. At the top of the printout, write down the number of links the Publisher Help system found.
3. One at a time, click two additional links in the Search Results task pane and print the information. Hand in the printouts to your instructor. Use the Back and Forward buttons to return to the original page.
4. Use the Type a question for help box to search for information on alignment. Click the Align or distribute objects link in the Search Results task pane. When the Microsoft Office Publisher Help window is displayed, maximize the window. Read and print the information. One at a time, click the links on the page and print the information for any new page that displays. Close the Microsoft Office Publisher Help window.
5. For each of the following words and phrases, click one link in the Search Results task pane, click the Show All link, and then print the page: text, date, curves, print resolution, shadows, 3-D effects, and create a logo.

2 Expanding on the Publisher Help System Basics

Instructions: Use the Publisher Help system to understand the topics better and answer the questions listed below. Answer the questions on your own paper, or hand in the printed Help information to your instructor.

1. Show the Office Assistant. Right-click the Office Assistant and then click Animate! on the shortcut menu. Repeat invoking the Animate! command to see various animations. Right-click the Office Assistant, click Options on the shortcut menu, click the Reset my tips button, and then click the OK button. When you see a lightbulb above the Office Assistant, it indicates that the Office Assistant has a tip to share with you. Click the lightbulb to display the tip.
2. Use the Office Assistant to find help on undoing tasks. Print the Help information for three links in the Search Results task pane. Close the Microsoft Office Publisher Help window. Hand in the printouts to your instructor. Hide the Office Assistant.
3. Press the F1 key. Search for information on Help. Click the first two links in the Search Results task pane. Read and print the information for both.
4. One at a time, invoke the first three commands in Table A-1. Print each page. Click two links on one of the pages and print the information. Hand in the printouts to your instructor.
5. Click About Microsoft Office Publisher on the Help menu. Click the Tech Support button and print the resulting page. Click the System Info button. If necessary, click the plus sign next to Components in the System Summary pane to expand its contents. Below the Components category, click CD-ROM. Click File on the menu bar and then click Print. Click Display in the list. Print the information. Hand in the printouts to your instructor.

Appendix B

Speech and Handwriting Recognition and Speech Playback

Introduction

This appendix discusses the Office capability that allows users to create and modify publications using its alternative input technologies available through **text services**. Office provides a variety of text services, which enable you to speak commands and enter text in an application. The most common text service is the keyboard. Other text services include speech recognition and handwriting recognition.

The Language Bar

The **Language bar** allows you to use text services in the Office applications. You can utilize the Language bar in one of three states: (1) in a restored state as a floating toolbar in the Publisher window (Figure B-1a or Figure B-1b if Text Labels are enabled); (2) in a minimized state docked next to the notification area on the Windows taskbar (Figure B-1c); or (3) hidden (temporarily closed and out of the way). If the Language bar is hidden, you can activate it by right-clicking the Windows taskbar, pointing to Toolbars on the shortcut menu (Figure B-1d), and then clicking Language bar on the Toolbars submenu. If you want to close the Language bar, right-click the Language bar and then click Close the Language bar on the shortcut menu (Figure B-1e).

(a) Language Bar with Text Labels Disabled

(b) Language Bar with Text Labels Enabled

(c) Minimized Language Bar Docked on Windows Taskbar next to Notification Area

FIGURE B-1

(d) Windows Taskbar Shortcut Menu and Toolbars Submenu

(e) Language Bar Shortcut Menu

When Windows was installed on your computer, the installer specified a default language. For example, most users in the United States select English (United States) as the default language. You can add more than 90 additional languages and varying dialects such as Basque, English (Zimbabwe), French (France), French (Canada), German (Germany), German (Austria), and Swahili. With multiple languages available, you can switch from one language to another while working in Publisher. If you change the language or dialect, then text services may change the functions of the keys on the keyboard, adjust speech recognition, and alter handwriting recognition. If a second language is activated, then a Language icon appears immediately to the right of the move handle on the Language bar and the language name is displayed on the Publisher status bar. This appendix assumes that English (United States) is the only language installed. Thus, the Language icon does not appear in the examples in Figure B-1 on the previous page.

Buttons on the Language Bar

The Language bar shown in Figure B-2a contains seven buttons. The number of buttons on your Language bar may be different. These buttons are used to select the language, customize the Language bar, control the microphone, control handwriting, and obtain help.

The first button on the left is the Microphone button, which enables and disables the microphone. When the microphone is enabled, text services adds two buttons and a balloon to the Language bar (Figure B-2b). These additional buttons and the balloon will be discussed shortly.

The second button from the left is the Speech Tools button. The Speech Tools button displays a menu of commands (Figure B-2c) that allow you to scan the current document looking for words to add to the speech recognition dictionary; hide or show the balloon on the Language bar; train the Speech Recognition service so that it can interpret your voice better; add and delete specific words to and from its dictionary, such as names and other words not understood easily; and change the user profile so more than one person can use the microphone on the same computer.

The third button from the left on the Language bar is the Handwriting button. The Handwriting button displays the Handwriting menu (Figure B-2d), which lets you choose the Writing Pad (Figure B-2e), Write Anywhere (Figure B-2f), or the on-screen Standard keyboard (Figure B-2g). The On-Screen Symbol Keyboard command on the Handwriting menu displays an on-screen keyboard that allows you to enter special symbols that are not available on a standard keyboard. You can choose only one form of handwriting at a time.

The fourth button indicates which one of the handwriting forms is active. For example, in Figure B-2a, the Writing Pad is active. The handwriting recognition capabilities of text services will be discussed shortly.

The fifth button from the left on the Language bar is the Help button. The Help button displays the Help menu. If you click the Language Bar Help command on the Help menu, the Language Bar Help window appears (Figure B-2h). On the far right of the Language bar are two buttons stacked above and below each other. The top button is the Minimize button and the bottom button is the Options button. The Minimize button minimizes the Language bar so that it appears on the Windows taskbar. The next section discusses the Options button.

Customizing the Language Bar

The down arrow icon immediately below the Minimize button in Figure B-2a is called the Options button. The Options button displays a menu of text services options (Figure B-2i). You can use this menu to hide the Speech Tools, Handwriting, and Help buttons on the Language bar by clicking their names to remove the check mark to the left of each button. You also can show the Correction, Speak Text, and Pause Speaking buttons on the Language bar by clicking their names to place a check mark to the left of the respective command. When you select text and then click the Correction button, a list of correction alternatives is displayed in the Publisher window. You can use the Corrections button to correct both speech recognition and handwriting recognition errors. The Speak Text and Pause Speaking buttons are discussed at the end of this Appendix. The Settings command on the Options menu displays a dialog box that lets you customize the Language bar. This command will be discussed shortly. The Restore Defaults command redisplays hidden buttons on the Language bar.

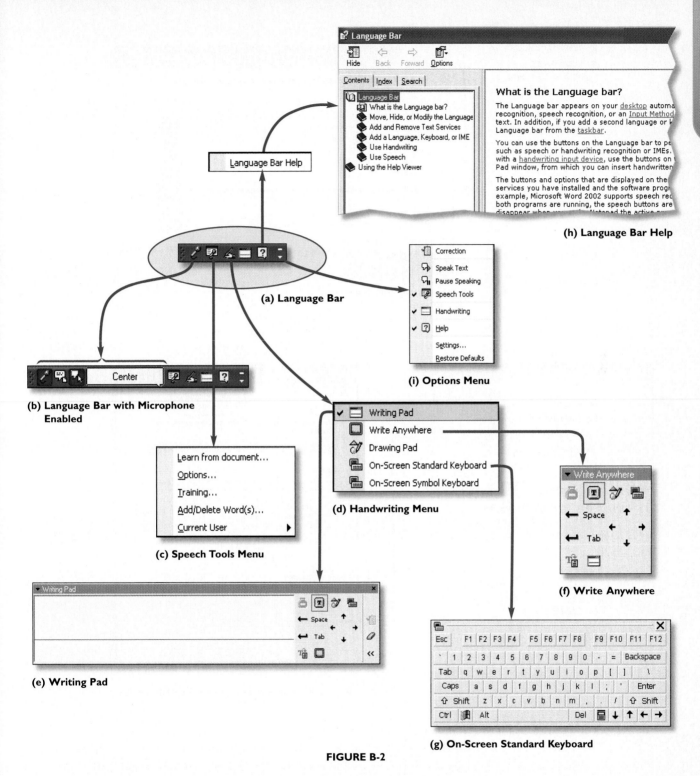

(a) Language Bar

(b) Language Bar with Microphone Enabled

(c) Speech Tools Menu

(d) Handwriting Menu

(e) Writing Pad

(f) Write Anywhere

(g) On-Screen Standard Keyboard

(h) Language Bar Help

(i) Options Menu

FIGURE B-2

If you right-click the Language bar, a shortcut menu appears (Figure B-3a on the next page). This shortcut menu lets you further customize the Language bar. The Minimize command on the shortcut menu docks the Language bar on the Windows taskbar. The Transparency command in Figure B-3a toggles the Language bar between being solid and transparent. You can see through a transparent Language bar (Figure B-3b). The Text Labels command toggles on text labels on the Language bar (Figure B-3c) and off (Figure B-3b). The Vertical command displays the Language bar vertically on the screen (Figure B-3d).

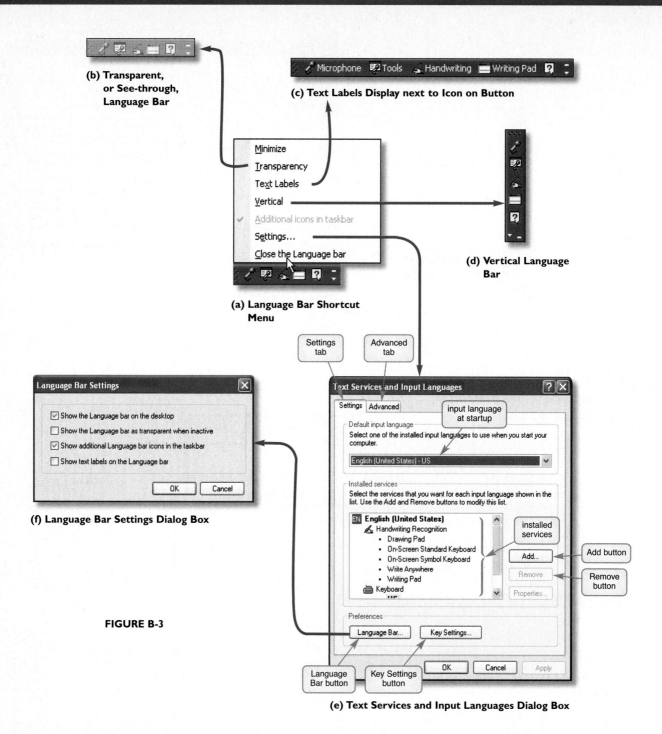

(b) Transparent, or See-through, Language Bar

(c) Text Labels Display next to Icon on Button

(a) Language Bar Shortcut Menu

(d) Vertical Language Bar

(f) Language Bar Settings Dialog Box

FIGURE B-3

(e) Text Services and Input Languages Dialog Box

The Settings command in Figure B-3a displays the Text Services and Input Languages dialog box (Figure B-3e). The Text Services and Input Languages dialog box allows you to add additonal languages, add and remove text services, modify keys on the keyboard, modify the Language bar, and extend support of advanced text services to all programs, including Notepad and other programs that normally do not support text services (through the Advanced tab). If you want to remove any one of the services in the Installed services list, select the service, and then click the Remove button. If you want to add a service, click the Add button. The Key Settings button allows you to modify the keyboard. If you click the Language Bar button in the Text Services and Input Languages dialog box, the Language Bar Settings dialog box appears (Figure B-3f). This dialog box contains Language bar options, some of which are the same as the commands on the Language bar shortcut menu shown in Figure B-3a.

The Close the Language bar command on the shortcut menu shown in Figure B-3a closes or hides the Language bar. If you close the Language bar and want to redisplay it, see Figure B-1d on page APP 11.

Speech Recognition

The **Speech Recognition service** available with Office enables your computer to recognize human speech through a microphone. The microphone has two modes: dictation and voice command (Figure B-4). You switch between the two modes by clicking the Dictation button and the Voice Command button on the Language bar. These buttons appear only when you turn on Speech Recognition by clicking the Microphone button on the Language bar (Figure B-5a on the next page). If you are using the Microphone button for the very first time in Publisher, it will require that you check your microphone settings and step through voice training before activating the Speech Recognition service.

The Dictation button places the microphone in Dictation mode. In **Dictation mode,** whatever you speak is entered as text in the active text box. The Voice Command button places the microphone in Voice Command mode. In **Voice Command mode,** whatever you speak is interpreted as a command. If you want to turn off the microphone, click the Microphone button on the Language bar or in Voice Command mode say, "Mic off" (pronounced mike off). It is important to remember that minimizing the Language bar does not turn off the microphone.

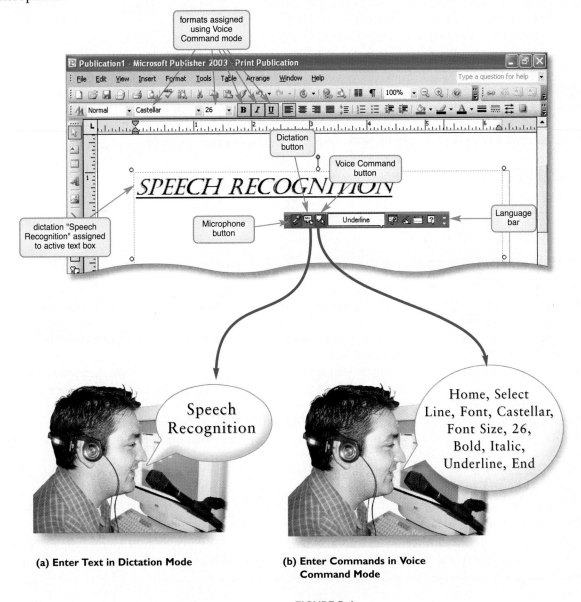

(a) **Enter Text in Dictation Mode**

(b) **Enter Commands in Voice Command Mode**

FIGURE B-4

The Language bar speech message balloon shown in Figure B-5b displays messages that may offer help or hints. In Voice Command mode, the name of the last recognized command you said appears. If you use the mouse or keyboard instead of the microphone, a message will appear in the Language bar speech message balloon indicating the word you could say. In Dictation mode, the message, Dictating, usually appears. The Speech Recognition service, however, will display messages to inform you that you are talking too soft, too loud, too fast, or to ask you to repeat what you said by displaying, What was that?

Getting Started with Speech Recognition

For the microphone to function properly, you should follow these steps:

1. Make sure your computer meets the minimum requirements.
2. Start Publisher. Activate Speech Recognition by clicking Tools on the menu bar and then clicking Speech.
3. Set up and position your microphone, preferably a close-talk headset with gain adjustment support.
4. Train Speech Recognition.

The following sections describe these steps in more detail.

(a) Microphone Off

(b) Microphone On

FIGURE B-5

SPEECH RECOGNITION SYSTEM REQUIREMENTS   For Speech Recognition to work on your computer, it needs the following:

1. Microsoft Windows 98 or later or Microsoft Windows NT 4.0 or later
2. At least 128 MB RAM
3. 400 MHz or faster processor
4. Microphone and sound card

SETUP AND POSITION YOUR MICROPHONE   Set up your microphone as follows:

1. Connect your microphone to the sound card in the back of the computer.
2. Position the microphone approximately one inch out from and to the side of your mouth. Position it so you are not breathing into it.
3. On the Language bar, with the Microphone button on, click the Speech Tools button and then click Options on the Speech Tools menu (Figure B-6a).
4. When text services displays the Speech input settings dialog box (Figure B-6b), click the Advanced Speech button. When text services displays the Speech Properties dialog box (Figure B-6c), click the Speech Recognition tab.
5. Click the Configure Microphone button. Follow the Microphone Wizard directions as shown in Figures B-6d, B-6e, and B-6f. The Next button will remain dimmed in Figure B-6e until the volume meter consistently stays in the green area.
6. If someone else installed Speech Recognition, click the New button in the Speech Properties dialog box and enter your name. Click the Train Profile button and step through the Voice Training dialog box. The Voice Training dialog box will require that you enter your gender and age group. It then will step you through voice training.

You can adjust the microphone further by clicking the Settings button in the Speech Properties dialog box (Figure B-6c). The Settings button displays the Recognition Profile Settings dialog box that allows you to adjust the pronunciation sensitivity and accuracy versus recognition response time.

Language bar

Speech Tools button

Options command

(a) Speech Tools Menu

Learn from document...
Options...
Training...
Add/Delete Word(s)...
Current User

Speech input settings

Dictation

Mode Keys
Assign mode keys   Settings...

You can assign a button to switch quickly between dictation and voice command modes when using speech recognition software. Click Settings to assign the keyboard or mouse action you want to use to switch between modes.

Advanced settings
☑ Show speech messages
☑ Automatically recognize new words in documents temporarily
☑ Require high confidence for short words
☐ Save speech data with the document in supporting applications
☑ Automatically remove whitespace for punctuation
☑ Disable dictation while typing
☐ Playback original audio when correcting
☑ Allow dictation when correction window is open
☑ Enable commands in dictation mode

speech input options

Advanced Speech button

Voice Command...   Advanced Speech...   Language Bar...

OK   Cancel   Apply

(b) Speech Input Settings Dialog Box

(d) Adjust Microphone

Microphone Wizard - Welcome

The Microphone Wizard adjusts your microphone volume for use with speech recognition.

Before you begin, make sure that your microphone and speakers are properly connected to your computer. Refer to your microphone and speaker instructions for more information.

If you are using a headset microphone, adjust the headset microphone as shown. Position the microphone so that it is about an inch from the side of your mouth and so that you are not breathing directly into it.

If you change the room in which you use Microsoft Speech Recognition and your accuracy drops, run the Microphone Wizard again.

Speech Recognition tab

Speech Properties

Speech Recognition   Text To Speech

Language
Microsoft English (U.S.) v6.1 Recognizer   Settings...

Recognition Profiles
Profiles store information about how to recognize your voice. Change a profile to recognize a different voice or a different noise environment.

☑ James Quasney

Training your profile will improve your speech recognition accuracy.

New...
Delete...
Settings...
Train Profile...

New button

Settings button

Microphone
Level
Audio Input...   Configure Microphone...

Train Profile button

OK   Cancel   Apply

(c) Speech Properties Dialog Box

Configure Microphone button

Microphone Wizard - Adjust Volume

Read the following sentence in your everyday tone of voice until the volume meter level consistently stays in the green area:

"I am using the Microphone Wizard. It is adjusting the volume of my microphone."

Help   Click Help for microphone tips if the volume meter does not move as you are speaking.

Your microphone volume level is now tuned to your voice. Click Next to continue.

(e) Adjust Volume

Microphone Wizard - Test Positioning

Read the following sentence in your everyday tone of voice:

"This papaya tastes perfect"

After a pause, a recording will be played back to you. If it sounds like you are blowing into the microphone, reposition the microphone, and repeat the above sentence.

If you do not hear anything played back, you may wish to check your speaker or headset audio output is connected properly and the volume is set appropriately.

If you repositioned your microphone, click Back and repeat the microphone volume adjustment.

< Back   Finish   Cancel

(f) Test Microphone

FIGURE B-6

TRAIN THE SPEECH RECOGNITION SERVICE   The Speech Recognition service will understand most commands and some dictation without any training at all. It will recognize much more of what you speak, however, if you take the time to train it. After one training session, it will recognize 85 to 90 percent of your words. As you do more training, accuracy will rise to 95 percent. If you feel that too many mistakes are being made, then continue to train the service. The more training you do, the more accurately it will work for you. Follow these steps to train the Speech Recognition service:

(a) Speech Tools Menu

(b) Voice Training Dialog Box

FIGURE B-7

1. Click the Speech Tools button on the Language bar and then click Training (Figure B-7a).
2. When the Voice Training dialog box appears (Figure B-7b), click one of the sessions and then click the Next button.
3. Complete the training session, which should take less than 15 minutes.

If you are serious about using a microphone to speak to your computer, you need to take the time to go through at least three of the eight training sessions listed in Figure B-7b.

Using Speech Recognition

Speech recognition lets you enter text into a publication similarly to speaking into a tape recorder. Instead of typing, you can dictate text that you want to be displayed in the document, and you can issue voice commands. In Voice Command mode, you can speak menu names, commands on menus, toolbar button names, and dialog box option buttons, check boxes, list boxes, and button names. Speech recognition, however, is not a completely hands-free form of input. Speech recognition works best if you use a combination of your voice, the keyboard, and the mouse. You soon will discover that Dictation mode is far less accurate than Voice Command mode. Table B-1 lists some tips that will improve the Speech Recognition service's accuracy considerably.

Table B-1	Tips to Improve Speech Recognition
NUMBER	**TIP**
1	The microphone hears everything. Though the Speech Recognition service filters out background noise, it is recommended that you work in a quiet environment.
2	Try not to move the microphone around once it is adjusted.
3	Speak in a steady tone and speak clearly.
4	In Dictation mode, do not pause between words. A phrase is easier to interpret than a word. Sounding out syllables in a word will make it more difficult for the Speech Recognition service to interpret what you are saying.
5	If you speak too loudly or too softly, it makes it difficult for the Speech Recognition service to interpret what you said. Check the Language bar speech message balloon for an indication that you may be speaking too loudly or too softly.
6	If you experience problems after training, adjust the recognition options that control accuracy and rejection by clicking the Settings button shown in Figure B-6c on the previous page.
7	When you are finished using the microphone, turn it off by clicking the Microphone button on the Language bar or in Voice Command mode, say "Mic off." Leaving the microphone on is the same as leaning on the keyboard.
8	If the Speech Recognition service is having difficulty with unusual words, then add the words to its dictionary by using the Learn from document and Add/Delete Word(s) commands on the Speech Tools menu (Figure B-8a). The last names of individuals and the names of companies are good examples of the types of words you should add to the dictionary.
9	Training will improve accuracy; practice will improve confidence.

The last command on the Speech Tools menu is the Current User command (Figure B-8a). The Current User command is useful for multiple users who share a computer. It allows them to configure their own individual profiles, and then switch between users as they use the computer.

For additional information about the Speech Recognition service, enter speech recognition in the Type a question for help box on the menu bar.

Handwriting Recognition

Using the Office **Handwriting Recognition service**, you can enter text and numbers into Publisher by writing instead of typing. You can write using a special handwriting device that connects to your computer or you can write on the screen using your mouse. Four basic methods of handwriting are available by clicking the Handwriting button on the Language bar: Writing Pad; Write Anywhere; Drawing Pad; and On-Screen Keyboard. Although the on-screen keyboard does not involve handwriting recognition, it is part of the Handwriting menu and, therefore, will be discussed in this section.

If your Language bar does not include the Handwriting button, then for installation instructions, enter install handwriting recognition in the Type a question for help box on the menu bar.

(a) Speech Tools Menu

(b) Add/Delete Word(s) Dialog Box

FIGURE B-8

Writing Pad

To display the Writing Pad, click the Handwriting button on the Language bar and then click Writing Pad (Figure B-9). The **Writing Pad** resembles a notepad with one or more lines on which you can use freehand to print or write in cursive. With the Text button enabled, you can form letters on the line by dragging the mouse. To the right of the notepad is a rectangular toolbar. Use the buttons on this toolbar to adjust the Writing Pad, insert spaces and tabs, and perform other handwriting activities.

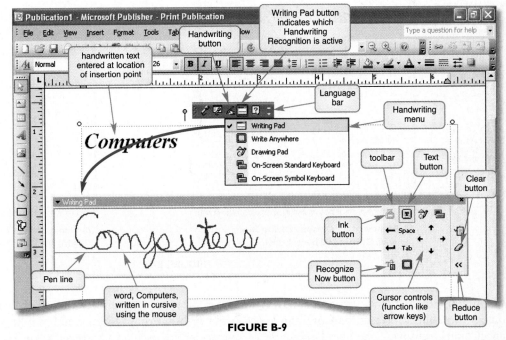

FIGURE B-9

Consider the example in Figure B-9 on the previous page. With a text box selected in the publication, the word, Computers, is written in cursive on the **Pen line** in the Writing Pad. As soon as the word is complete, the Handwriting Recognition service automatically converts the handwriting to typed characters and inserts the text at the location of the insertion point. With the Ink button enabled, instead of the Text button, the text is inserted in handwritten form in the document.

You can customize the Writing Pad by clicking the Options button on the left side of the Writing Pad title bar and then clicking the Options command (Figure B-10a). Invoking the Options command causes the Handwriting Options dialog box to be displayed. The Handwriting Options dialog box contains two sheets: Common and Writing Pad. The Common sheet lets you change the pen color and pen width, adjust recognition, and customize the toolbar area of the Writing Pad. The Writing Pad sheet allows you to change the background color and the number of lines that are displayed in the Writing Pad. Both sheets contain a Restore Default button to restore the settings to what they were when the software was installed initially.

(a) Writing Pad Options Menu

(b) Handwriting Options Dialog Box with Common Sheet Active

(c) Handwriting Options Dialog Box with Writing Pad Sheet Active

FIGURE B-10

When you first start using the Writing Pad, you may want to remove the check mark from the Automatic recognition check box in the Common sheet in the Handwriting Options dialog box (Figure B-10b). With the check mark removed, the Handwriting Recognition service will not interpret what you write in the Writing Pad until you click the Recognize Now button on the toolbar (Figure B-9 on the previous page). This allows you to pause and adjust your writing.

The best way to learn how to use the Writing Pad is to practice with it. Also, for more information, enter handwriting recognition in the Type a question for help box on the menu bar.

Write Anywhere

Rather than use Writing Pad, you can write anywhere on the screen by invoking the Write Anywhere command on the Handwriting menu (Figure B-11) that displays when you click the Handwriting button on the Language bar. In this case, the entire window is your writing pad.

In Figure B-11, the word, Budget, is written in cursive using the mouse button. Shortly after the word is written, the Handwriting Recognition service interprets it, assigns it to the active text box, and erases what was written.

It is recommended that when you first start using the Write Anywhere service, you remove the check mark from the Automatic recognition check box in the Common sheet in the Handwriting Options dialog box (Figure B-10b). With the check mark removed, the Handwriting Recognition service will not interpret what you write on the screen until you click the Recognize Now button on the toolbar (Figure B-11).

Write Anywhere is more difficult to use than the Writing Pad, because when you click the mouse button, Publisher may interpret the action as an object rather than starting to write. For this reason, it is recommended that you use the Writing Pad.

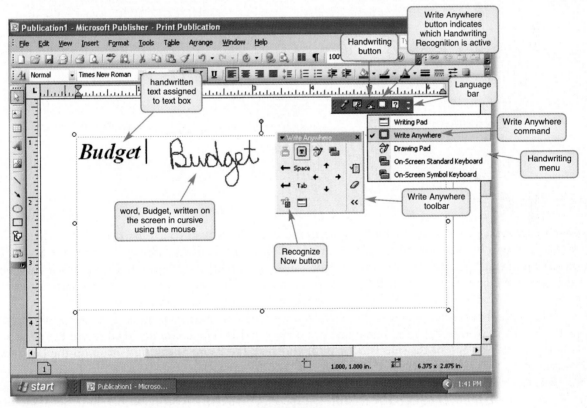

FIGURE B-11

On-Screen Keyboard

The On-Screen Standard Keyboard command on the Handwriting menu (Figure B-12) displays an on-screen keyboard. The **on-screen keyboard** lets you enter data at the location of the insertion point by using your mouse to click the keys. The on-screen keyboard is similar to the type found on handheld computers or PDAs.

The On-Screen Symbol Keyboard command on the Handwriting menu displays a special on-screen keyboard that allows you to enter symbols that are not on your keyboard, as well as Unicode characters. **Unicode characters** use a coding scheme capable of representing all the world's current languages.

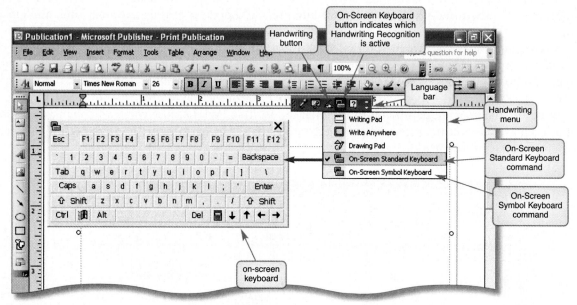

FIGURE B-12

Speech Playback

Using **speech playback**, you can have your computer read back the text in your publication's text boxes. Publisher provides two buttons for speech playback: Speak Text and Pause Speaking. To show the Speak Text button on the Language bar, click the Options button on the Language bar (Figure B-13) and then click Speak Text on the Options menu. Similarly, click the Options button on the Language bar and then click Pause Speaking on the Options menu to show the Pause Speaking button on the Language bar.

To use speech playback, select the text you want the computer to start reading back in the publication and then click the Speak Text button on the Language bar (Figure B-13). The computer reads from the beginning of the selected text, until the end of the selection or until you click the Pause Speaking button on the Language bar. After the computer reads back the selected text, it stops speech playback.

When you click the Speak Text button on the Language bar, it changes to a Stop Speaking button. Click the Stop Speaking button on the Language bar to stop the speech playback. If you click the Pause Speaking button on the Language bar to stop speech playback, the Pause Speaking button changes to a Resume Speaking button that you click when you want the computer to continue reading the document from the location at which it stopped reading.

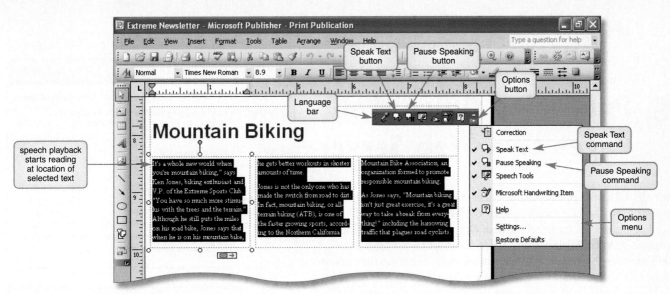

FIGURE B-13

Customizing Speech Playback

You can customize speech playback through the Speech Properties dialog box. With the Microphone button off, click the Speech Tools button on the Language bar and then click Options on the Speech Tools menu (Figure B-2c on page APP 13). When text services displays the Speech Properties dialog box, click the Text To Speech tab (Figure B-14). The Text To Speech sheet has two areas: Voice selection and Voice speed. The Voice selection area lets you choose between two male voices and one female voice. You can click the Preview Voice button to hear a sample of the voice. The Voice speed area contains a slider. Drag the slider to slow down or speed up the pace of the speaking voice.

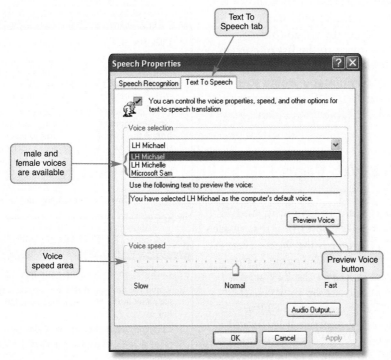

FIGURE B-14

Appendix C

Publishing Office Web Pages to a Web Server

With the Office applications, you use the Save as Web Page command on the File menu to save the Web page to a Web server using one of two techniques: Web folders or File Transfer Protocol. A **Web folder** is an Office shortcut to a Web server. **File Transfer Protocol** (**FTP**) is an Internet standard that allows computers to exchange files with other computers on the Internet.

You should contact your network system administrator or technical support staff at your ISP to determine if their Web server supports Web folders, FTP, or both, and to obtain necessary permissions to access the Web server. If you decide to publish Web pages using a Web folder, you must have the Office Server Extensions (OSE) installed on your computer.

Using Web Folders to Publish Office Web Pages

When publishing to a Web folder, someone first must create the Web folder before you can save to it. If you are granted permission to create a Web folder, you must obtain the URL of the Web server, a user name, and possibly a password that allows you to access the Web server. You also must decide on a name for the Web folder. Table C-1 explains how to create a Web folder.

Office adds the name of the Web folder to the list of current Web folders. You can save to this folder, open files in the folder, rename the folder, or perform any operations you would to a folder on your hard disk. You can use your Office program or Windows Explorer to access this folder. Table C-2 explains how to save to a Web folder.

Using FTP to Publish Office Web Pages

When publishing a Web page using FTP, you first must add the FTP location to your computer before you can save to it. An FTP location, also called an **FTP site**, is a collection of files that reside on an FTP server. In this case, the FTP server is the Web server.

To add an FTP location, you must obtain the name of the FTP site, which usually is the address (URL) of the FTP server, and a user name and a password that allows you to access the FTP server. You save and open the Web pages on the FTP server using the name of the FTP site. Table C-3 explains how to add an FTP site.

Office adds the name of the FTP site to the FTP locations list in the Save As and Open dialog boxes. You can open and save files using this list. Table C-4 explains how to save to an FTP location.

Table C-1 Creating a Web Folder

1. Click File on the menu bar and then click Save As (or Open).
2. When the Save As dialog box (or Open dialog box) appears, click My Network Places on the My Places bar, and then click the Create New Folder button on the toolbar.
3. When the Add Network Place Wizard dialog box appears, click the Next button. If necessary, click Choose another network location. Click the Next button. Click the View some examples link, type the Internet or network address, and then click the Next button. Click Log on anonymously to deselect the check box, type your user name in the User name text box, and then click the Next button. Enter the name you want to call this network place and then click the Next button. Click the Finish button.

Table C-2 Saving to a Web Folder

1. Click File on the menu bar and then click Save As.
2. When the Save As dialog box appears, type the Web page file name in the File name text box. Do not press the ENTER key.
3. Click My Network Places on the My Places bar.
4. Double-click the Web folder name in the Save in list.
5. If the Enter Network Password dialog box appears, type the user name and password in the respective text boxes and then click the OK button.
6. Click the Save button in the Save As dialog box.

Table C-3 Adding an FTP Location

1. Click File on the menu bar and then click Save As (or Open).
2. In the Save As dialog box, click the Save in box arrow and then click Add/Modify FTP Locations in the Save in list; or in the Open dialog box, click the Look in box arrow and then click Add/Modify FTP Locations in the Look in list.
3. When the Add/Modify FTP Locations dialog box appears, type the name of the FTP site in the Name of FTP site text box. If the site allows anonymous logon, click Anonymous in the Log on as area; if you have a user name for the site, click User in the Log on as area and then enter the user name. Enter the password in the Password text box. Click the OK button.
4. Close the Save As or the Open dialog box.

Table C-4 Saving to an FTP Location

1. Click File on the menu bar and then click Save As.
2. When the Save As dialog box appears, type the Web page file name in the File name text box. Do not press the ENTER key.
3. Click the Save in box arrow and then click FTP Locations.
4. Double-click the name of the FTP site to which you wish to save.
5. When the FTP Log On dialog box appears, enter your user name and password and then click the OK button.
6. Click the Save button in the Save As dialog box.

Appendix D

Changing Screen Resolution and Resetting the Publisher Toolbars and Menus

Changing Screen Resolution

The **screen resolution** indicates the number of pixels (dots) that your system uses to display the letters, numbers, graphics, and background you see on your screen. The screen resolution usually is stated as the product of two numbers, such as 800 × 600. An 800 × 600 screen resolution results in a display of 800 distinct pixels on each of 600 lines, or about 480,000 pixels. The figures in this book were created using a screen resolution of 800 × 600.

The screen resolutions most commonly used today are 800 × 600 and 1024 × 768, although some Office specialists operate their computers at a much higher screen resolution, such as 2048 × 1536. The following steps show how to change the screen resolution from 1024 × 768 to 800 × 600.

To Change the Screen Resolution

1

• **If necessary, minimize all applications so that the Windows desktop appears.**

• **Right-click the Windows desktop.**

Windows displays the Windows desktop shortcut menu (Figure D-1).

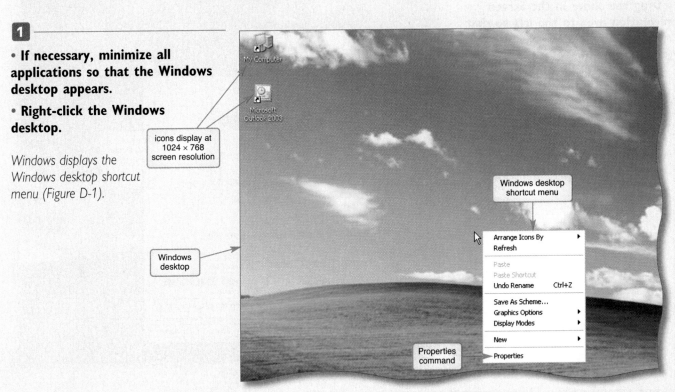

icons display at 1024 × 768 screen resolution

Windows desktop shortcut menu

Windows desktop

Properties command

FIGURE D-1

2

• **Click Properties on the shortcut menu.**

• **When Windows displays the Display Properties dialog box, click the Settings tab.**

Windows displays the Settings sheet in the Display Properties dialog box (Figure D-2). The Settings sheet shows a preview of the Windows desktop using the current screen resolution (1024 × 768). The Settings sheet also shows the screen resolution and the color quality settings.

FIGURE D-2

3

• **Drag the slider in the Screen resolution area to the left so that the screen resolution changes to 800 × 600.**

The screen resolution in the Screen resolution area changes to 800 × 600 (Figure D-3). The Settings sheet shows a preview of the Windows desktop using the new screen resolution (800 × 600).

FIGURE D-3

4

• **Click the OK button.**

• **If Windows displays the Monitor Settings dialog box, click the Yes button.**

Windows changes the screen resolution from 1024 x 768 to 800 x 600 (Figure D-4).

icons display at 800 × 600 screen resolution

FIGURE D-4

As shown in the previous steps, as you decrease the screen resolution, Windows displays less information on your screen, but the information increases in size. The icons are slightly larger in Figure D-4 than they are in previous figures. The reverse also is true: as you increase the screen resolution, Windows displays more information on your screen, but the information decreases in size.

Resetting the Publisher Toolbars and Menus

Publisher customization capabilities allow you to create custom toolbars by adding and deleting buttons and to personalize menus based on their usage. Each time you start Publisher, the toolbars and menus display using the same settings as the last time you used it. The figures in this book were created with the Publisher toolbars and menus set to the original, or installation, settings.

Resetting the Standard and Formatting Toolbars

The steps on the next page show how to reset the Standard and Formatting toolbars.

To Reset the Standard and Formatting Toolbars

1

• **If necessary, start Publisher for your system as described in Project 1.**

• **Click the Toolbar Options button on the Standard toolbar and then point to Add or Remove Buttons on the Toolbar Options menu.**

Publisher displays the Toolbar Options menu and the Add or Remove Buttons submenu (Figure D-5).

FIGURE D-5

2

• **Point to Standard on the Add or Remove Buttons submenu.**

• **When the Standard submenu displays, scroll down and then point to Reset Toolbar.**

Publisher displays the Standard submenu, which lists the buttons and boxes that can be displayed on the Standard toolbar (Figure D-6). To remove a button from the Standard toolbar, click a button name with a check mark to the left of the name to remove the check mark.

FIGURE D-6

3

• **Click Reset Toolbar.**

• **If Publisher displays the Microsoft Publisher dialog box, click Yes.**

Publisher resets the Standard toolbar to its original settings.

4

• **Reset the Formatting toolbar by following Steps 1 through 3 and replacing any reference to the Standard toolbar with the Formatting toolbar.**

Not only can you use the Standard submenu shown in Figure D-6 to reset the Standard toolbar to its original settings, but you also can use it to customize the Standard toolbar by adding and deleting buttons. To add or delete buttons, click the button name on the Standard submenu to add or remove the check mark. Buttons with a check mark to the left currently are displayed on the Standard toolbar; buttons without a check mark are not displayed on the Standard toolbar. You can complete the same tasks for the Formatting toolbar, using the Formatting submenu to add or delete buttons on the Formatting toolbar.

Resetting the Publisher Menus

The following steps show how to reset the Publisher menus to their original settings.

To Reset the Publisher Menus

Other Ways

1. On View menu point to Toolbars, click Customize on Toolbars submenu, click Toolbars tab, click toolbar name, click Reset button, click OK button, click Close button
2. Right-click toolbar, click Customize on shortcut menu, click Toolbars tab, click toolbar name, click Reset button, click OK button, click Close button
3. In Voice Command mode, say "View, Toolbars, Customize, Toolbars, [desired toolbar name], Reset, OK, Close"

1

• **Click the Toolbar Options button on the Standard toolbar and then point to Add or Remove Buttons on the Toolbar Options menu.**

The Toolbar Options menu and the Add or Remove Buttons submenu are displayed (Figure D-7).

FIGURE D-7

• **Click Customize on the Add or Remove Buttons submenu. When Publisher displays the Customize dialog box, click the Options tab.**

Publisher displays the Customize dialog box (Figure D-8). The Customize dialog box contains three sheets used for customizing the Publisher toolbars and menus.

3

• **Click the Reset menu and toolbar usage data button. When Publisher displays the Microsoft Publisher dialog box, click the Yes button.**

• **Click the Close button in the Customize dialog box.**

Publisher resets the menus to the original settings.

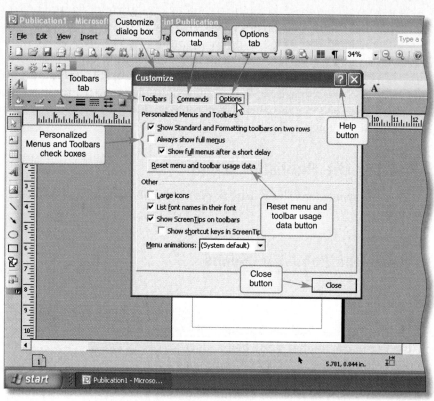

FIGURE D-8

Other Ways

1. On View menu point to Toolbars, click Customize on Toolbars submenu, click Options tab, click Reset menu and toolbar usage data button, click Yes button, click Close button
2. Right-click toolbar, click Customize on shortcut menu, click Options tab, click Reset menu and toolbar usage data button, click Yes button, click Close button
3. In Voice Command mode, say "View, Toolbars, Customize, Options, Reset menu and toolbar usage data, Yes, Close"

Using the Options sheet in the Customize dialog box, as shown in Figure D-8 on the previous page, you can select options to personalize menus and toolbars. For example, you can place or remove a check mark that instructs Publisher to display the Standard and Formatting toolbars on two rows. You also can select whether Publisher always displays full menus or displays short menus followed by full menus, after a short delay. Other options available on the Options sheet include settings to instruct Publisher to display toolbars with large icons; to use the appropriate font to display font names in the Font list; and to display a ScreenTip when a user points to a toolbar button. Clicking the Help button on the title bar in the Customize dialog box displays the Microsoft Office Publisher Help window with more information about each of the customize features.

Using the Commands sheet in the Customize dialog box, you can add buttons to toolbars and commands to menus. Recall that the menu bar at the top of the Publisher window is a special toolbar. To add buttons to a toolbar, click a category name in the Categories list and then drag the command name in the Commands list to a toolbar. To add commands to a menu, click a category name in the Categories list, drag the command name in the Commands list to a menu name on the menu bar, and then, when the menu is displayed, drag the command to the desired location in the list of menu commands.

Using the Toolbars sheet in the Customize dialog box, you can add new toolbars and reset existing toolbars and the menu. To add a new toolbar, click the New button, enter a toolbar name in the New Toolbar dialog box, and then click the OK button. Once the new toolbar is created, you can use the Command sheet to add or remove buttons, as you would with any other toolbar. If you add one or more buttons to an existing toolbar and want to reset the toolbar to its original settings, click the toolbar name in the Toolbars list so a check mark displays to the left of the name and then click the Reset button. If you add commands to one or more menus and want to reset the menus to their default settings, click Menu Bar in the Toolbars list so a check mark displays to the left of the name and then click the Reset button. When you have finished, click the Close button to close the Customize dialog box.

Index

Quick Reference Summary

In Microsoft Office Publisher 2003, you can accomplish a task in a number of ways. The following table provides a quick reference to each task presented in this textbook. The first column identifies the task. The second column indicates the page number on which the task is discussed in the book. The subsequent four columns list the different ways the task in column one can be carried out. Besides using the mouse or keyboard, you can invoke the commands listed in the MOUSE, MENU BAR, and SHORTCUT MENU columns using Voice commands.

Microsoft Office Publisher 2003 Quick Reference Summary

TASK	PAGE NUMBER	MOUSE	MENU BAR	SHORTCUT MENU	KEYBOARD SHORTCUT
Align Objects	PUB 166		Arrange | Align or Distribute	Align or Distribute	ALT+R | A
Attention Getters	PUB 90	Design Gallery Object button on Objects toolbar	Insert | Design Gallery Object | Attention Getters		ALT+I | D
AutoFit Text	PUB 31		Format | AutoFit Text	Change Text | AutoFit Text	ALT+O | X
Automatic Page Numbering	PUB 111	Insert Page Number button on Header and Footer toolbar	Insert | Page Numbers		ALT+I | U
AutoShapes	PUB 158	AutoShapes button on Objects toolbar	Arrange | Change AutoShape		ALT+R | C
Bold	PUB 145	Bold button on Formatting toolbar	Format | Font	Change Text | Font	CTRL+B
Bullets	PUB 23	Bullets button on Formatting toolbar	Format | Indents and Lists	Change Text | Bullets and Numbering	ALT+F | B
Center	PUB 161	Center button on Formatting toolbar	Arrange | Align or Distribute	Change Text | Font	CTRL+E
Change Pages	PUB 73	Page icon on status bar	Edit | Go to Page		CTRL+G or F5
Copy and Paste	PUB 109	Copy button and Paste button on Standard toolbar	Edit | Copy; Edit | Paste	Copy; Paste	CTRL+C; CTRL+V
Convert to Web Site	PUB 51		File | Convert to Web Publication		
Custom Color Schemes	PUB 136	Color Schemes button on Formatting toolbar	Format | Color Schemes		ALT+O | C
Delete Objects	PUB 26	Cut button on Standard toolbar	Edit | Delete Object	Delete Object	DELETE
Delete Pages	PUB 73		Edit | Delete Page	Delete Page	ALT+E | A
Design Checker	PUB 48		Tools | Design Checker		ALT+T | K
Edit a Story in Microsoft Word	PUB 86		Edit | Edit Story in Microsoft Word		ALT+E | W
Edit Graphics	PUB 36	Double-click graphic	Format | Picture	Format Picture	ALT+O | E
Edit Style	PUB 92	Style box on Formatting toolbar	Format | Styles and Formatting		ALT+O | S
Font	PUB 11	Font box on Formatting toolbar	Format | Font	Change Text | Font	CTRL+SHIFT+F
Font Color	PUB 136	Font Color button on Formatting toolbar	Format | Font	Change Text | Font	ALT+O | F

Microsoft Office Publisher 2003 Quick Reference Summary *(continued)*

TASK	PAGE NUMBER	MOUSE	MENU BAR	SHORTCUT MENU	KEYBOARD SHORTCUT
Font Effect	PUB 148	Font button on Formatting toolbar	Format | Font	Change Text | Font	ALT+O | F
Font Size	PUB 145	Font Size box on Formatting toolbar	Format | Font	Change Text | Font	CTRL+SHIFT+P
Forms	PUB 133	Design Gallery Object button on Objects toolbar	Insert | Design Gallery Object | Reply Forms		ALT+I | D
Group	PUB 167	Group button	Arrange | Group	Group	CTRL+SHIFT+G
Help	PUB 54 and Appendix A	Microsoft Office Publisher Help button on Standard toolbar	Help | Microsoft Office Publisher Help		F1
Import Text	PUB 78	Drag and drop text	Insert | Text File	Change Text | Text File	ALT+I | E
Insert Hyperlink	PUB 47	Insert Hyperlink button on Standard toolbar	Insert | Hyperlink	Hyperlink	CTRL+K
Insert Pages	PUB 75		Insert | Page		CTRL+SHIFT+N
Language Bar	APP 11	Language indicator button in tray status area			
Line Spacing	PUB 150	Line Spacing button on Formatting toolbar	Format | Paragraph	Change Text | Paragraph	ALT+O | P
Master Page	PUB 111		View | Master Page		CTRL+M
Mastheads	PUB 75	Design Gallery Object button on Objects toolbar	Insert | Design Gallery Object | Mastheads		ALT+I | D
Move	PUB 39	Point to border and drag	Edit | Cut; Edit | Paste	Cut; Paste	CTRL+X; CTRL+V
New Publication	PUB 8	New button on Standard toolbar	File | New		CTRL+N
Open Publication	PUB 43	Open button on Standard toolbar	File | Open		CTRL+O
OverFlow Text	PUB 89		Format | AutoFit Text	Change Text | AutoFit Text	ALT+O | X
Pack and Go	PUB 175		File | Pack and Go		ALT+F | K
Photographs	PUB 154	Picture Frame button on Objects toolbar	Insert | Picture | From File	Change Picture | From File	ALT+I | P | F
Preview Publication	PUB 171	Print Preview button on Standard toolbar	File | Print Preview		ALT+F | V
Print Publication	PUB 41	Print button on Standard toolbar	File | Print		CTRL+P
Publish to the Web	PUB 52		File | Publish to the Web		ALT+F, T
Pull Quotes	PUB 105	Design Gallery Object button on Objects toolbar	Insert | Design Gallery Object | Pull Quotes		ALT+I | D
Quit Publisher	PUB 56	Close button on title bar	File | Exit		ALT+F4
Resize Graphic	PUB 39	Drag sizing handle	Format | Picture | Size	Format Picture | Size	ALT+O | E | S
Save Publication - New Name	PUB 33		File | Save As		ALT+F | A
Save Publication - Same Name	PUB 41	Save button on Standard toolbar	File | Save		CTRL+S
Select All Text	PUB 30		Edit | Select All		CTRL+A
Send a Publication via E-Mail	PUB 205	Send This Page as Message button on Standard toolbar	File | Send E-Mail		ALT+F | D
Sidebars	PUB 99	Design Gallery Object button on Objects toolbar	Insert | Design Gallery Object | Sidebars		ALT+I | D
Shortcut Menu	PUB 27	Right-click object			SHIFT+F10
Smart Tags	PUB 106	Click Smart Tag button	Tools | AutoCorrect Options		ALT+T | A

Microsoft Office Publisher 2003 Quick Reference Summary

TASK	PAGE NUMBER	MOUSE	MENU BAR	SHORTCUT MENU	KEYBOARD SHORTCUT
Special Characters	PUB 199	Special Characters button on Standard toolbar			
Spell Check	PUB 114	Spelling button on Standard toolbar	Tools | Spelling	Proofing Tools | Spelling	F7
Task Pane	PUB 8		View | Task Pane		CTRL+F1
Tear-offs	PUB 23	Design Gallery Object button on Objects toolbar	Insert | Design Gallery Object | Phone Tear-Offs		ALT+I | D
Text Boxes	PUB 22	Text Box button on Objects toolbar	Insert | Text Box		ALT+I | X
Toolbar, Dock	PUB 20	Drag toolbar to dock			
Toolbar, Reset	APP 28	Toolbar Options button, Add or Remove Buttons, Customize, Toolbars tab	View | Toolbars | Customize | Toolbars |	Customize | Toolbars tab	ALT+V | T | C | B
Toolbar, Show Entire	PUB 9	Double-click move handle			
Toolbar, Show or Hide	PUB 9	Right-click toolbar, click toolbar name	View | Toolbars	Toolbars	ALT+V | T
Undo	PUB 28	Undo button on Standard toolbar	Edit | Undo	Undo	CTRL+Z
Ungroup	PUB 168	Ungroup button	Arrange | Ungroup	Ungroup	CTRL+SHIFT+G
Web Page Preview	PUB 53	Web Page Preview button on Standard toolbar	File | Web Page Preview		ALT+F | B
WordArt	PUB 94	Insert WordArt button on Objects toolbar	Insert | Picture | WordArt		ALT+I | P | W
Zoom	PUB 22	Zoom box on Standard toolbar	View | Zoom	Zoom	F9